taste of home
slow cooker
Classics

taste of home
B O O K S

REIMAN MEDIA GROUP, INC. • GREENDALE, WISCONSIN

A TASTE OF HOME/READER'S DIGEST BOOK

EDITORS
Jan Briggs, Jennifer Olski

ART DIRECTOR
Edwin Robles, Jr.

LAYOUT DESIGNER
Catherine Fletcher

PROOFREADERS
Linne Bruskewitz, Jean Steiner

EDITORIAL ASSISTANT
Barb Czysz

FOOD DIRECTOR
Diane Werner RD

RECIPE TESTING & EDITING
Taste of Home Test Kitchen

FOOD PHOTOGRAPHY
Reiman Photo Studio

SENIOR EDITOR, RETAIL BOOKS
Jennifer Olski

VICE PRESIDENT, EXECUTIVE EDITOR/BOOKS
Heidi Reuter Lloyd

CREATIVE DIRECTOR
Ardyth Cope

SENIOR VICE PRESIDENT, EDITOR IN CHIEF
Catherine Cassidy

PRESIDENT AND CHIEF EXECUTIVE OFFICER
Mary G. Berner

PRESIDENT, FOOD & ENTERTAINING
Suzanne M. Grimes

Pictured on the front cover (clockwise from top left):
Tangy Pulled Pork Sandwiches (p. 42), Easy Minestrone (p. 90),
Strawberry Rhubarb Sauce (p. 310) and Busy Day Beef Stew (p. 198)

Pictured on spine:
Chicken Cacciatore (p. 216)

Pictured on back cover (from left to right): Buffet Meatballs
(p. 12), Sirloin Roast with Gravy (p. 152), Asparagus Berry Salad
(p. 334) and Chocolate Bread Pudding (p. 298)

International Standard Book Number (10): 0-89821-657-5
International Standard Book Number (13): 978-0-89821-657-8
Library of Congress Control Number: 2007929917

For other Taste of Home books and products,
visit www.tasteofhome.com.

For more Reader's Digest products and information,
visit www.rd.com (in the United States).
www.rd.ca (in Canada)

Printed in China
5 7 9 10 8 6 4

TABLE OF CONTENTS

28
PEPPERED MEATBALLS

142
SLOW-COOKER PIZZA

308
CHUNKY APPLESAUCE

252
SWEET 'N' SOUR RIBS

introduction

Turn to your slow cooker for unbeatable mix-it-and-forget-it convenience. With a slow cooker, it's easy to put a hot, home-cooked meal on the table at the end of the day, even when you've been away.

Enjoy delicious, from-scratch fare even on your most hurried days!

If your idea of a quick meal on a hectic evening is a call to the pizza delivery guy, think again! Simply fill your slow cooker in the morning, turn it on and head out the door. When you return later, you'll be greeted with the wonderful aroma of a hearty, simmering supper.

Your slow cooker makes the ideal kitchen companion. Use it to free up oven space when preparing food for a large gathering or holiday meal. On hot summer days, use a slow cooker in place of the oven and avoid heating up the kitchen!

With a slow cooker you can save on your food budget. The low and slow cooking process is ideal for less tender cuts, fork-tender stews, chili and pot roasts...without spending lots of money on expensive meats.

Discover these and all the tasty benefits of the slow cooker with *Slow Cooker Classics*. It's chock-full of useful tips and family-favorite recipes from the readers of *Taste of Home*, America's #1 cooking magazine. You'll find entrees, soups, side dishes, appetizers and even desserts! A special bonus chapter helps round out your meals with easy breads and scrumptious salads.

You can make every one of the recipes in this full-color volume with confidence because each is a tried-and-true favorite of a fellow busy cook. Plus, every recipe has been tested and approved by the Taste of Home Test Kitchen staff.

Take a moment to browse the handy tips included here, then satisfy your family with these slow-cooked, home-style meals.

The Difference Between a Crock-Pot® And a Slow Cooker

The original slow cooker, called a Crock-Pot, was introduced in 1971 by Rival®. The term "slow cooker" and the name Crock-Pot are frequently used interchangeably when referring to this appliance.

The most popular slow cookers have heat coils circling a crockery insert. With this type, the heat surrounds the food to help it cook evenly. These models have two heat settings: "high" (equal to 300°F) and "low" (equal to 200°F).

Other types of slow cookers have heat coils on the bottom and have an adjustable thermostat.

All the recipes in this cookbook are cooked on either "high" or "low" for a certain amount of time.

When a time range is provided, this accounts for variables such as thickness of meat, how full the slow cooker is, temperature of the food going into the cooker, etc.

As you become more familiar with your slow cooker, you'll be better able to judge which end of the range to use for cooking food.

A handy attribute of slow cookers is that if you can't get home at exactly the time the food should be done, it generally doesn't hurt to leave the slow cooker cooking on low for an extra hour.

Selecting the Right Size Slow Cooker

Slow cookers come in a range of sizes, from 1 quart to 6 quarts. It's important to use the right size for the amount of food you're making.

To cook food properly and safely, manufacturers and the USDA recommend slow cookers be filled at least half full but no more than two-thirds full. Check the chart at right to find the proper size slow cooker for your needs.

In general, to serve a dip from a buffet, the smallest slow cookers are ideal. To entertain or cook for a potluck dinner, the larger cookers work best.

Many slow cookers have a removable stoneware insert. That handy feature allows you to assemble the food the night before, when it's convenient for you. Uncooked meats should be stored separately from other ingredients and added when you're ready to cook.

Cover and store the insert in the refrigerator. Then in the morning, you can just put in the insert, turn on the cooker and go.

Note: Don't preheat the base unit. An insert that has been in the refrigerator overnight should always be put into a

cold base unit. Stoneware is sensitive to dramatic temperature changes and cracking or breakage could occur with preheating.

Another option, especially for recipes that require additional preparation like browning meat, is to assemble your recipe in the evening, put everything in the slow cooker and turn it on. Let it cook overnight while you sleep.

In the morning, when the recipe has cooked for the required amount of time, store your finished dish in the refrigerator and reheat it in the microwave at dinnertime.

SLOW COOKER SIZE RECOMMENDATIONS:
1 person household 1 to 1-1/2 quarts
2 people 2 to 3-1/2 quarts
3 or 4 people 3-1/2 to 4-1/2 quarts
4 or 5 people 4-1/2 to 5 quarts
6 or more people 5 to 6 quarts

Preparing Foods for The Slow Cooker

Meats. For enhanced flavor and appearance, meat may be browned before going into the slow cooker, but it's not necessary. If you decide not to brown the meat, you may want to add color when serving by sprinkling on some chopped parsley or shredded cheese. Garnishes such as fresh herbs and lemon wedges can also help.

Vegetables. Vegetables, especially root vegetables like carrots and potatoes, tend to cook slower than meat. Place these vegetables on the bottom and around the sides of the slow cooker and put meat on top of the vegetables. Add tender vegetables like peas and zucchini, or those you'd prefer to be crisp-tender, during the last 15 to 60 minutes of cooking.

Dairy. Most milk-based products tend to break down during slow cooking. If possible, add items like milk, sour cream, cream cheese or cream during the last hour of cooking. Cheeses don't generally hold up over extended periods of cooking, so they should be added near the end of cooking—or use processed cheeses instead.

Seasonings. Whole herbs and spices are better than the crushed forms in the slow cooker. The whole berry or leaf is firmer and stands up better over long cooking times. They'll be at their peak at serving time. Add fresh herbs just before the end of cooking.

Beans. Dried beans can be tricky to work with in the slow cooker. Minerals in the water and variations in voltage affect different types of beans in different ways. As a result, dried beans should always be soaked before adding to a slow cooker recipe. Here's how:

Place beans in a Dutch oven or soup kettle; add water to cover by 2 inches. Bring to a boil; boil for 2 minutes. Remove from the heat; cover and let stand for 1 to 4 hours or until beans are softened. Drain and rinse beans, discarding liquid.

Note: Lentils and split peas do not need to be soaked. After dried beans are completely cooked, they can be combined with sugar and/or acidic foods, such as tomato sauce. Sugar and acid have a hardening effect on beans and will prevent them from becoming tender. An alternative is to use canned beans that have been rinsed and drained.

Pasta. If added to a slow cooker when dry, pasta becomes very sticky. Partially cook pasta until it's almost tender but not completely cooked before adding. Or, boil pasta until it's completely tender and add it at the end of cooking just to heat it through and blend it with the other ingredients.

Fish. Fish is very tender and turns into flakes if slow cooked for long periods. Add fish during the last 20 minutes of cooking.

SLOW COOKER BASICS:

- No peeking! Refrain from lifting the lid while the slow cooker is cooking unless you're instructed in a recipe to stir or add ingredients. The loss of steam can mean an additional 15 to 30 minutes of cooking time each time you lift the lid.

- Be sure the lid is seated properly—not tilted or askew. The steam during cooking creates a seal.

- Remove food from the slow cooker within 1 hour after it's finished cooking. Promptly refrigerate leftovers.

- Slow cooking may take longer at higher altitudes.

Converting Recipes For the Slow Cooker

Almost any recipe that bakes in the oven or simmers on the stovetop can be converted for the slow cooker. Here are some guidelines:

Using this book or the manufacturer's instruction booklet, locate a recipe similar to the one you want to convert. Use it as a guide. Note the quantity and size of meat and vegetable pieces, heat setting, cooking time and amount of liquid.

Note: Since there is no evaporation, foods tend to water down. If your recipe calls for 6 to 8 cups of water, you might want to start with 5 cups. Conversely, recipes should include some liquid. If a recipe doesn't include liquid, add 1/2 cup of water or broth.

In general, 1 hour of simmering on the range or baking at 350°F in the oven is equal to 8-10 hours on low or 4-5 hours on high in a slow cooker. Check the chart above.

CONVENTIONAL COOKING TIMES:	SLOW COOKER COOKING TIMES:
15 to 30 min.	Low: 4 to 6 hours High: 1-1/2 to 2 hours
35 to 45 min.	Low: 6 to 8 hours High: 3 to 4 hours
50 min. or more	Low: 8 to 10 hours High: 4 to 5 hours

Thickeners such as flour, cornstarch and tomato paste are used to give texture to foods cooked in the slow cooker.

Before converting recipes, check manufacturer's guidelines for your particular slow cooker.

HELPFUL FOIL HANDLES

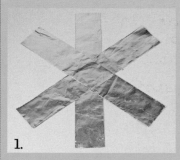

1.

2.

3.

Meat loaves and some layered dishes are easier to get out of the slow cooker using foil handles. Here's how:

1. Cut three 20- x 3-inch strips of heavy-duty aluminum foil. Crisscross the strips so they resemble the spokes of a wheel.

2. Place the meat loaf in the center of the strips, and pull them up and bend the edges to form handles.

3. Grasp the foil handles to lift the loaf and lower it into the slow cooker. Leave the foil in while cooking so you can easily lift the meat out to serve.

Note: For a layered dish, place the strips in the cooker and up the sides before putting in the food. Leave them in. Once the food is cooked, pull the strips together as a handle to neatly remove the food in one piece.

CHECK YOUR SLOW COOKER'S OPERATION:
Did you inherit a used slow cooker or find one at a garage sale and want to see if it's working properly?

To be considered safe, a slow cooker must be able to cook slow enough so that it can be left unattended, yet it must be fast enough to keep the food at a safe temperature. Here's how to check:

1. Fill the slow cooker with 2 quarts of lukewarm water.

2. Heat on low with the lid covered for 8 hours.

3. Using a thermometer, check the temperature of the water quickly since the temperature can drop quite a bit once the lid is removed.

4. The temperature should be at 185°F. If it's too hot, your meal cooked for 8 hours would likely be overdone. If the temperature is below 185°, it could be the cooker does not heat food to an adequate temperature to avoid the growth of harmful bacteria.

Cleaning Your Slow Cooker

Removable stoneware inserts make cleanup a breeze. Be sure to cool the insert before adding water for cleaning to avoid cracking.

Wash the insert in the dishwasher or in warm, soapy water. Avoid using abrasive cleansers since they may scratch the stoneware.

To remove mineral stains on a crockery insert, fill the cooker with hot water and 1 cup white vinegar; cover. Turn heat control to high for 2 hours. Then empty. When cool, wash with hot, sudsy water and a cloth or sponge. Rinse well and dry with a towel.

To remove water marks from a highly glazed crockery insert, rub the surface with vegetable oil and allow to stand for 2 hours before washing with hot sudsy water.

Do not immerse the metal base unit. Clean it with a damp sponge.

Special Uses

Don't forget your slow cooker when you go camping, provided electricity is available. It's a handy appliance when space is limited and you want "set-it-and-forget-it" meals.

Reheating foods in a slow cooker is not recommended. Cooked food can be brought to steaming on the stovetop or in the microwave and then put into a preheated slow cooker to keep hot for serving.

Use a slow cooker on a buffet table to keep soup, stew or mashed potatoes hot.

appetizers & beverages

Whether you're planning a family feast or a casual get-together for friends, set up your slow cooker to handle the appetizers and beverages. While you focus on the final details of your meal, simple starters—like this Pizza Dip on page 16— can simmer and finish cooking.

The dips, salsas, fondues, finger foods and drinks featured here call for everyday ingredients and little prep. So it's easy and affordable to add an extra course to a weeknight dinner or a Saturday celebration!

hot bacon cheese dip

COOK TIME: 2 HOURS

Suzanne Whitaker
Knoxville, Tennessee

I've tried several appetizers before, but this one is a surefire people-pleaser. The thick dip has lots of bacon flavor and keeps friends happily munching. I serve it with tortilla chips or sliced French bread.

> 2 packages (8 ounces *each*) cream cheese, cubed
>
> 4 cups (16 ounces) shredded cheddar cheese
>
> 1 cup half-and-half cream
>
> 2 teaspoons Worcestershire sauce
>
> 1 teaspoon dried minced onion
>
> 1 teaspoon prepared mustard
>
> 16 bacon strips, cooked and crumbled

Tortilla chips *and/or* French bread slices

■ In a 1-1/2-qt. slow cooker, combine the first six ingredients. Cover and cook for 2 hours on high or until cheeses are melted, stirring occasionally. Just before serving, stir in bacon. Serve warm with tortilla chips and/or bread.

YIELD: 4 cups.

SLOW COOKER TIP:
Avoid peeking into the slow cooker during the cooking process to check on your food. Taking the lid off, even one time, causes the slow cooker to lose a significant amount of heat, requiring a longer cooking time.

sweet-and-sour smokies

COOK TIME: 4 HOURS

Debi Hetland
Rochelle, Illinois

This warm appetizer is so simple to make but so tasty. I use cherry pie filling, chunks of pineapple and a little brown sugar to create a fruity sauce that's just perfect for mini smoked sausage links. These smokies have been a hit at potlucks and parties for every occasion.

> 2 packages (16 ounces *each*) miniature smoked sausages
>
> 2 cans (21 ounces *each*) cherry pie filling
>
> 1 can (20 ounces) pineapple chunks, drained
>
> 3 tablespoons brown sugar

■ Place the sausages in a 3-qt. slow cooker. In a large bowl, combine the pie filling, pineapple and brown sugar and pour over sausages. Cover and cook on low for 4 hours.

YIELD: 16-20 servings.

buffet meatballs

COOK TIME: 4 HOURS

Janet Anderson
Carson City, Nevada

I need only five ingredients to fix these easy appetizers. Grape juice and apple jelly are the secrets behind the sweet yet tangy sauce that complements convenient packaged meatballs.

> 1 cup grape juice
>
> 1 cup apple jelly
>
> 1 cup ketchup
>
> 1 can (8 ounces) tomato sauce
>
> 4 pounds frozen Italian-style meatballs

■ In a small saucepan, combine the juice, jelly, ketchup and tomato sauce. Cook and stir over medium heat until jelly is melted; remove from the heat. Place meatballs in a 5-qt. slow cooker. Pour sauce over the top and gently stir to coat. Cover and cook on low for 4 hours or until heated through.

YIELD: about 11 dozen.

HOT BACON CHEESE DIP

BUFFET MEATBALLS

reuben spread

COOK TIME: 2 HOURS

Rosalie Fuchs
Paynesville, Minnesota

I received the recipe for this hearty spread from my daughter. It tastes just like a Reuben sandwich. I keep the slow cooker plugged in while serving it, so it stays warm.

- **1 jar (16 ounces) sauerkraut, rinsed and drained**
- **1 package (8 ounces) cream cheese, cubed**
- **2 cups (8 ounces) shredded Swiss cheese**
- **1 package (3 ounces) deli corned beef, chopped**
- **3 tablespoons Thousand Island salad dressing**

Snack rye bread *or* crackers

- In a 1-1/2-qt. slow cooker, combine the first five ingredients. Cover and cook for 2 hours or until cheeses are melted; stir to blend. Serve warm with bread or crackers.

YIELD: 3-1/2 cups.

hearty broccoli dip

COOK TIME: 2 TO 3 HOURS

Sue Call
Beech Grove, Indiana

You'll need just five ingredients to stir up this no-fuss appetizer. People often ask me to bring this creamy dip to potlucks and parties. I never leave with leftovers.

- **1 pound ground beef**
- **1 pound process cheese (Velveeta), cubed**
- **1 can (10-3/4 ounces) condensed cream of mushroom soup, undiluted**
- **1 package (10 ounces) frozen chopped broccoli, thawed**
- **2 tablespoons salsa**

Tortilla chips

- In a skillet, cook beef over medium heat until no longer pink; drain. Transfer to a 3-qt. slow cooker. Add cheese, soup, broccoli and salsa; mix well.
- Cover and cook on low for 2-3 hours or until heated through, stirring after 1 hour. Serve with tortilla chips.

YIELD: 5-1/2 cups.

mulled grape cider

COOK TIME: 3 HOURS

Sharon Harmon
Orange, Massachusetts

I created this recipe one year when I tried to make grape jelly and ended up with jars of grape syrup instead. So I simmered it up like hot apple cider, and my friends raved over it.

- **5 pounds Concord grapes**
- **8 cups water, *divided***

1-1/2 cups sugar

- **8 whole cloves**
- **4 cinnamon sticks (4 inches)**

Dash ground nutmeg

- In a large saucepan or Dutch oven, combine grapes and 2 cups water; bring to a boil, stirring constantly. Press through a strainer; reserve juice and discard skins and seeds.
- Pour juice through a double layer of cheesecloth into a 3-qt. slow cooker. Add sugar, cloves, cinnamon sticks, nutmeg and remaining water. Heat on low for 3 hours. Discard cloves and cinnamon sticks before serving.

YIELD: 10-12 servings (2-3/4 quarts).

SLOW COOKER TIP: Fill the slow cooker no less than half full and no more than two-thirds full. Keep the lid in place, removing it only to stir the food or check for doneness.

REUBEN SPREAD

pizza dip

COOK TIME: 1-1/2 TO 2 HOURS

Sara Nowacki
Franklin, Wisconsin

Everybody loves this simple dip. It has all the cheesy goodness of real pizza. If you have any left over, spoon it on toasted English muffins for a great open-faced sandwich.

> 2 packages (8 ounces *each*) cream cheese, cubed
>
> 1 can (14 ounces) pizza sauce
>
> 1 package (8 ounces) sliced pepperoni, chopped
>
> 1 can (3.8 ounces) chopped ripe olives, drained
>
> 2 cups (8 ounces) shredded part-skim mozzarella cheese

Bagel chips *or* garlic toast

■ Place the cream cheese in a 3-qt. slow cooker. Combine the pizza sauce, pepperoni and olives; pour over cream cheese. Top with mozzarella cheese.

■ Cover and cook on low for 1-1/2 to 2 hours or until cheese is melted. Stir; serve warm with bagel chips or garlic toast.

YIELD: 5-1/2 cups.

old-fashioned peach butter

COOK TIME: 9 TO 11 HOURS

Marilou Robinson
Portland, Oregon

Using the slow cooker eliminates much of the stirring required when simmering fruit butter on the stovetop. It's great on toast.

> 14 cups coarsely chopped peeled fresh *or* frozen peaches (about 5-1/2 pounds)
>
> 2-1/2 cups sugar
>
> 4-1/2 teaspoons lemon juice
>
> 1-1/2 teaspoons ground cinnamon
>
> 3/4 teaspoon ground cloves
>
> 1/2 cup quick-cooking tapioca

■ In a large bowl, combine the peaches, sugar, lemon juice, cinnamon and cloves; mix well. Transfer to a 5-qt. slow cooker. Cover and cook on low for 8-10 hours or until peaches are very soft, stirring occasionally.

■ Stir in tapioca. Cook, uncovered, on high for 1 hour or until thickened. Pour into jars or freezer containers; cool to room temperature, about 1 hour. Refrigerate or freeze.

YIELD: 9 cups.

moist 'n' tender wings

COOK TIME: 8 HOURS

Sharon Morcilio
Joshua Tree, California

These no-fuss wings are fall-off-the-bone tender. Chili sauce offers a bit of spice while molasses lends a hint of sweetness. They're great for parties or a meal with a side dish of rice.

> 25 whole chicken wings (about 5 pounds)
>
> 1 bottle (12 ounces) chili sauce
>
> 1/4 cup lemon juice
>
> 1/4 cup molasses
>
> 2 tablespoons Worcestershire sauce
>
> 6 garlic cloves, minced
>
> 1 tablespoon chili powder
>
> 1 tablespoon salsa
>
> 1 teaspoon garlic salt
>
> 3 drops hot pepper sauce

■ Cut chicken wings into three sections; discard wing tips. Place the wings in a 5-qt. slow cooker.

■ In a bowl, combine the remaining ingredients; pour over chicken. Stir to coat. Cover and cook on low for 8 hours or until chicken is tender.

YIELD: about 4 dozen.

EDITOR'S NOTE: 5 pounds of uncooked chicken wing sections (wingettes) may be substituted for the whole chicken wings. Omit the first step.

> **SLOW COOKER TIP:**
> Let your slow cooker insert cool before washing. As sturdy as stoneware seems, the shock of pouring cold water into a hot insert could cause it to crack.

PIZZA DIP

MOIST 'N' TENDER WINGS

fruit salsa

COOK TIME: 2 HOURS

Florence Buchkowsky
Prince Albert, Saskatchewan

I serve this fruity salsa anywhere I use ordinary salsa. My son and I experimented with different ingredients to find the combination we liked best. Using the slow cooker minimizes prep time and maximizes the flavor.

- **1 can (11 ounces) mandarin oranges, undrained**
- **1 can (8-1/2 ounces) sliced peaches, undrained**
- **1 can (8 ounces) pineapple tidbits, undrained**
- **1 medium onion, chopped**
- **1/2 *each* medium green, sweet red and yellow pepper, chopped**
- **3 garlic cloves, minced**
- **3 tablespoons cornstarch**
- **4 teaspoons vinegar**

Tortilla chips

- In a 3-qt. slow cooker, combine the fruit, onion, peppers, garlic, cornstarch and vinegar; stir well.

- Cover and cook on high for 2 hours or until thickened and heated through, stirring occasionally. Serve with tortilla chips.

YIELD: 4 cups.

orange spiced cider

COOK TIME: 2 TO 3 HOURS

Erika Reinhard
Colorado Springs, Colorado

Every time I serve this wonderful hot beverage, someone asks for the recipe. Orange juice adds a bit of sweetness while red-hot candies are a fun substitute for traditional cinnamon sticks.

- **4 cups unsweetened apple juice**
- **1 can (12 ounces) orange juice concentrate, thawed**
- **1/2 cup water**
- **1 tablespoon red-hot candies**
- **1/2 teaspoon ground nutmeg**
- **1 teaspoon whole cloves**

Fresh orange slices and cinnamon sticks, optional

- In a 3-qt. slow cooker, combine the first five ingredients. Place cloves in a double thickness of cheesecloth; bring up corners of cloth and tie with kitchen string to form a bag. Add bag to slow cooker.

- Cover and cook on low for 2-3 hours or until heated through. Before serving, discard spice bag and stir cider. Garnish with orange slices and cinnamon sticks if desired.

YIELD: 8 servings.

party sausages

COOK TIME: 1 TO 2 HOURS

Jo Ann Renner
Xenia, Ohio

Don't want any leftovers after a party? Serve these sausages! I've never had even one end up uneaten.

- **2 pounds fully cooked smoked sausage links**
- **1 bottle (8 ounces) Catalina salad dressing**
- **1 bottle (8 ounces) Russian salad dressing**
- **1/2 cup packed brown sugar**
- **1/2 cup pineapple juice**

- Cut sausages diagonally into 1/2-in. slices; cook in a skillet over medium heat until lightly browned.

- Transfer sausages to a 3-qt. slow cooker; discard drippings. Add dressings, sugar and juice to skillet; cook and stir over medium-low heat until sugar is dissolved. Pour over sausages.

- Heat on low for 1-2 hours or until heated through. Serve hot.

YIELD: 16 servings.

EDITOR'S NOTE: French salad dressing may be substituted for one or both dressings.

SLOW COOKER TIP: Slow cooker inserts are fairly easy to clean with hot, soapy water. For even faster cleaning, coat the bottom and sides of the insert with nonstick cooking spray before putting in the food.

FRUIT SALSA

nacho rice dip

SERVE IN A SLOW COOKER

Audra Hungate
Holt, Missouri

Spanish rice mix adds an interesting twist to this effortless appetizer. Every time I serve this dip at get-togethers, my guests gobble it up.

> 1 package (6.8 ounces) Spanish rice and vermicelli mix
>
> 2 tablespoons butter
>
> 2 cups water
>
> 1 can (14-1/2 ounces) diced tomatoes, undrained
>
> 1 pound ground beef
>
> 1 pound (16 ounces) process American cheese, cubed
>
> 1 can (14-1/2 ounces) stewed tomatoes
>
> 1 jar (8 ounces) process cheese sauce

Tortilla chips

- In a large saucepan, cook rice mix in butter until golden. Stir in water and diced tomatoes; bring to a boil. Reduce heat; cover and simmer for 15-20 minutes or until rice is tender.

- Meanwhile, in a skillet, cook beef until no longer pink. Drain and add to the rice. Stir in cheese, stewed tomatoes and cheese sauce; cook and stir until cheese is melted. Transfer to a 3-qt. slow cooker; cover and keep warm on low. Serve with tortilla chips.

YIELD: about 8 cups.

SLOW COOKER TIP:
Because of how a slow cooker works, it is not necessary to stir the food unless a recipe specifically calls for stirring.

barbecue sausage bites

COOK TIME: 2-1/2 TO 3 HOURS

Rebekah Randolph
Greer, South Carolina

A popular, sweet-and-tangy appetizer, this dish pairs pineapple chunks with barbecue sauce and three kinds of sausage.

> 1 package (1 pound) miniature smoked sausages
>
> 3/4 pound fully cooked bratwurst
>
> 3/4 pound smoked kielbasa *or* Polish sausage
>
> 1 bottle (18 ounces) barbecue sauce
>
> 2/3 cup orange marmalade
>
> 1/2 teaspoon ground mustard
>
> 1/8 teaspoon ground allspice
>
> 1 can (20 ounces) pineapple chunks, drained

- In a 3-qt. slow cooker, combine the sausages. In a small bowl, whisk the barbecue sauce, marmalade, mustard and allspice. Pour over sausage mixture; stir to coat.

- Cover and cook on high for 2-1/2 to 3 hours or until heated through. Stir in pineapple. Serve with toothpicks.

YIELD: 12-14 servings.

BARBECUE SAUSAGE BITES

hot spiced lemon drink

COOK TIME: 2 TO 3 HOURS

Mandy Wright
Springville, Utah

I received this recipe from a lady in our church who is an excellent cook. She has shared several slow cooker recipes with us. We really enjoy the tropical flavor of this warm citrus punch. This is great for a special cool-weather meal or holiday brunch. Garnish each glass with a cinnamon stick.

> 2-1/2 quarts water
>
> 2 cups sugar
>
> 1-1/2 cups orange juice
>
> 1/2 cup plus 2 tablespoons lemon juice
>
> 1/4 cup pineapple juice
>
> 1 cinnamon stick (3 inches)
>
> 1/2 teaspoon whole cloves

- In a 5-qt. slow cooker, combine the water, sugar and juices. Place cinnamon stick and cloves on a double thickness of cheesecloth; bring up corners of cloth and tie with kitchen string to form a bag. Place in slow cooker.

- Cover and cook on low for 2-3 hours or until heated through. Discard spice bag.

YIELD: about 3 quarts.

HOT SPICED LEMON DRINK

taco joe dip

COOK TIME: 5 TO 7 HOURS

Lang Secrest
Sierra Vista, Arizona

This recipe was given to us by our daughter. My husband and I love it. Because it's made in a slow cooker, it's great for parties or busy days.

- 1 can (16 ounces) kidney beans, rinsed and drained
- 1 can (15-1/4 ounces) whole kernel corn, drained
- 1 can (15 ounces) black beans, rinsed and drained
- 1 can (14-1/2 ounces) stewed tomatoes
- 1 can (8 ounces) tomato sauce
- 1 can (4 ounces) chopped green chilies, drained
- 1 envelope taco seasoning
- 1/2 cup chopped onion

Tortilla chips

- In a 3-qt. slow cooker, combine the first eight ingredients. Cover and cook on low for 5-7 hours. Serve with tortilla chips.

YIELD: about 7 cups.

EDITOR'S NOTE: To make Taco Joe Soup, add a 29-ounce can of tomato sauce to the slow cooker. It will serve 6-8.

tangy pork meatballs

SERVE IN A SLOW COOKER

Katie Koziolek
Hartland, Minnesota

Buffet "grazers" stampede for these meatballs! The mouth-watering morsels go so fast, I often make several batches at once. Barbecue sauce adds a nice bite to the mildly seasoned ground pork.

- 2 eggs, beaten
- 2/3 cup dried bread crumbs
- 2 tablespoons dried minced onion
- 2 teaspoons seasoned salt
- 2 pounds ground pork

SAUCE:

- 1-1/2 cups ketchup
- 1 can (8 ounces) tomato sauce
- 3 tablespoons Worcestershire sauce
- 2 to 3 tablespoons cider vinegar
- 2 teaspoons Liquid Smoke, optional

- In a bowl, combine the eggs, bread crumbs, onion and salt. Crumble pork over mixture and mix well. Shape into 3/4-in. balls; place on a greased 15-in. x 10-in. x 1-in. baking pan. Bake at 400° for 15 minutes or until the meat is no longer pink.

- Meanwhile in a large saucepan, combine sauce ingredients. Simmer, uncovered, for 10 minutes, stirring occasionally. Add meatballs. Serve in a 3-qt. slow cooker.

YIELD: about 1-1/2 dozen.

cheddar fondue

SERVE IN A SLOW COOKER

Norene Wright
Manilla, Indiana

This cheesy blend, sparked with mustard and Worcestershire sauce, is yummy. It's great with bread, veggies or ham!

- 1/4 cup butter
- 1/4 cup all-purpose flour
- 1/2 teaspoon salt
- 1/4 teaspoon pepper
- 1/4 teaspoon ground mustard
- 1/4 teaspoon Worcestershire sauce
- 1-1/2 cups milk
- 2 cups (8 ounces) shredded cheddar cheese

Bread cubes, ham cubes, bite-size sausage *and/or* broccoli florets

- In a saucepan, melt butter; stir in flour, salt, pepper, mustard and Worcestershire sauce until smooth. Gradually add milk. Bring to a boil; cook and stir for 2 minutes or until thickened. Reduce heat. Add the cheese; cook and stir until melted.

- Transfer to a 3-qt. slow cooker; keep warm. Serve with bread, ham, sausage and/or broccoli.

YIELD: 2-1/2 cups.

TACO JOE DIP

paddy's reuben dip

COOK TIME: 2 HOURS

Mary Jane Kimmes
Hastings, Minnesota

This slow-cooked spread tastes just like the popular Reuben sandwich. Even when I double the recipe, I end up with an empty dish.

- **4 packages (4-1/2 ounces *each*) deli corned beef, finely chopped**
- **1 package (8 ounces) cream cheese, cubed**
- **1 can (8 ounces) sauerkraut, rinsed and drained**
- **1 cup (8 ounces) sour cream**
- **1 cup (4 ounces) shredded Swiss cheese**

Rye bread *or* crackers

- In a mini slow cooker, combine the first five ingredients. Cover and cook on low for 2 hours or until cheese is melted; stir until blended. Serve warm with bread or crackers.

YIELD: about 4 cups.

slow-cooked smokies

COOK TIME: 6 TO 7 HOURS

Sundra Hauck
Bogalusa, Louisiana

I like to include these little smokies smothered in barbecue sauce on all my appetizer buffets since they're popular with both children and adults.

- **1 package (1 pound) miniature smoked sausages**
- **1 bottle (28 ounces) barbecue sauce**
- **1-1/4 cups water**
- **3 tablespoons Worcestershire sauce**
- **3 tablespoons steak sauce**
- **1/2 teaspoon pepper**

- In a 3-qt. slow cooker, combine all ingredients; mix well. Cover and cook on low for 6-7 hours. Serve with a slotted spoon.

YIELD: 8 servings.

tangy barbecue wings

COOK TIME: 3 TO 4 HOURS

Sherry Pitzer
Troy, Missouri

When I took these savory, slow-cooked appetizers to work, they were gone before I even got a bite!

- **25 whole chicken wings (about 5 pounds)**
- **2-1/2 cups hot and spicy ketchup**
- **2/3 cup white vinegar**
- **1/2 cup plus 2 tablespoons honey**
- **1/2 cup molasses**
- **1 teaspoon salt**
- **1 teaspoon Worcestershire sauce**
- **1/2 teaspoon onion powder**
- **1/2 teaspoon chili powder**
- **1/2 to 1 teaspoon Liquid Smoke, optional**

- Cut chicken wings into three sections; discard wing tip sections.

- Place chicken wings in two greased 15-in. x 10-in. x 1-in. baking pans. Bake, uncovered, at 375° for 30 minutes; drain. Turn wings; bake 20-25 minutes longer or until juices run clear.

- Meanwhile, in a large saucepan, combine the remaining ingredients. Bring to a boil. Reduce heat; simmer, uncovered, for 25-30 minutes. Drain wings; place a third of them in a 5-qt. slow cooker. Top with about 1 cup sauce. Repeat layers twice. Cover and cook on low for 3-4 hours. Stir before serving.

YIELD: about 4 dozen.

EDITOR'S NOTE: 5 pounds of uncooked chicken wing sections (wingettes) may be substituted for the whole chicken wings. Omit the first step.

PADDY'S REUBEN DIP

RIVAL LITTLE DIPPER

TANGY BARBECUE WINGS

hot crab dip

COOK TIME: 3 TO 4 HOURS

Teri Rasey-Bolf
Cadillac, Michigan

I have six children and one grandchild, work full time, and coach soccer and football. So I appreciate recipes like this one that are easy to assemble. The rich, creamy dip is a fun appetizer for any gathering.

- 1/2 cup milk
- 1/3 cup salsa
- 3 packages (8 ounces *each*) cream cheese, cubed
- 2 packages (8 ounces *each*) imitation crabmeat, flaked
- 1 cup thinly sliced green onions
- 1 can (4 ounces) chopped green chilies

Assorted crackers

- ■ Combine milk and salsa. Transfer to a 3-qt. slow cooker coated with nonstick cooking spray. Stir in the cream cheese, crab, onions and chilies.

- ■ Cover and cook on low for 3-4 hours, stirring every 30 minutes. Serve with crackers.

YIELD: about 5 cups.

tropical tea

COOK TIME: 2 TO 4 HOURS

Irene Helen Zundel
Carmichaels, Pennyslvania

I like to brew a batch of this fragrant, flavorful tea in a slow cooker for my family gatherings. It's always a hit!

- 6 cups boiling water
- 6 individual tea bags
- 1-1/2 cups orange juice
- 1-1/2 cups unsweetened pineapple juice
- 1/3 cup sugar
- 1 medium navel orange, sliced and halved
- 2 tablespoons honey

- ■ In a 5-qt. slow cooker, combine boiling water and tea bags. Cover and let stand for 5 minutes. Discard tea bags. Stir in the remaining ingredients.

- ■ Cover and cook on low for 2-4 hours or until heated through. Serve warm.

YIELD: about 2-1/2 quarts.

parmesan fondue

SERVE IN A SLOW COOKER

Gwynne Fleener
Coeur d'Alene, Idaho

This recipe was given to me many years ago at a New Year's potluck. Since then, it has been a tradition to serve it at our holiday open house. The creamy mixture is always a hit.

- 1-1/2 to 2 cups milk
- 2 packages (8 ounces *each*) cream cheese, cubed
- 1-1/2 cups grated Parmesan cheese
- 1/2 teaspoon garlic salt
- 1 loaf (1 pound) French bread, cubed

- ■ In a large saucepan, cook and stir the milk and cream cheese over low heat until cheese is melted. Stir in Parmesan cheese and garlic salt; cook and stir until heated through.

- ■ Transfer to a mini slow cooker; keep warm. Serve with bread cubes.

YIELD: about 3-1/2 cups.

SLOW COOKER TIP: Natural cheeses should be avoided because they tend to break down. You can use process cheese or add natural cheese late in cooking. Milk will curdle over long cooking times, so substitute evaporated milk or stir in heavy whipping cream or sour cream near the end of cooking.

HOT CRAB DIP

peppered meatballs

COOK TIME: 2-1/2 HOURS

Darla Schroeder
Stanley, North Dakota

Plenty of ground pepper gives these saucy meatballs their irresistible zest. They're so hearty, I sometimes serve them over noodles as a main course.

- 1/2 cup sour cream
- 2 teaspoons grated Parmesan *or* Romano cheese
- 2 to 3 teaspoons pepper
- 1 teaspoon salt
- 1 teaspoon dry bread crumbs
- 1/2 teaspoon garlic powder
- 1-1/2 pounds ground beef

SAUCE:

- 1 cup (8 ounces) sour cream
- 1 can (10-3/4 ounces) condensed cream of mushroom soup, undiluted
- 2 teaspoons dill weed
- 1/2 teaspoon sugar
- 1/2 teaspoon pepper
- 1/4 teaspoon garlic powder

■ In a bowl, combine sour cream and Parmesan cheese. Add pepper, salt, bread crumbs and garlic powder. Crumble meat over mixture and mix well. Shape into 1-in. balls. Place in a greased 15-in. x 10-in. x 1-in. baking pan. Bake at 350° for 20-25 minutes or until no longer pink.

■ Transfer meatballs to a 3-qt. slow cooker. Combine the sauce ingredients; pour over meatballs. Cover and cook on high for 2 hours or until heated through.

YIELD: 1-1/2 dozen (2 cups sauce).

hot chili dip

COOK TIME: 1 TO 2 HOURS

Nikki Rosati
Franksville, Wisconsin

I first made this zippy dip for my husband's birthday party. So many people asked for the recipe that I made photocopies to pass out.

- 1 jar (24 ounces) salsa
- 1 can (15 ounces) chili with beans
- 2 cans (2-1/4 ounces *each*) sliced ripe olives, drained
- 12 ounces process cheese (Velveeta), cubed

Tortilla chips

■ In a small slow cooker, combine the salsa, chili and olives. Stir in cheese.

■ Cover and cook on low for 1-2 hours or until cheese is melted, stirring halfway through. Serve with chips.

YIELD: about 2 cups.

tomato fondue

SERVE IN A SLOW COOKER

Marlene Muckenhirn
Delano, Minnesota

Both the young and young at heart will gobble up this cheesy tomato fondue when served alongside hot dogs and bread cubes.

- 1 garlic clove, halved
- 1/2 cup condensed tomato soup, undiluted
- 1-1/2 teaspoons ground mustard
- 1-1/2 teaspoons Worcestershire sauce
- 10 slices process American cheese, cubed
- 1/4 to 1/3 cup milk
- 1 package (16 ounces) miniature hot dogs *or* smoked sausage, warmed

Cubed French bread

■ Rub garlic clove over the bottom and sides of a small slow cooker; discard garlic and set slow cooker aside.

■ In a small saucepan, combine the tomato soup, mustard and Worcestershire sauce; heat through. Stir in cheese until melted. Stir in milk; heat through.

■ Transfer to prepared slow cooker and keep warm. Serve with hot dogs and bread cubes.

YIELD: about 1 cup.

PEPPERED MEATBALLS

sweet 'n' spicy meatballs

SERVE IN A SLOW COOKER

Genie Brown
Roanoke, Virginia

You'll usually find a batch of these meatballs in my freezer. The slightly sweet sauce nicely complements the spicy pork sausage.

- 2 pounds bulk hot pork sausage
- 1 egg, lightly beaten
- 1 cup packed brown sugar
- 1 cup red wine vinegar
- 1 cup ketchup
- 1 tablespoon soy sauce
- 1 teaspoon ground ginger

- In a large bowl, combine the sausage and egg. Shape into 1-in. balls. Place in a greased 15-in. x 10-in. x 1-in. baking pan. Bake at 400° for 15-20 minutes or until meat is no longer pink.

- Meanwhile, in a saucepan, combine the brown sugar, vinegar, ketchup, soy sauce and ginger. Bring to a boil. Reduce heat; simmer, uncovered, until sugar is dissolved.

- Transfer meatballs to a 3-qt. slow cooker. Add the sauce and stir gently to coat. Cover and keep warm on low until serving.

YIELD: about 4 dozen.

SLOW COOKER TIP:
To boost color and eye appeal of slow-cooked foods, use bright garnishes such as cheese, sour cream, tomatoes, fresh parsley and red peppers.

spiced apricot cider

COOK TIME: 2 HOURS

Connie Cummings
Gloucester, New Jersey

You'll need just six ingredients to simmer together this hot spiced beverage. Each delicious mugful is rich with apricot flavor. It's a real treat to serve at any occasion.

- 2 cans (12 ounces *each*) apricot nectar
- 2 cups water
- 1/4 cup lemon juice
- 1/4 cup sugar
- 2 whole cloves
- 2 cinnamon sticks (3 inches)

- In a 3-qt. slow cooker, combine all ingredients; mix well. Cover and cook on low for 2 hours or until cider reaches desired temperature. Remove cloves and cinnamon sticks before serving.

YIELD: 6 servings.

SPICED APRICOT CIDER

slow-cooked salsa

COOK TIME: 2-1/2 TO 3 HOURS

Toni Menard
Lompoc, California

I love the fresh taste of homemade salsa, but as a working mother, I don't have much time to make it. So I came up with this slow-cooked version that practically makes itself!

- 10 plum tomatoes, cored
- 2 garlic cloves
- 1 small onion, cut into wedges
- 2 jalapeno peppers
- 1/4 cup cilantro leaves
- 1/2 teaspoon salt, optional

- Cut a small slit in two tomatoes; insert a garlic clove into each slit. Place tomatoes and onion in a 3-qt. slow cooker.

- Cut stem off jalapenos; remove seeds if a milder salsa is desired. Place jalapenos in the slow cooker.

- Cover and cook on high for 2-1/2 to 3 hours or until vegetables are softened (some may brown slightly); cool.

- In a blender or food processor, combine the tomato mixture, cilantro and salt if desired; cover and process until smooth. Refrigerate leftovers.

YIELD: about 2 cups.

EDITOR'S NOTE: When cutting or seeding hot peppers, use rubber or plastic gloves to protect your hands. Avoid touching your face.

SLOW COOKER TIP:
A good rule of thumb is to assume that 1 hour of cooking on high is equal to about 2 to 2-1/2 hours on low.

SLOW-COOKED SALSA

cranberry apple cider

COOK TIME: 2 HOURS

Jennifer Naboka
North Plainfield, New Jersey
I love to start this soothing cider in the slow cooker on nights before my husband goes hunting. Then he can fill his thermos and take it with him out into the cold. The cider has a terrific fruit flavor we both enjoy.

> 4 cups water
>
> 4 cups apple juice
>
> 1 can (12 ounces) frozen apple juice concentrate, thawed
>
> 1 medium apple, peeled and sliced
>
> 1 cup fresh *or* frozen cranberries
>
> 1 medium orange, peeled and sectioned
>
> 1 cinnamon stick

■ In a 3-qt. slow cooker, combine all ingredients; mix well. Cover and cook on low for 2 hours or until cider reaches desired temperature.

■ Discard cinnamon stick. If desired, remove fruit with a slotted spoon before serving.

YIELD: 10 servings (about 2-1/2 quarts).

cheesy pizza fondue

COOK TIME: 4 TO 6 HOURS

Nel Carver
Moscow, Idaho
I keep these dip ingredients on hand for spur-of-the-moment gatherings. Folks can't resist chewy bread cubes coated with a savory sauce.

> 1 jar (29 ounces) meatless spaghetti sauce
>
> 2 cups (8 ounces) shredded mozzarella cheese
>
> 1/4 cup shredded Parmesan cheese
>
> 2 teaspoons dried oregano
>
> 1 teaspoon dried minced onion
>
> 1/4 teaspoon garlic powder
>
> 1 unsliced loaf (1 pound) Italian bread, cut into cubes

■ In a 1-1/2-qt. slow cooker, combine the spaghetti sauce, cheeses, oregano, onion and garlic powder.

■ Cook for 4-6 hours or until cheese is melted and sauce is hot. Serve with bread cubes.

YIELD: 12 servings (4 cups).

meaty chili dip

SERVE IN A SLOW COOKER

Karen Kiel
Camdenton, Missouri
A meaty dish like this is a must for the men in my family. They scrape the serving bowl clean! For the best dipping, use large corn chips.

> 1 pound ground beef
>
> 1 medium green pepper, chopped
>
> 1 cup water
>
> 1 can (6 ounces) tomato paste
>
> 1 package (3 ounces) cream cheese, cubed
>
> 1 envelope chili seasoning mix

Corn chips

■ In a large skillet, cook beef and green pepper over medium heat until meat is no longer pink; drain. Add the water, tomato paste, cream cheese and chili seasoning mix. Bring to a boil. Reduce heat; simmer, uncovered, until cheese is melted.

■ Transfer to a small slow cooker to keep warm. Serve with corn chips.

YIELD: 3 cups.

SLOW COOKER TIP: Store leftovers in shallow, covered containers and refrigerate within two hours after cooking is finished. Reheating leftovers in a slow cooker is not recommended. However, cooked food can be reheated on the stovetop or in a microwave and then put into a preheated slow cooker to keep hot for serving.

CRANBERRY APPLE CIDER

marinated chicken wings

COOK TIME: 3-1/2 TO 4 HOURS

Janie Botting
Sultan, Washington

I've made these nicely flavored wings many times for get-togethers. They're so moist and tender...I always get lots of compliments and many requests for the recipe.

> 20 whole chicken wings (about 4 pounds)
>
> 2 cups soy sauce
>
> 1/2 cup white wine *or* chicken broth
>
> 1/2 cup vegetable oil
>
> 2 to 3 garlic cloves, minced
>
> 2 tablespoons sugar
>
> 2 teaspoons ground ginger

■ Cut chicken wings into three sections; discard wing tips. Place wings in a large resealable heavy-duty plastic bag or 13-in. x 9-in. x 2-in. baking dish.

■ In a bowl, combine remaining ingredients; mix well. Pour half of the sauce over chicken; turn to coat. Seal or cover the chicken and remaining sauce; refrigerate overnight. Drain chicken, discarding the marinade.

■ Place chicken in a 5-qt. slow cooker; top with reserved sauce. Cover and cook on low for 3-1/2 to 4 hours or until chicken juices run clear. Transfer wings to a serving dish; discard cooking juices.

YIELD: 18-20 servings.

EDITOR'S NOTE: 4 pounds of uncooked chicken wing sections may be substituted for the whole chicken wings. Omit the first step of the recipe.

slow-cooker cheese dip

COOK TIME: 4 HOURS

Marion Bartone
Conneaut, Ohio

I brought this slightly spicy cheese dip to a gathering with friends, and it was a huge hit!

> 1 pound ground beef
>
> 1/2 pound bulk hot pork sausage
>
> 2 pounds process cheese (Velveeta), cubed
>
> 2 cans (10 ounces *each*) diced tomatoes and green chilies, undrained

Tortilla chips

■ In a skillet, cook beef and sausage over medium heat until no longer pink; drain. Transfer to a 5-qt. slow cooker. Add cheese and tomatoes; mix well.

■ Cover and cook on low for 4 hours or until the cheese is melted, stirring occasionally. Serve with tortilla chips.

YIELD: 3 quarts.

pizza spread

SERVE IN A SLOW COOKER

Beverly Mons
Middletown, New York

For a satisfying snack, spread slices of French bread with this thick, cheesy mixture. It's a very adaptable recipe. It would also be good with Italian sausage instead of ground beef.

> 1 pound ground beef
>
> 1 jar (26 ounces) marinara *or* spaghetti sauce
>
> 1 teaspoon dried oregano
>
> 4 cups (16 ounces) shredded mozzarella cheese
>
> 1 loaf Italian *or* French bread, cubed *or* sliced

■ In a saucepan, cook beef over medium heat until no longer pink; drain. Stir in marinara sauce and oregano. Gradually stir in cheese until melted.

■ Pour into a small slow cooker to keep warm. Serve with bread.

YIELD: 8-10 servings.

MARINATED CHICKEN WINGS

creamy chipped beef fondue

SERVE IN A SLOW COOKER

Beth Fox
Lawrence, Kansas
My mother often served fondue during the holidays and I've since followed in that tradition. It's nice to offer a hearty appetizer that requires very little work.

1-1/3 to 1-1/2 cups milk

2 packages (8 ounces *each*) cream cheese, cubed

1 package (2-1/2 ounces) thinly sliced dried beef, chopped

1/4 cup chopped green onions

2 teaspoons ground mustard

1 loaf (1 pound) French bread, cubed

- In a saucepan, heat milk and cream cheese over medium heat; stir until smooth. Stir in beef, onions and mustard; heat through.

- Transfer to a fondue pot or small slow cooker; keep warm. Serve with bread cubes.

YIELD: about 4 cups.

slow-cooker party mix

COOK TIME: 3 HOURS

Dana Hughes
Gresham, Oregon
This mildly seasoned snack mix is always a party favorite. Served warm from a slow cooker, the munchable mixture is very satisfying.

4 cups Wheat Chex

4 cups Cheerios

3 cups pretzel sticks

1 can (12 ounces) salted peanuts

1/4 cup butter, melted

2 to 3 tablespoons grated Parmesan cheese

1 teaspoon celery salt

1/2 to 3/4 teaspoon seasoned salt

- In a 5-qt. slow cooker, combine cereals, pretzels and peanuts. Combine butter, Parmesan cheese, celery salt and seasoned salt; drizzle over cereal mixture and mix well.

- Cover and cook on low for up to 3 hours, stirring every 30 minutes. Serve warm or at room temperature.

YIELD: about 3 quarts.

simmered smoked links

COOK TIME: 4 HOURS

Maxine Cenker
Weirton, West Virginia
A tasty, sweet-sour sauce glazes bite-size sausages in this recipe. Serve these effortless appetizers with toothpicks at parties or get-togethers.

2 packages (16 ounces *each*) miniature smoked sausage links

1 cup packed brown sugar

1/2 cup ketchup

1/4 cup prepared horseradish

- Place sausages in a 3-qt. slow cooker. Combine brown sugar, ketchup and horseradish; pour over sausages. Cover and cook on low for 4 hours.

YIELD: 16-20 servings.

SLOW COOKER TIP: Long cooking can dilute the strength of herbs and spices. So you should always taste the finished dish before serving to adjust seasonings. Consider adding a dash of pepper, salt, lemon juice or minced fresh herbs.

CREAMY CHIPPED BEEF FONDUE

soups & sandwiches

Savory, home-style soups and super sandwiches will satisfy hungry appetites. Try this tempting two-handed creation, Hearty Italian Sandwiches on page 78, for dinner or get-togethers on game day.

Plug in your slow cooker before you leave in the morning, toss in some fresh ingredients and then look forward to the enticing aromas later that day. Your one-pot recipe will be ready to serve and enjoy when you return home.

french dip sandwiches

COOK TIME: 7 TO 9 HOURS

Florence Robinson
Lenox, Iowa

When I want to impress company, I put these satisfying sandwiches on the menu. I serve the au jus sauce in individual bowls for dipping. It's delicious.

> 2 large onions, cut into 1/4-inch slices
>
> 1/4 cup butter, cubed
>
> 1 beef bottom round roast (3 to 4 pounds)
>
> 5 cups water
>
> 1/2 cup soy sauce
>
> 1 envelope onion soup mix
>
> 1-1/2 teaspoons browning sauce, optional
>
> 1 garlic clove, minced
>
> 12 to 14 French rolls, split
>
> 1 cup (4 ounces) shredded Swiss cheese

- In a large skillet, saute onions in butter until tender; transfer to a 5-qt. slow cooker. Cut the roast in half; place over onions.

- In a large bowl, combine the water, soy sauce, soup mix, browning sauce if desired and garlic; pour over roast. Cover and cook on low for 7-9 hours or until the meat is tender.

- Remove roast with a slotted spoon and let stand for 15 minutes. Thinly slice meat across the grain. Place on rolls; sprinkle with Swiss cheese.

- Broil 3-4 in. from the heat for 1 minute or until the cheese is melted. Skim fat from juices; strain and serve as a dipping sauce.

YIELD: 12-14 servings.

hearty black bean soup

COOK TIME: 9 TO 10 HOURS

Amy Chop
Oak Grove, Louisiana

Cumin and chili powder give spark to this thick, hearty soup. If you have leftover meat—smoked sausage, browned ground beef or roast—toss it in for the last 30 minutes of cooking. I know this dish will bring you lots of compliments.

> 3 medium carrots, halved and thinly sliced
>
> 2 celery ribs, thinly sliced
>
> 1 medium onion, chopped
>
> 4 garlic cloves, minced
>
> 1 can (30 ounces) black beans, rinsed and drained
>
> 2 cans (14-1/2 ounces *each*) chicken broth
>
> 1 can (15 ounces) crushed tomatoes
>
> 1-1/2 teaspoons dried basil
>
> 1/2 teaspoon dried oregano
>
> 1/2 teaspoon ground cumin
>
> 1/2 teaspoon chili powder
>
> 1/2 teaspoon hot pepper sauce
>
> Hot cooked rice

- In a 3-qt. slow cooker, combine the first 12 ingredients. Cover and cook on low for 9-10 hours or until vegetables are tender. Serve over rice.

YIELD: 8 servings.

spicy pork chili

COOK TIME: 6 HOURS

Taste of Home Test Kitchen
Slow-cooked boneless pork makes a tasty chili.

> 2 pounds boneless pork, cut into 1/2-inch cubes
>
> 1 tablespoon vegetable oil
>
> 1 can (28 ounces) crushed tomatoes
>
> 2 cups frozen corn
>
> 1 can (15 ounces) black beans, rinsed and drained
>
> 1 cup chopped onion
>
> 1 cup beef broth
>
> 1 can (4 ounces) chopped green chilies
>
> 1 tablespoon chili powder
>
> 1 teaspoon minced garlic
>
> 1/2 teaspoon *each* salt, cayenne pepper and pepper
>
> 1/4 cup minced fresh cilantro
>
> Shredded cheddar cheese, optional

- In a large skillet, cook pork in oil over medium-high heat for 5-6 minutes or until browned. Transfer pork and drippings to a 5-qt. slow cooker.

- Stir in remaining ingredients except cilantro and cheese. Cover and cook on low for 6 hours or until pork is tender. Stir in cilantro. Serve with cheese if desired.

YIELD: 6 servings.

FRENCH DIP SANDWICHES

SPICY PORK CHILI

hearty chicken noodle soup

COOK TIME: 5-1/2 TO 6-1/2 HOURS

Norma Reynolds
Overland Park, Kansas

This satisfying homemade soup with a hint of cayenne is chock-full of vegetables, chicken and noodles.

- 12 fresh baby carrots, cut into 1/2-inch pieces
- 4 celery ribs, cut into 1/2-inch pieces
- 3/4 cup finely chopped onion
- 1 tablespoon minced fresh parsley
- 1/2 teaspoon pepper
- 1/4 teaspoon cayenne pepper
- 1-1/2 teaspoons mustard seed
- 2 garlic cloves, peeled and halved
- 1-1/4 pounds boneless skinless chicken breast halves
- 1-1/4 pounds boneless skinless chicken thighs
- 4 cans (14-1/2 ounces *each*) chicken broth
- 1 package (9 ounces) refrigerated linguine

■ In a 5-qt. slow cooker, combine the first six ingredients. Place mustard seed and garlic on a double thickness of cheesecloth; bring up corners of cloth and tie with kitchen string to form a bag. Place in slow cooker. Add chicken and broth. Cover and cook on low for 5-6 hours or until chicken juices run clear.

■ Discard spice bag. Remove chicken; cool slightly. Stir linguine into soup; cover and cook for 30 minutes or until tender. Cut chicken into pieces and return to soup; heat through.

YIELD: 12 servings (3 quarts).

shrimp chowder

COOK TIME: 3-1/2 HOURS

Will Zunio
Gretna, Louisiana

This chowder cooks in 3 hours, so it can be made in the afternoon and served to guests that night.

- 1/2 cup chopped onion
- 2 teaspoons butter
- 2 cans (12 ounces *each*) evaporated milk
- 2 cans (10-3/4 ounces *each*) condensed cream of potato soup, undiluted
- 2 cans (10-3/4 ounces *each*) condensed cream of chicken soup, undiluted
- 1 can (11 ounces) white *or* shoepeg corn, drained
- 1 teaspoon Creole seasoning
- 1/2 teaspoon garlic powder
- 2 pounds cooked small shrimp, peeled and deveined
- 1 package (3 ounces) cream cheese, cubed

■ In a small skillet, saute onion in butter until tender. In a 5-qt. slow cooker, combine the onion mixture, milk, soups, corn, Creole seasoning and garlic powder.

■ Cover and cook on low for 3 hours. Stir in shrimp and cream cheese. Cook 30 minutes longer or until shrimp are heated through and cheese is melted. Stir to blend.

YIELD: 12 servings (3 quarts).

tangy pulled pork sandwiches

COOK TIME: 4 TO 5 HOURS

Beki Kosydar-Krantz
Clarks Summit, Pennsylvania

The slow cooker not only makes this an easy meal, but it keeps the pork tender, moist and loaded with flavor. The sandwiches are so comforting, it's hard to believe they're lighter. Try this recipe for your next gathering.

- 1 pork tenderloin (1 pound)
- 1 cup ketchup
- 2 tablespoons plus 1-1/2 teaspoons brown sugar
- 2 tablespoons plus 1-1/2 teaspoons cider vinegar
- 1 tablespoon plus 1-1/2 teaspoons Worcestershire sauce
- 1 tablespoon spicy brown mustard
- 1/4 teaspoon pepper
- 4 kaiser rolls, split

■ Cut the tenderloin in half; place in a 3-qt. slow cooker. Combine the ketchup, brown sugar, vinegar, Worcestershire sauce, mustard and pepper; pour over pork.

■ Cover and cook on low for 4-5 hours or until meat is tender. Remove meat; shred with two forks. Return to the slow cooker; heat through. Serve on rolls.

YIELD: 4 servings.

SHRIMP CHOWDER

TANGY PULLED PORK SANDWICHES

savory winter soup

COOK TIME: 8 HOURS

Dana Simmons
Lancaster, Ohio

Even my father, who doesn't particularly like soup, enjoys my full-flavored version of traditional vegetable soup. He asked me to share the recipe with Mom, and I gladly obliged!

2 pounds ground beef

3 medium onions, chopped

1 garlic clove, minced

3 cans (10-1/2 ounces *each*) condensed beef broth, undiluted

1 can (28 ounces) diced tomatoes, undrained

3 cups water

1 cup *each* diced carrots and celery

1 cup fresh *or* frozen cut green beans

1 cup cubed peeled potatoes

2 tablespoons minced fresh parsley *or* 2 teaspoons dried parsley flakes

1 teaspoon dried basil

1/2 teaspoon dried thyme

Salt and pepper to taste

■ In a skillet, cook beef, onions and garlic over medium heat until the meat is no longer pink; drain.

■ Transfer to a 5-qt. slow cooker. Add the remaining ingredients and mix well. Cover and cook on high for 8 hours or until heated through.

YIELD: 14 servings (3-1/2 quarts).

seafood chowder

COOK TIME: 4 TO 5 HOURS

Marlene Muckenhirm
Delano, Minnesota

Our family often requests this creamy chowder. We enjoy it with raw veggies, breadsticks and an array of baked goodies. It's an easy-to-serve and easy-to-clean-up meal.

1 can (10-3/4 ounces) condensed cream of potato soup, undiluted

1 can (10-3/4 ounces) condensed cream of mushroom soup, undiluted

2-1/2 cups milk

4 medium carrots, finely chopped

2 medium potatoes, peeled and cut into 1/4-inch cubes

1 large onion, finely chopped

2 celery ribs, finely chopped

1 can (6-1/2 ounces) chopped clams, drained

1 can (6 ounces) medium shrimp, drained

4 ounces imitation crabmeat, flaked

5 bacon strips, cooked and crumbled

■ In a 3-qt. slow cooker, combine soups and milk. Stir in the vegetables. Cover and cook on low for 4-5 hours. Stir in clams, shrimp and crab; cover and heat through, about 20 minutes. Garnish each serving with bacon.

YIELD: 8 servings.

beef fajitas

COOK TIME: 7 TO 8 HOURS

Twila Burkholder
Middleburg, Pennsylvania

My family loves beef, and I love to use the slow cooker, so this dish pleases everyone. The meat comes out nice and tender.

1 beef flank steak (2 pounds), thinly sliced

1 cup tomato juice

2 garlic cloves, minced

1 tablespoon minced fresh cilantro

1 teaspoon chili powder

1 teaspoon ground cumin

1/2 teaspoon salt

1/2 teaspoon ground coriander

1 medium onion, sliced

1 *each* medium green and sweet red pepper, julienned

1 medium jalapeno, cut into thin strips

12 flour tortillas (6 inches)

Sour cream, guacamole, salsa *or* shredded cheddar cheese, optional

■ Place beef in a 3-qt. slow cooker. Combine the next seven ingredients; pour over beef. Cover and cook on low for 6-7 hours. Add onion, peppers and jalapeno. Cover and cook 1 hour longer or until meat and vegetables are tender.

■ Using a slotted spoon, place about 1/2 cup of meat-vegetable mixture on each tortilla. Add desired toppings. Roll up.

YIELD: 12 servings.

EDITOR'S NOTE: When cutting or seeding hot peppers, use rubber or plastic gloves to protect your hands. Avoid touching your face.

SAVORY WINTER SOUP

shredded beef barbecue

COOK TIME: 8 TO 10 HOURS

Lori Bergquist
Wilton, North Dakota

This beef roast simmers for hours in a homemade barbecue sauce, so it's very tender and easy to shred for sandwiches. The mixture freezes well, too.

- **1 boneless beef sirloin tip roast (2-1/2 pounds)**
- 1/2 teaspoon salt
- 1/4 teaspoon pepper
- 1 tablespoon vegetable oil
- 1 cup *each* ketchup and water
- 1/2 cup chopped onion
- 1/3 cup packed brown sugar
- 3 tablespoons Worcestershire sauce
- 2 tablespoons lemon juice
- 2 tablespoons cider vinegar
- 2 tablespoons Dijon mustard
- 2 teaspoons celery seed
- 2 teaspoons chili powder
- 12 kaiser rolls, split

- Sprinkle roast with salt and pepper. In a nonstick skillet, brown roast in oil on all sides over medium-high heat; drain.

- Transfer roast to a 5-qt. slow cooker. Combine the ketchup, water, onion, brown sugar, Worcestershire sauce, lemon juice, vinegar, mustard, celery seed and chili powder; pour over roast.

- Cover and cook on low for 8-10 hours or until meat is tender. Remove meat; shred with two forks and return to slow cooker. Spoon 1/2 cup meat mixture onto each roll.

YIELD: 12 servings.

chicken bean soup

COOK TIME: 4 HOURS

Phyllis Shaughnessy
Livonia, New York

This easy soup is tasty and nutritious, too. I like to top individual bowls with a few sprigs of fresh parsley. Home-baked rolls—I use frozen bread dough—are an added treat.

- **1 pound boneless skinless chicken breasts, cubed**
- 2 cans (14-1/2 ounces *each*) chicken broth
- 2 cans (14-1/2 ounces *each*) diced Italian tomatoes, undrained
- 1 can (16 ounces) kidney beans, rinsed and drained
- 1 can (15-1/4 ounces) whole kernel corn, drained *or* 1-1/2 cups frozen corn
- 1 can (15 ounces) lima beans, rinsed and drained *or* 1-1/2 cups frozen lima beans
- 1 cup frozen peas and pearl onions
- 1 tablespoon snipped fresh dill *or* 1 teaspoon dill weed
- 1/2 teaspoon ground ginger, optional

- In a 5-qt. slow cooker, combine all ingredients. Cover and cook on low for 4 hours or until chicken juices run clear.

YIELD: 12 servings (3 quarts).

SLOW COOKER TIP:

Certain dairy ingredients, such as milk, cream and sour cream, tend to break down during the long slow cooker process. Be sure to add those ingredients toward the end of the cooking time.

slow-cooked sauerkraut soup

COOK TIME: 5 TO 6 HOURS

Linda Lohr
Lititz, Pennsylvania

We live in Lancaster County, Pennsylvania, which has a rich heritage of German culture. Dishes that include sauerkraut, potatoes and sausage abound here. We enjoy this recipe on cold winter evenings, along with muffins and fruit. The "mmm's" start with the first whiff as the door opens after school, work or a day outdoors.

- **1 medium potato, cut into 1/4-inch cubes**
- 1 pound smoked kielbasa, cut into 1/2-inch cubes
- 1 can (32 ounces) sauerkraut, rinsed and drained
- 4 cups chicken broth
- 1 can (10-3/4 ounces) condensed cream of mushroom soup, undiluted
- 1/2 pound fresh mushrooms, sliced
- 1 cup cubed cooked chicken
- 2 medium carrots, cut into 1/4-inch slices
- 2 celery ribs, sliced
- 2 tablespoons white vinegar
- 2 teaspoons dill weed
- 1/2 teaspoon pepper
- 3 to 4 bacon strips, cooked and crumbled

- In a 5-qt. slow cooker, combine the first 12 ingredients. Cover and cook on high for 5-6 hours or until the vegetables are tender. Skim fat. Garnish individual servings with bacon.

YIELD: 10-12 servings (about 3 quarts).

fiesta pork sandwiches

COOK TIME: 8 TO 10 HOURS

Yvette Massey
La Luz, New Mexico

This is an easy dish that my family really enjoys. When I fix it for company, I prepare the meat the day before so I can relax with my friends.

1 boneless pork shoulder roast (3 to 4 pounds)

1/3 cup lime juice

2 tablespoons grapefruit juice

2 tablespoons water

1 bay leaf

6 garlic cloves, minced

1/2 teaspoon salt

1/2 teaspoon dried oregano

1/2 teaspoon chili powder

2 tablespoons olive oil

1 large onion, thinly sliced

12 to 14 sandwich rolls, split

■ Cut roast in half; pierce several times with a fork. Place in a large resealable plastic bag or shallow glass container. Combine the next eight ingredients; pour over roast. Cover; refrigerate overnight, turning occasionally. Drain, reserving marinade.

■ In a skillet over medium heat, brown the roast in oil on all sides. Place onion, roast and marinade in a 5-qt. slow cooker. Cover and cook on high for 2 hours. Reduce heat to low; cook 6-8 hours longer or until the meat is tender. Remove roast; shred or thinly slice. Discard bay leaf. Skim fat from cooking juices and transfer to a saucepan; bring to a rolling boil. Serve pork on rolls with juices as a dipping sauce.

YIELD: 12-14 servings.

slow-cooked chowder

COOK TIME: 6 TO 7 HOURS

Pam Leonard
Aberdeen, South Dakota

The hectic holidays often leave little time for cooking. That's why this slow cooker recipe is a favorite. I just combine the ingredients, flip a switch and forget it!

5 cups water

5 teaspoons chicken bouillon granules

8 medium potatoes, cubed

2 medium onions, chopped

1 medium carrot, thinly sliced

1 celery rib, thinly sliced

1/4 cup butter, cubed

1 teaspoon salt

1/4 teaspoon pepper

1 can (12 ounces) evaporated milk

1 tablespoon minced fresh parsley

■ In a 5-qt. slow cooker, combine the first nine ingredients. Cover and cook on high for 1 hour. Reduce heat to low; cover and cook for 5-6 hours or until vegetables are tender. Stir in milk and parsley; heat through.

YIELD: 12 servings (about 3 quarts).

summer's bounty soup

COOK TIME: 7 TO 8 HOURS

Victoria Zmarzley-Hahn
Northampton, Pennsylvania

Lots of wonderfully fresh-tasting vegetables are showcased in this chunky soup. It's a great way to use up summer's excess produce. And you can add or delete just about any vegetable you like.

4 medium tomatoes, chopped

2 medium potatoes, peeled and cubed

2 cups halved fresh green beans

2 small zucchini, cubed

1 medium yellow summer squash, cubed

4 small carrots, thinly sliced

2 celery ribs, thinly sliced

1 cup cubed peeled eggplant

1 cup sliced fresh mushrooms

1 small onion, chopped

1 tablespoon minced fresh parsley

1 tablespoon salt-free garlic and herb seasoning

4 cups V8 juice

■ Combine all ingredients in a 5-qt. slow cooker. Cover and cook on low for 7-8 hours or until the vegetables are tender.

YIELD: 12-14 servings (about 3-1/2 quarts).

FIESTA PORK SANDWICHES

beef vegetable soup

COOK TIME: 9 TO 11 HOURS

Jean Hutzell
Dubuque, Iowa

This nicely seasoned soup tastes so good. It's convenient, too, since it simmers all day.

- **1 pound ground beef**
- **1 medium onion, chopped**
- **1/2 teaspoon salt**
- **1/4 teaspoon pepper**
- **3 cups water**
- **3 medium potatoes, peeled and cut into 3/4-inch cubes**
- **1 can (14-1/2 ounces) Italian diced tomatoes, undrained**
- **1 can (11-1/2 ounces) V8 juice**
- **1 cup chopped celery**
- **1 cup sliced carrots**
- **2 tablespoons sugar**
- **1 tablespoon dried parsley flakes**
- **2 teaspoons dried basil**
- **1 bay leaf**

■ In a nonstick skillet, cook beef and onion over medium heat until meat is no longer pink; drain. Stir in salt and pepper.

■ Transfer to a 5-qt. slow cooker. Add the remaining ingredients. Cover and cook on low for 9-11 hours or until vegetables are tender. Discard bay leaf before serving.

YIELD: 7 servings.

smoked sausage soup

COOK TIME: 5 TO 8 HOURS

Rachel Lyn Grasmick
Rocky Ford, Colorado

This rich soup is packed with vegetables, sausage and chicken. I guarantee it's unlike any other soup you've ever eaten.

- **2 cups chopped onion**
- **2 tablespoons butter**
- **2 cups cubed cooked chicken**
- **1 pound cooked smoked sausage, cut into bite-size pieces**
- **3 cups sliced celery**
- **3 cups sliced summer squash**
- **2 cups chicken broth**
- **1-1/2 cups minced fresh parsley**
- **1 can (8 ounces) tomato sauce**
- **2 tablespoons cornstarch**
- **2 tablespoons poultry seasoning**
- **1 teaspoon dried oregano**
- **1 teaspoon ground cumin**
- **1 teaspoon Liquid Smoke, optional**
- **1/2 teaspoon pepper**

■ In a skillet or microwave, cook onion in butter until softened. Transfer to a 3-qt. or larger slow cooker. Add remaining ingredients, stirring to blend. Cook on high for 5-8 hours.

YIELD: 6-8 servings (2-1/2 quarts).

turkey sloppy joes

COOK TIME: 4 HOURS

Marylin LaRue
Freeland, Michigan

This tangy sandwich filling is so easy to prepare in the slow cooker, and it goes over well at gatherings large and small. I frequently take it to potlucks, and I'm always asked for my secret ingredient.

- **1 pound ground turkey breast**
- **1 small onion, chopped**
- **1/2 cup chopped celery**
- **1/4 cup chopped green pepper**
- **1 can (10-3/4 ounces) condensed tomato soup, undiluted**
- **1/2 cup ketchup**
- **1 tablespoon brown sugar**
- **2 tablespoons prepared mustard**
- **1/4 teaspoon pepper**
- **8 hamburger buns, split**

■ In a large saucepan coated with nonstick cooking spray, cook the turkey, onion, celery and green pepper over medium heat until the meat is no longer pink; drain if necessary. Stir in the soup, ketchup, brown sugar, mustard and pepper.

■ Transfer to a 3-qt. slow cooker. Cover and cook on low for 4 hours. Serve on buns.

YIELD: 8 servings.

SLOW COOKER TIP: For the best color and flavor, cook ground beef or turkey until no longer pink before using it in a slow cooker recipe (unless preparing meat loaf or a similar dish). Browning other cuts of meat or poultry, while not necessary, can enhance the flavor and appearance and may reduce the fat in the finished dish.

BEEF VEGETABLE SOUP

savory cheese soup

COOK TIME: 7-1/2 TO 8-1/2 HOURS

Ann Huseby
Lakeville, Minnesota

This creamy soup is great at parties. Let guests serve themselves and choose from fun garnishes such as popcorn, croutons, green onions and bacon bits.

> 3 cans (14-1/2 ounces *each*) chicken broth
>
> 1 small onion, chopped
>
> 1 large carrot, chopped
>
> 1 celery rib, chopped
>
> 1/4 cup chopped sweet red pepper
>
> 2 tablespoons butter
>
> 1 teaspoon salt
>
> 1/2 teaspoon pepper
>
> 1/3 cup all-purpose flour
>
> 1/3 cup cold water
>
> 1 package (8 ounces) cream cheese, cubed and softened
>
> 2 cups (8 ounces) shredded cheddar cheese
>
> 1 can (12 ounces) beer, optional

Optional toppings: croutons, popcorn, cooked crumbled bacon, sliced green onions

■ In a 3-qt. slow cooker, combine the first eight ingredients. Cover and cook on low for 7-8 hours. Combine flour and water until smooth; stir into soup. Cover and cook on high 30 minutes longer or until soup is thickened.

■ Stir in cream cheese and cheddar cheese until blended. Stir in beer if desired. Cover and cook on low until heated through. Serve with desired toppings.

YIELD: 6-8 servings.

beef barbecue

COOK TIME: 6-1/2 TO 8-1/2 HOURS

Karen Walker
Sterling, Virginia

We like to keep our freezer stocked with plenty of beef roasts. When we're not in the mood for pot roast, I fix these satisfying sandwiches instead. The meat cooks in a tasty sauce while I'm at work. Then I just slice it thinly and serve it on rolls.

> 1 boneless chuck roast (3 pounds)
>
> 1 cup barbecue sauce
>
> 1/2 cup apricot preserves
>
> 1/3 cup chopped green *or* sweet red pepper
>
> 1 small onion, chopped
>
> 1 tablespoon Dijon mustard
>
> 2 teaspoons brown sugar
>
> 12 sandwich rolls, split

■ Cut the roast into quarters; place in a greased 5-qt. slow cooker. In a bowl, combine the barbecue sauce, preserves, green pepper, onion, mustard and brown sugar; pour over roast.

■ Cover and cook on low for 6-8 hours or until meat is tender. Remove roast and thinly slice; return meat to slow cooker and stir gently. Cover and cook 20-30 minutes longer. Skim fat from sauce. Serve beef and sauce on rolls.

YIELD: 12 servings.

spicy tomato chicken soup

COOK TIME: 4 HOURS

Margaret Bailey
Coffeeville, Mississippi

Cumin, chili powder and cayenne pepper give this slow-cooked specialty its kick. I serve bowls of it with crunchy tortilla strips that bake in no time. Leftover soup freezes well for nights I don't feel like cooking.

> 2 cans (14-1/2 ounces *each*) chicken broth
>
> 3 cups cubed cooked chicken
>
> 2 cups frozen corn
>
> 1 can (10-3/4 ounces) tomato puree
>
> 1 can (10 ounces) diced tomatoes and green chilies
>
> 1 large onion, finely chopped
>
> 2 garlic cloves, minced
>
> 1 bay leaf
>
> 1 to 2 teaspoons ground cumin
>
> 1 teaspoon salt
>
> 1/2 to 1 teaspoon chili powder
>
> 1/8 teaspoon pepper
>
> 1/8 teaspoon cayenne pepper
>
> 4 white *or* yellow corn tortillas (6 inches), cut into 1/4-inch strips

■ In a 3-qt. slow cooker, combine the first 13 ingredients. Cover and cook on low for 4 hours.

■ Place the tortilla strips on an ungreased baking sheet. Bake at 375° for 5 minutes; turn. Bake 5 minutes longer. Discard bay leaf from soup. Serve with tortilla strips.

YIELD: 8 servings.

SAVORY CHEESE SOUP

chili with an italian twist

COOK TIME: 6 HOURS

Sandra McKenzie
Braham, Minnesota

This slow cooker chili is hearty. I use home-canned tomatoes and pizza sauce to give it my own unique flavor.

- 2 pounds ground beef
- 4 cans (16 ounces *each*) kidney beans, rinsed and drained
- 1 can (28 ounces) stewed tomatoes, undrained
- 1 can (15 ounces) pizza sauce
- 1 can (4 ounces) chopped green chilies
- 1/4 cup chopped onion
- 4 to 5 teaspoons chili powder
- 2 garlic cloves, minced
- 1 teaspoon dried basil
- 1/2 teaspoon salt
- 1/8 teaspoon pepper

■ In a large skillet, cook beef over medium heat until no longer pink; drain. Transfer to a 5-qt. slow cooker. Stir in the remaining ingredients. Cover and cook on low for 6 hours.

YIELD: 12 servings.

hearty split pea soup

COOK TIME: 4 TO 5 HOURS

Deanna Waggy
South Bend, Indiana

This slow cooker soup is one of my favorite meals to make during a busy workweek. When I get home, I just add the milk and supper is served!

- 1 package (16 ounces) dried split peas
- 2 cups diced fully cooked lean ham
- 1 cup diced carrots
- 1 medium onion, chopped
- 2 garlic cloves, minced
- 2 bay leaves
- 1/2 teaspoon salt
- 1/2 teaspoon pepper
- 5 cups boiling water
- 1 cup hot milk

■ In a 3-qt. slow cooker, layer the first nine ingredients in order listed (do not stir). Cover and cook on high for 4-5 hours or until vegetables are tender. Stir in milk. Discard bay leaves before serving.

YIELD: 9 servings.

teriyaki pulled pork sandwiches

COOK TIME: 8 TO 9 HOURS

Taste of Home Test Kitchen

The aroma of pork roast slowly simmering in pineapple juice and teriyaki sauce is a nice way to come home at the end of a busy day! You'll love these easy, change-of-pace sandwiches.

- 1 boneless pork shoulder roast (3 pounds), trimmed
- 2 teaspoons olive oil
- 1 cup finely chopped onion
- 1 cup teriyaki sauce, *divided*
- 1/2 cup unsweetened pineapple juice
- 3 tablespoons all-purpose flour
- 8 whole wheat hamburger buns, split
- 1 can (20 ounces) sliced pineapple, drained

■ In a large skillet, brown roast in oil over medium-high heat. Cut in half; place in a 5-qt. slow cooker. Add the onion, 1/2 cup teriyaki sauce and pineapple juice. Cover and cook on low for 7-8 hours or until meat is tender.

■ Remove roast; set aside. In a small bowl, combine the flour and remaining teriyaki sauce until smooth; stir into cooking juices. Cover and cook on high for 30-40 minutes or until thickened.

■ Shred meat with two forks; return to the slow cooker and heat through. Spoon 1/2 cup onto each bun; top with a slice of pineapple.

YIELD: 8 servings.

CHILI WITH AN ITALIAN TWIST

tangy barbecue sandwiches

COOK TIME: 8 TO 9 HOURS

Debbi Smith
Crossett, Arkansas

Since I prepare the beef for these robust sandwiches in the slow cooker, it's easy to fix a meal for a hungry bunch.

- 3 cups chopped celery
- 1 cup chopped onion
- 1 cup ketchup
- 1 cup barbecue sauce
- 1 cup water
- 2 tablespoons white vinegar
- 2 tablespoons Worcestershire sauce
- 2 tablespoons brown sugar
- 1 teaspoon chili powder
- 1 teaspoon salt
- 1/2 teaspoon pepper
- 1/2 teaspoon garlic powder
- 1 boneless chuck roast (3 to 4 pounds), trimmed
- 14 to 18 hamburger buns, split

- In a 5-qt. slow cooker, combine the first 12 ingredients; mix well. Add roast. Cover and cook on high for 1 hour. Reduce heat to low and cook 7-8 hours longer or until meat is tender.

- Remove roast; cool. Shred meat and return to sauce; heat through. Use a slotted spoon to serve on buns.

YIELD: 14-18 servings.

southwestern chicken soup

COOK TIME: 7 TO 8 HOURS

Harold Tartar
West Palm Beach, Florida

This zippy, satisfying slow cooker recipe brings people back for seconds.

- 1-1/4 pounds boneless skinless chicken breasts, cut into thin strips
- 1 to 2 tablespoons vegetable oil
- 2 cans (14-1/2 ounces *each*) chicken broth
- 1 package (16 ounces) frozen corn, thawed
- 1 can (14-1/2 ounces) diced tomatoes, undrained
- 1 medium onion, chopped
- 1 medium green pepper, chopped
- 1 medium sweet red pepper, chopped
- 1 can (4 ounces) chopped green chilies
- 1-1/2 teaspoons seasoned salt, optional
- 1 teaspoon ground cumin
- 1/2 teaspoon garlic powder

- In a large skillet, saute the chicken in oil until lightly browned. Transfer to a 5-qt. slow cooker with a slotted spoon. Stir in the remaining ingredients. Cover and cook on low for 7-8 hours. Stir before serving.

YIELD: 10 servings.

beef barley lentil soup

COOK TIME: 8 HOURS

Judy Metzentine
The Dalles, Oregon

It's easy for me to fill my slow cooker and forget about supper...until the kitchen is filled with wonderful aroma, that is! I've served this soup often to family and friends on cold nights, along with homemade rolls and a green salad. For variety, substitute jicama (a starchy root vegetable found in the produce department of many grocery stores) for the potatoes.

- 1 pound ground beef
- 1 medium onion, chopped
- 2 cups cubed red potatoes (1/4-inch pieces)
- 1 cup chopped celery
- 1 cup chopped carrot
- 1 cup dried lentils, rinsed
- 1/2 cup medium pearl barley
- 8 cups water
- 2 teaspoons beef bouillon granules
- 1 teaspoon salt
- 1/2 teaspoon lemon-pepper seasoning
- 2 cans (14-1/2 ounces *each*) stewed tomatoes

- In a nonstick skillet, cook beef and onion over medium heat until meat is no longer pink; drain.

- Transfer to a 5-qt. slow cooker. Layer with the potatoes, celery, carrots, lentils and barley. Combine the water, bouillon, salt and lemon-pepper; pour over vegetables. Cover and cook on low for 6 hours or until vegetables and barley are tender. Add the tomatoes; cook 2 hours longer.

YIELD: 10 servings.

TANGY BARBECUE SANDWICHES

BEEF BARLEY LENTIL SOUP

steak burritos

COOK TIME: 8 TO 9 HOURS

Valerie Jones
Portland, Maine

I spice up flank steak with convenient taco seasoning packets. Slowly simmered all day, the beef is tender and a snap to shred. Just fill flour tortillas and add toppings for a tasty, time-easing meal.

- **2 beef flank steaks (about 1 pound *each*)**
- **2 envelopes taco seasoning**
- **1 medium onion, chopped**
- **1 can (4 ounces) chopped green chilies**
- **1 tablespoon vinegar**
- **10 flour tortillas (6 inches)**
- **1-1/2 cups (6 ounces) shredded Monterey Jack cheese**
- **1-1/2 cups chopped seeded plum tomatoes**
- **3/4 cup sour cream**

■ Cut steaks in half; rub with taco seasoning. Place in a 3-qt. slow cooker coated with nonstick cooking spray. Top with onion, chilies and vinegar.

■ Cover and cook on low for 8-9 hours or until meat is tender. Remove steaks and cool slightly; shred meat with two forks. Return to slow cooker; heat through.

■ Spoon about 1/2 cup meat mixture down the center of each tortilla. Top with cheese, tomato and sour cream. Fold ends and sides over filling.

YIELD: 10 servings.

hamburger vegetable soup

COOK TIME: 8 TO 9 HOURS

Theresa Jackson
Cicero, New York

I work full time and have a family of four. We sit down to a home-cooked meal just about every night, many times thanks to my slow cooker. This hearty soup is often on the menu.

- **1 pound ground beef**
- **1 medium onion, chopped**
- **2 garlic cloves, minced**
- **4 cups V8 juice**
- **1 can (14-1/2 ounces) stewed tomatoes**
- **2 cups coleslaw mix**
- **2 cups frozen green beans**
- **2 cups frozen corn**
- **2 tablespoons Worcestershire sauce**
- **1 teaspoon dried basil**
- **1/2 teaspoon salt**
- **1/4 teaspoon pepper**

■ In a saucepan, cook beef, onion and garlic over medium heat until meat is no longer pink; drain.

■ In a 3-qt. slow cooker, combine the remaining ingredients. Stir in beef mixture. Cover and cook on low for 8-9 hours or until the vegetables are tender.

YIELD: 10 servings.

meatball subs

COOK TIME: 4 TO 5 HOURS

Jean Glacken
Elkton, Maryland

Flavorful sauce and meatballs make a hearty sandwich filling or pasta topping.

- **2 eggs, beaten**
- **1/4 cup milk**
- **1/2 cup dry bread crumbs**
- **2 tablespoons grated Parmesan cheese**
- **1 teaspoon salt**
- **1/4 teaspoon pepper**
- **1/8 teaspoon garlic powder**
- **1 pound ground beef**
- **1/2 pound bulk Italian sausage**

SAUCE:

- **1 can (15 ounces) tomato sauce**
- **1 can (6 ounces) tomato paste**
- **1 small onion, chopped**
- **1/2 cup chopped green pepper**
- **1/2 cup red wine *or* beef broth**
- **1/3 cup water**
- **2 garlic cloves, minced**
- **1 teaspoon dried oregano**
- **1 teaspoon salt**
- **1/2 teaspoon sugar**
- **1/2 teaspoon pepper**
- **6 to 7 Italian rolls, split**

■ In a bowl, combine eggs and milk; add next five ingredients. Add beef and sausage; mix well. Shape into 1-in. balls. Broil 4 in. from heat for 4 minutes; turn and broil 3 minutes longer. Transfer to a 3-qt. slow cooker.

■ Combine first 11 sauce ingredients; pour over meatballs. Cover; cook on low for 4-5 hours or until meatballs are no longer pink. Serve on rolls.

YIELD: 6-7 servings.

STEAK BURRITOS

big red soup

COOK TIME: 10 HOURS

Shelly Korell
Bayard, Nebraska

We're Nebraska Cornhusker football fans, and on the days when the "Big Red" team is playing, I make up a big pot of this savory soup.

- 2 tablespoons vegetable oil
- 2 pounds beef stew meat, cut into 1-inch cubes
- 3/4 cup chopped onion
- 2 garlic cloves, minced
- 2 cans (14-1/2 ounces *each*) diced tomatoes in sauce
- 1 can (10-1/2 ounces) *each* condensed beef broth and chicken broth, undiluted
- 1 can (10-3/4 ounces) condensed tomato soup, undiluted
- 1/4 cup water
- 1 teaspoon ground cumin
- 1 teaspoon chili powder
- 1 teaspoon salt
- 1/2 teaspoon lemon-pepper seasoning
- 2 teaspoons Worcestershire sauce
- 1/3 cup picante sauce
- 8 corn tortillas, cut into quarters
- 1 cup (4 ounces) shredded cheddar cheese

■ Heat oil in skillet; brown beef stew meat. Place meat in 5-qt. slow cooker; add remaining ingredients except for tortillas and cheese. Cook on low for at least 10 hours. When serving, place enough tortilla quarters to cover bottom of each bowl. Pour soup over tortilla pieces; sprinkle with the cheese.

YIELD: 10-12 servings.

manhattan clam chowder

COOK TIME: 8 TO 10 HOURS

Mary Dixon
Northville, Michigan

I came up with this simple, delicious soup years ago when my husband and I both worked. It's easy to dump all the ingredients into the slow cooker in the morning...and wonderful to come home to the aroma of dinner ready.

- 3 celery ribs, sliced
- 1 large onion, chopped
- 1 can (14-1/2 ounces) sliced potatoes, drained
- 1 can (14-1/2 ounces) sliced carrots, drained
- 2 cans (6-1/2 ounces *each*) chopped clams
- 2 cups tomato juice
- 1-1/2 cups water
- 1/2 cup tomato puree
- 1 tablespoon dried parsley flakes
- 1-1/2 teaspoons dried thyme
- 1 teaspoon salt, optional
- 1 bay leaf
- 2 whole black peppercorns

■ In a 3-qt. slow cooker, combine all ingredients; stir. Cover and cook on low for 8-10 hours or until the vegetables are tender. Remove bay leaf and peppercorns before serving.

YIELD: 9 servings.

tangy bean soup

COOK TIME: 4-1/2 TO 5-1/2 HOURS

Joan Hallford
North Richland Hills, Texas

This soup has a great Southwestern flavor and is a real winner with my family. I love it because I can have the soup cooking in my slow cooker, and when I get home from work, I can quickly make the dumplings and fix dinner in a jiffy.

- 2 cans (14-1/2 ounces *each*) chicken broth
- 1 package (16 ounces) frozen mixed vegetables
- 1 can (15 ounces) black beans, rinsed and drained
- 1 can (15 ounces) pinto beans, rinsed and drained
- 1 can (14-1/2 ounces) diced tomatoes, undrained
- 1 medium onion, chopped
- 1 tablespoon chili powder
- 1 tablespoon minced fresh cilantro
- 4 garlic cloves, minced
- 1/4 teaspoon pepper

CORNMEAL DUMPLINGS:

- 1/2 cup all-purpose flour
- 1/2 cup shredded cheddar cheese
- 1/3 cup cornmeal
- 1 tablespoon sugar
- 1 teaspoon baking powder
- 1 egg
- 2 tablespoons milk
- 2 teaspoons vegetable oil

■ In a 5-qt. slow cooker, combine the first 10 ingredients. Cover and cook on high for 4-5 hours.

■ For dumplings, combine the flour, cheese, cornmeal, sugar and baking powder in a large bowl. In another bowl, combine the egg, milk and oil; add to dry ingredients just until moistened (batter will be stiff).

■ Drop by heaping tablespoons onto soup. Cover and cook on high 30 minutes longer (without lifting cover) or until a toothpick inserted in a dumpling comes out clean.

YIELD: 6 servings.

TANGY BEAN SOUP

italian turkey sandwiches

COOK TIME: 5 TO 6 HOURS

Carol Riley
Galva, Illinois

I hope you enjoy these tasty turkey sandwiches as much as our family does. The recipe makes plenty, so it's great for potlucks. Leftovers are just as good reheated the next day.

> 1 bone-in turkey breast (5-1/2 pounds), skin removed
>
> 1/2 cup chopped green pepper
>
> 1 medium onion, chopped
>
> 1/4 cup chili sauce
>
> 3 tablespoons white vinegar
>
> 2 tablespoons dried oregano *or* Italian seasoning
>
> 4 teaspoons beef bouillon granules
>
> 11 kaiser *or* hard sandwich rolls, split

■ Place the turkey breast, green pepper and onion in a 5-qt. slow cooker coated with nonstick cooking spray. Combine the chili sauce, vinegar, oregano and bouillon; pour over turkey and vegetables. Cover and cook on low for 5-6 hours or until meat juices run clear and vegetables are tender.

■ Remove turkey with a slotted spoon, reserving cooking liquid. Shred the turkey with two forks; return to cooking juices. Spoon 1/2 cup onto each roll.

YIELD: 11 servings.

tomato hamburger soup

COOK TIME: 4 HOURS

Julie Kruger
St. Cloud, Minnesota

As a full-time teacher, I only have time to cook from scratch a few nights each week. This recipe makes a big enough batch to feed my family for two nights.

> 1 can (46 ounces) V8 juice
>
> 2 packages (16 ounces *each*) frozen mixed vegetables
>
> 1 pound ground beef, cooked and drained
>
> 1 can (10-3/4 ounces) condensed cream of mushroom soup, undiluted
>
> 2 teaspoons dried minced onion

Salt and pepper to taste

■ In a 5-qt. slow cooker, combine the first five ingredients; mix well. Cover and cook on high for 4 hours or until heated through. Season with salt and pepper.

YIELD: 12 servings (3 quarts).

beef 'n' black bean soup

COOK TIME: 6 TO 7 HOURS

Vickie Gibson
Gardendale, Alabama

I'm always trying to come up with time-saving recipes. This zippy and colorful soup is one of my husband's favorites. It has been a hit at family gatherings, too.

> 1 pound ground beef
>
> 2 cans (14-1/2 ounces *each*) chicken broth
>
> 1 can (14-1/2 ounces) diced tomatoes, undrained
>
> 8 green onions, thinly sliced
>
> 3 medium carrots, thinly sliced
>
> 2 celery ribs, thinly sliced
>
> 2 garlic cloves, minced
>
> 1 tablespoon sugar
>
> 1-1/2 teaspoons dried basil
>
> 1/2 teaspoon salt
>
> 1/2 teaspoon dried oregano
>
> 1/2 teaspoon ground cumin
>
> 1/2 teaspoon chili powder
>
> 2 cans (15 ounces *each*) black beans, rinsed and drained
>
> 1-1/2 cups cooked rice

■ In a skillet over medium heat, cook beef until no longer pink; drain. Transfer to a 5-qt. slow cooker. Add the next 12 ingredients.

■ Cover and cook on high for 1 hour. Reduce heat to low; cook for 4-5 hours or until vegetables are tender. Add the beans and rice; cook 1 hour longer or until heated through.

YIELD: 10 servings (2-1/2 quarts).

ITALIAN TURKEY SANDWICH

rich french onion soup

COOK TIME: 5 TO 7 HOURS

Linda Adolph
Edmonton, Alberta

When entertaining guests, I bring out this savory soup while we're waiting for the main course. It's simple to make—just saute the onions early in the day and let the soup simmer until dinnertime. In winter, big bowls of it make a warming supper with a salad and biscuits.

- 6 large onions, chopped
- 1/2 cup butter
- 6 cans (10-1/2 ounces *each*) condensed beef broth, undiluted
- 1-1/2 teaspoons Worcestershire sauce
- 3 bay leaves
- 10 slices French bread, toasted

Shredded Parmesan and mozzarella cheeses

- In a large skillet, saute onions in butter until crisp-tender. Transfer to an ungreased 5-qt. slow cooker. Add the broth, Worcestershire sauce and bay leaves.

- Cover and cook on low for 5-7 hours or until the onions are tender. Discard bay leaves. Top each serving with French bread and cheeses.

YIELD: 10 servings.

hominy pork soup

COOK TIME: 4 HOURS

Raquel Walkup
San Pedro, California

Tender pork and hominy make this chili-like soup different from the usual offerings. For a satisfying meal, I serve it with sliced green onions, shredded cheese, lime wedges and warm flour tortillas.

- 1 pound pork chop suey meat, cut into 1/2-inch cubes
- 2 cans (15 ounces *each*) chili without beans
- 1 can (15-1/2 ounces) hominy, drained
- 1 can (8 ounces) tomato sauce
- 1 medium onion, chopped
- 1 bay leaf
- 1 tablespoon chili powder
- 1 teaspoon *each* dried basil, oregano and parsley flakes
- 1 teaspoon ground cumin

Warmed flour tortillas, shredded Monterey Jack cheese, sliced green onions and lime wedges, optional

- In a 3-qt. slow cooker, combine the pork, chili, hominy, tomato sauce, onion and seasonings.

- Cover and cook on high for 4 hours or until meat is tender. Discard bay leaf. Serve with tortillas, cheese, green onions and lime wedges if desired.

YIELD: 7 servings.

shredded barbecued beef sandwiches

COOK TIME: 7 TO 8 HOURS

Fran Frerichs
Gurley, Nebraska

Our family loves these tasty sandwiches. The recipe makes a lot, so it's a nice choice for parties.

- 3 pounds beef stew meat, cut into 1-inch cubes
- 3 medium green peppers, diced
- 2 large onions, diced
- 1 can (6 ounces) tomato paste
- 1/2 cup packed brown sugar
- 1/4 cup cider vinegar
- 3 tablespoons chili powder
- 2 teaspoons salt
- 2 teaspoons Worcestershire sauce
- 1 teaspoon ground mustard
- 14 to 16 sandwich buns, split

- In a 3-qt. slow cooker, combine the beef, green peppers and onions. In a small bowl, combine tomato paste, brown sugar, vinegar, chili powder, salt, Worcestershire sauce and mustard. Stir into meat mixture.

- Cover and cook on high for 7-8 hours or until meat is tender.

- Skim the fat from cooking juices. Shred beef, using two forks. With a slotted spoon, place about 1/2 cup beef mixture on each bun.

YIELD: 14-16 servings.

SLOW COOKER TIP: For the best results when shredding meat, remove cooked meat from the slow cooker (use a slotted spoon if necessary). Place meat in a shallow pan or platter. With two forks, pull meat into thin shreds. Return shredded meat to the slow cooker to warm or use as the recipe directs.

RICH FRENCH ONION SOUP

hot ham sandwiches

COOK TIME: 4 TO 5 HOURS

Susan Rehm
Grahamsville, New York

I came up with this crowd-pleasing recipe when trying to re-create a favorite sandwich from a restaurant near my hometown. Flavored with sweet relish, these ham sandwiches are oh-so-easy.

- **3 pounds thinly sliced deli ham (about 40 slices)**
- **2 cups apple juice**
- **2/3 cup packed brown sugar**
- **1/2 cup sweet pickle relish**
- **2 teaspoons prepared mustard**
- **1 teaspoon paprika**
- **12 kaiser rolls, split**

Additional sweet pickle relish, optional

- Separate ham slices and place in a 3-qt. slow cooker. In a bowl, combine the apple juice, brown sugar, relish, mustard and paprika. Pour over ham.

- Cover and cook on low for 4-5 hours or until heated through. Place 3-4 slices of ham on each roll. Serve with additional relish if desired.

YIELD: 12 servings.

brisket for a bunch

COOK TIME: 7 TO 8 HOURS

Dawn Fagerstrom
Warren, Minnesota

This makes tender slices of beef in a delicious au jus. To easily get very thin slices, chill the brisket before slicing, then reheat in the juices.

- **1 beef brisket (2-1/2 pounds), cut in half**
- **1 tablespoon vegetable oil**
- **1/2 cup chopped celery**
- **1/2 cup chopped onion**
- **3/4 cup beef broth**
- **1/2 cup tomato sauce**
- **1/4 cup water**
- **1/4 cup sugar**
- **2 tablespoons onion soup mix**
- **1 tablespoon vinegar**
- **12 hamburger buns, split**

- In a large skillet, brown the brisket on all sides in oil; transfer to a 3-qt. slow cooker. In the same skillet, saute celery and onion for 1 minute. Gradually add broth, tomato sauce and water; stir to loosen the browned bits from pan. Add sugar, soup mix and vinegar; bring to a boil. Pour over brisket.

- Cover and cook on low for 7-8 hours or until meat is tender. Let stand for 5 minutes before slicing. Skim fat from cooking juices. Serve meat in buns with cooking juices.

YIELD: 12 servings.

EDITOR'S NOTE: This recipe is for fresh beef brisket, not corned beef.

minestrone

COOK TIME: 8 HOURS

Paula Zsiray
Logan, Utah

With this savory soup, I just add bread and a salad to have dinner ready. For a thicker soup, mash half of the garbanzo beans and add to the slow cooker.

- **2 cans (14-1/2 ounces each) chicken broth**
- **1 can (28 ounces) crushed tomatoes**
- **1 can (16 ounces) kidney beans, rinsed and drained**
- **1 can (15 ounces) garbanzo beans or chickpeas, rinsed and drained**
- **1 can (14-1/2 ounces) beef broth**
- **2 cups frozen cubed hash brown potatoes, thawed**
- **1 tablespoon dried minced onion**
- **1 tablespoon dried parsley flakes**
- **1 teaspoon salt**
- **1 teaspoon dried oregano**
- **1/2 teaspoon garlic powder**
- **1/2 teaspoon dried basil**
- **1/2 teaspoon dried marjoram**
- **1 package (10 ounces) frozen chopped spinach, thawed and drained**
- **2 cups frozen peas and carrots, thawed**

- In a 5-qt. slow cooker, combine the first 13 ingredients. Cover and cook on low for 8 hours. Stir in the spinach, peas and carrots; heat through.

YIELD: 12 servings (about 3 quarts).

SLOW COOKER TIP: Root vegetables, like potatoes, carrots and turnips, should be cut in small pieces (about 1 inch) and layered on the bottom of the slow cooker so they will start to cook as soon as the liquid heats.

HOT HAM SANDWICHES

shredded steak sandwiches

COOK TIME: 6 TO 8 HOURS

Lee Deneau
Lansing, Michigan

I received this recipe when I was a newlywed over 30 years ago, and it's been a favorite since then. The saucy steak barbecue makes a quick meal served on sliced buns or even over rice, potatoes or buttered noodles.

- **3 pounds boneless beef round steak, cut into large pieces**
- **2 large onions, chopped**
- **3/4 cup thinly sliced celery**
- **1-1/2 cups ketchup**
- **1/2 to 3/4 cup water**
- **1/3 cup lemon juice**
- **1/3 cup Worcestershire sauce**
- **3 tablespoons brown sugar**
- **3 tablespoons cider vinegar**
- **2 to 3 teaspoons salt**
- **2 teaspoons prepared mustard**
- **1-1/2 teaspoons paprika**
- **1 teaspoon chili powder**
- **1/2 teaspoon pepper**
- **1/8 to 1/4 teaspoon hot pepper sauce**
- **12 to 14 sandwich rolls, split**

- Place meat in a 5-qt. slow cooker. Add onions and celery. In a bowl, combine the ketchup, water, lemon juice, Worcestershire sauce, brown sugar, vinegar, salt, mustard, paprika, chili powder, pepper and hot pepper sauce. Pour over meat.

- Cover and cook on high for 6-8 hours. Remove meat; cool slightly. Shred with a fork. Return to the sauce and heat through. Serve on rolls.

YIELD: 12-14 servings.

minestrone soup

COOK TIME: 7 TO 9 HOURS

Kara de la Vega
Somerset, California

When this hearty minestrone has about 30 minutes left to cook, I add the macaroni. Then there's time to toss together a salad and slice some crusty French bread.

- **6 cups chicken broth**
- **1 can (15 ounces) garbanzo beans *or* chickpeas, rinsed and drained**
- **1 medium potato, peeled and cubed**
- **1 cup cubed deli ham**
- **1/3 cup chopped onion**
- **1 small carrot, chopped**
- **1 celery rib, chopped**
- **2 tablespoons minced fresh parsley**
- **1/2 teaspoon minced garlic**
- **1/2 cup uncooked elbow macaroni**
- **1 can (14-1/2 ounces) diced tomatoes, undrained**
- **1 package (10 ounces) frozen chopped spinach, thawed and squeezed dry**

- In a 5-qt. slow cooker, combine the first nine ingredients. Cover and cook on high for 1 hour. Reduce heat to low; cook for 6-8 hours or until vegetables are almost tender.

- During the last 30 minutes of cooking, stir in the macaroni. Cover and cook until macaroni is tender. Stir in the tomatoes and spinach; heat through.

YIELD: 10 servings.

flavorful white chili

COOK TIME: 8 TO 9 HOURS

Wilda Bensenhaver
Deland, Florida

For a tasty twist on conventional chili, try this low-fat version. It's packed with plenty of beans, tender grilled chicken and a zippy blend of spices.

- **1 pound dried great northern beans, rinsed and sorted**
- **4 cups chicken broth**
- **2 cups chopped onions**
- **3 garlic cloves, minced**
- **2 teaspoons ground cumin**
- **1-1/2 teaspoons dried oregano**
- **1 teaspoon ground coriander**
- **1/8 teaspoon ground cloves**
- **1/8 teaspoon cayenne pepper**
- **1 can (4 ounces) chopped green chilies**
- **1/2 pound boneless skinless chicken breast, grilled and cubed**
- **1 teaspoon salt**
- **3/4 cup shredded reduced-fat Mexican cheese blend**

- Place beans in a soup kettle or Dutch oven; add water to cover by 2 in. Bring to a boil; boil for 2 minutes. Remove from the heat; cover and let stand for 1 hour. Drain and rinse beans, discarding liquid.

- Place beans in a 3-qt. slow cooker. Add the broth, onions, garlic and seasonings. Cover and cook on low for 7-8 hours or until beans are almost tender. Add the chilies, chicken and salt; cover and cook for 1 hour or until the beans are tender. Serve with cheese.

YIELD: 6 servings.

FLAVORFUL WHITE CHILI

pork and veggie soup

COOK TIME: 7 TO 8 HOURS

Jennifer Honeycutt
Nashville, Tennessee

Looking for a change from typical vegetable soup? Try this hearty combination. A tasty broth has savory chunks of pork and a bounty of veggies, including carrots, green beans, diced tomatoes and corn.

- **2 pounds boneless pork, cubed**
- **2 tablespoons vegetable oil**
- **2 cups water**
- **4 medium carrots, cut into 1-inch pieces**
- **1 can (14-1/2 ounces) diced tomatoes, undrained**
- **1-1/2 cups frozen corn**
- **1-1/2 cups frozen cut green beans**
- **1 large onion, chopped**
- **1 jar (8 ounces) salsa**
- **1 can (4 ounces) chopped green chilies**
- **1 tablespoon minced fresh parsley**
- **2 garlic cloves, minced**
- **2 teaspoons beef bouillon granules**
- **2 teaspoons ground cumin**
- **1/2 teaspoon salt**
- **1/2 teaspoon pepper**

■ In a large skillet, brown pork in oil over medium heat; drain. Transfer to a 3-qt. slow cooker. Stir in the remaining ingredients. Cover and cook on low for 7-8 hours or until meat juices run clear and vegetables are tender.

YIELD: 9 servings.

slow-cooked chili

COOK TIME: 8 TO 10 HOURS

Sue Call
Beech Grove, Indiana

This chili can cook for up to 10 hours on low in the slow cooker. It's so good to come home to its wonderful aroma after a long day away.

- **2 pounds ground beef**
- **2 cans (16 ounces *each*) kidney beans, rinsed and drained**
- **2 cans (14-1/2 ounces *each*) diced tomatoes, undrained**
- **1 can (8 ounces) tomato sauce**
- **2 medium onions, chopped**
- **1 green pepper, chopped**
- **2 garlic cloves, minced**
- **2 tablespoons chili powder**
- **2 teaspoons salt, optional**
- **1 teaspoon pepper**
- **Shredded cheddar cheese, optional**

■ In a large skillet, cook beef over medium heat until no longer pink; drain.

■ Transfer to a 5-qt. slow cooker. Add the next nine ingredients. Cover and cook on low for 8-10 hours or on high for 4 hours. Garnish individual servings with cheese if desired.

YIELD: 10 servings.

shredded beef sandwiches

COOK TIME: 10 TO 12 HOURS

Myra Innes
Auburn, Kansas

I find it easy to feed a crowd with these tender and tasty sandwiches. The recipe came from my grandchildren's third grade teacher, and it remains one of our favorites.

- **1 boneless beef roast (3 pounds)**
- **1 medium onion, chopped**
- **1/3 cup white vinegar**
- **3 bay leaves**
- **1/2 teaspoon salt, optional**
- **1/4 teaspoon ground cloves**
- **1/8 teaspoon garlic powder**
- **12 hamburger buns, split**

■ Cut roast in half; place in a 3-qt. slow cooker. Combine onion, vinegar, bay leaves, salt if desired, cloves and garlic powder; pour over roast.

■ Cover and cook on low for 10-12 hours or until the meat is very tender. Discard bay leaves. Remove meat and shred with a fork. Serve on buns.

YIELD: 12 servings.

SLOW-COOKED CHILI

SHREDDED BEEF SANDWICHES

chicken vegetable soup

COOK TIME: 6 TO 8 HOURS

Connie Thomas
Jensen, Utah
This delicious chicken soup gets a special twist from tomato paste, lentils and Worcestershire sauce.

- **1 can (28 ounces) diced tomatoes, undrained**
- **2 cups reduced-sodium chicken broth**
- **2 cups cubed cooked chicken breast**
- **1 cup frozen corn**
- **2 celery ribs with leaves, chopped**
- **1 can (6 ounces) tomato paste**
- **1/4 cup dried lentils, rinsed**
- **1 tablespoon sugar**
- **1 tablespoon Worcestershire sauce**
- **2 teaspoons dried parsley flakes**
- **1 teaspoon dried marjoram**

■ In a 3-qt. slow cooker, combine all ingredients. Cover and cook on low for 6-8 hours or until vegetables are tender.

YIELD: 8 servings (2 quarts).

CHICKEN VEGETABLE SOUP

easy beef vegetable soup

COOK TIME: 8 HOURS

Heather Thurmeier
Pense, Saskatchewan
What a treat to come home from work and have this savory soup ready to eat. It's a nice traditional beef soup with old-fashioned goodness.

- **1 pound boneless beef top round steak, cut into 1/2-inch cubes**
- **1 can (14-1/2 ounces) no-salt added diced tomatoes, undrained**
- **3 cups water**
- **2 medium potatoes, peeled and cubed**
- **2 medium onions, diced**
- **3 celery ribs, sliced**
- **2 carrots, sliced**
- **3 reduced-sodium beef bouillon cubes**
- **1/2 teaspoon dried basil**
- **1/2 teaspoon dried oregano**
- **1/2 teaspoon salt-free seasoning blend**
- **1/4 teaspoon pepper**
- **1-1/2 cups frozen mixed vegetables**

■ In a 5-qt. slow cooker, combine the first 12 ingredients. Cover and cook on high for 6 hours. Add vegetables; cover and cook on high 2 hours longer or until the meat and vegetables are tender.

YIELD: 8-10 servings (about 2-1/2 quarts).

italian sausage hoagies

COOK TIME: 4 HOURS

Craig Wachs
Racine, Wisconsin
In southeastern Wisconsin, our cuisine is influenced by both Germans and Italians who immigrated to this area. When preparing this recipe, we usually substitute German bratwurst for the Italian sausage, so we blend the two influences with delicious results.

- **10 uncooked Italian sausage links**
- **2 tablespoons olive oil**
- **1 jar (26 ounces) meatless spaghetti sauce**
- **1/2 medium green pepper, julienned**
- **1/2 medium sweet red pepper, julienned**
- **1/2 cup water**
- **1/4 cup grated Romano cheese**
- **2 tablespoons dried oregano**
- **2 tablespoons dried basil**
- **2 loaves French bread (20 inches)**

■ In a large skillet over medium-high heat, brown sausage in oil; drain. Transfer to a 5-qt. slow cooker. Add the spaghetti sauce, peppers, water, cheese, oregano and basil. Cover and cook on low for 4 hours or until sausage is no longer pink.

■ Slice each French bread lengthwise but not all of the way through; cut each loaf widthwise into five pieces. Fill each with sausage, peppers and sauce.

YIELD: 10 servings.

ITALIAN SAUSAGE HOAGIES

potato chowder

COOK TIME: 8 TO 10 HOURS

Anna Mayer
Ft. Branch, Indiana

One of the ladies in our church quilting group brought this savory potato soup to a meeting. It's easy to assemble in the morning, then cook all day. Cream cheese and a sprinkling of bacon provide richness.

- **8 cups diced potatoes**
- **1/3 cup chopped onion**
- **3 cans (14-1/2 ounces *each*) chicken broth**
- **1 can (10-3/4 ounces) condensed cream of chicken soup, undiluted**
- **1/4 teaspoon pepper**
- **1 package (8 ounces) cream cheese, cubed**
- **1/2 pound sliced bacon, cooked and crumbled, optional**

Snipped chives, optional

■ In a 5-qt. slow cooker, combine the first five ingredients. Cover and cook on low for 8-10 hours or until potatoes are tender. Add cream cheese; stir until blended. Garnish with bacon and chives if desired.

YIELD: 12 servings (3 quarts).

spicy kielbasa soup

COOK TIME: 8 TO 9 HOURS

Carol Custer
Clifton Park, New York

Red pepper flakes bring a little zip to this hearty soup that's full of good-for-you ingredients. Should you have any left over, this soup is great reheated after the flavors have blended.

- **1/2 pound smoked turkey kielbasa, sliced**
- **1 medium onion, chopped**
- **1 medium green pepper, chopped**
- **1 celery rib with leaves, thinly sliced**
- **4 garlic cloves, minced**
- **2 cans (14-1/2 ounces *each*) chicken broth**
- **1 can (15-1/2 ounces) great northern beans, rinsed and drained**
- **1 can (14-1/2 ounces) stewed tomatoes, cut up**
- **1 small zucchini, sliced**
- **1 medium carrot, shredded**
- **1 tablespoon dried parsley flakes**
- **1/4 teaspoon crushed red pepper flakes**
- **1/4 teaspoon pepper**

■ In a nonstick skillet, cook kielbasa over medium heat until lightly browned. Add the onion, green pepper, celery and garlic. Cook and stir for 5 minutes or until vegetables are tender.

■ Transfer to a 3-qt. slow cooker. Stir in the remaining ingredients. Cover and cook on low for 8-9 hours.

YIELD: 5 servings.

savory chicken sandwiches

COOK TIME: 8 TO 9 HOURS

Joan Parker
Gastonia, North Carolina

This tender chicken tastes like you fussed but requires few ingredients. You can also thicken the juices and serve it over rice.

- **4 bone-in chicken breast halves**
- **4 chicken thighs**
- **1 envelope onion soup mix**
- **1/4 teaspoon garlic salt**
- **1/4 cup prepared Italian salad dressing**
- **1/4 cup water**
- **14 to 16 hamburger buns, split**

■ Remove skin from chicken if desired. Place chicken in a 5-qt. slow cooker. Sprinkle with soup mix and garlic salt. Pour dressing and water over chicken.

■ Cover and cook on low for 8-9 hours. Remove chicken; cool slightly. Skim the fat from cooking juices. Remove chicken from bones; cut into bite-size pieces and return to slow cooker. Serve with a slotted spoon on buns.

YIELD: 14-16 servings.

POTATO CHOWDER

barbecued chicken sandwiches

COOK TIME: 6 TO 8 HOURS

Roberta Brown
Waupaca, Wisconsin

These sandwiches are great for large gatherings. The chicken can be cooked ahead of time, then added to the home-made barbecue sauce for simmering hours before guests arrive.

- 2 broiler/fryer chickens (3 to 3-1/2 pounds *each*), cooked and shredded
- 1 large onion, chopped
- 2 cups water
- 1-1/4 cups ketchup
- 1/4 cup packed brown sugar
- 1/4 cup Worcestershire sauce
- 1/4 cup red wine vinegar
- 1 teaspoon *each* salt, celery seed and chili powder
- 1/4 teaspoon hot pepper sauce

Hamburger buns

- In a 3-qt. slow cooker or Dutch oven, combine all ingredients except buns; mix well.

- Cook on low for 6-8 hours in the slow cooker. Serve on buns.

YIELD: 8-10 servings.

EDITOR'S NOTE: 6 cups diced cooked chicken may be used instead of the shredded chicken.

beef au jus sandwiches

COOK TIME: 10 TO 12 HOURS

Dianne Joy Richardson
Colorado Springs, Colorado

I found this recipe in one of our local publications. It's great for an easy winter meal, since the meat cooks all day without any attention.

- 1 lean beef roast (3 to 4 pounds)
- 1/2 cup soy sauce
- 1 beef bouillon cube
- 1 bay leaf
- 3 to 4 whole peppercorns
- 1 teaspoon dried crushed rosemary
- 1 teaspoon dried thyme
- 1 teaspoon garlic powder

Hard rolls *or* French bread

- Remove and discard all visible fat from roast. Place in a 3-qt. slow cooker. Combine soy sauce, bouillon and spices; pour over roast. Add water to almost cover roast.

- Cover and cook over low heat 10-12 hours or until meat is very tender. Remove meat from broth; reserve broth. Shred meat with a fork. Serve on hard rolls or French bread slices with broth.

YIELD: 12 servings.

slow-cooked vegetable soup

COOK TIME: 9 TO 10 HOURS

Christina Till
South Haven, Michigan

You just have to try this hearty soup for its unique blend of flavors.

- 3/4 cup chopped onion
- 1/2 cup chopped celery
- 1/2 cup chopped green pepper
- 2 tablespoons olive oil
- 1 large potato, peeled and diced
- 1 medium sweet potato, peeled and diced
- 1 to 2 garlic cloves, minced
- 3 cups chicken broth *or* water
- 2 medium fresh tomatoes, chopped
- 1 can (16 ounces) kidney beans, rinsed and drained
- 1 can (15 ounces) garbanzo beans *or* chickpeas, rinsed and drained
- 2 teaspoons soy sauce
- 1 teaspoon paprika
- 1/2 teaspoon dried basil
- 1/4 teaspoon salt
- 1/4 teaspoon ground turmeric
- 1 bay leaf

Dash cayenne pepper

- In a large skillet, saute the onion, celery and green pepper in oil until crisp-tender. Add the potato, sweet potato and garlic; saute 3-5 minutes longer.

- Transfer to a 5-qt. slow cooker. Stir in remaining ingredients. Cover; cook on low for 9-10 hours or until vegetables are tender. Discard bay leaf before serving.

YIELD: 12 servings (about 3 quarts).

BARBECUED CHICKEN SANDWICHES

hearty italian sandwiches

COOK TIME: 6 HOURS

Elaine Krupsky
Las Vegas, Nevada

I've been making this sweet, spicy, satisfying sandwich filling for 35 years.

1-1/2 pounds ground beef

1-1/2 pounds bulk Italian sausage

2 *each* large onions, green peppers and sweet red peppers, sliced

1 teaspoon salt

1 teaspoon pepper

1/4 teaspoon crushed red pepper flakes

8 sandwich rolls, split

Shredded Monterey Jack cheese, optional

■In a Dutch oven, cook beef and sausage over medium heat until no longer pink; drain. Place a third of the onions and peppers in a 5-qt. slow cooker; top with half of the meat mixture. Repeat layers; top with remaining vegetables. Sprinkle with salt, pepper and pepper flakes.

■ Cover and cook on low for 6 hours or until vegetables are tender. With a slotted spoon, serve about 1 cup of meat and vegetables on each roll. Top with cheese if desired. Use pan juices for dipping if desired.

YIELD: 8 servings.

red bean vegetable soup

COOK TIME: 6 HOURS

Ronnie Lappe
Brownwood, Texas

The addition of Cajun seasoning boosts the flavor of this brothy soup. The easy recipe makes a big batch that's loaded with fresh vegetable chunks and canned beans.

3 large sweet red peppers, chopped

3 celery ribs, chopped

2 medium onions, chopped

4 cans (16 ounces *each*) red kidney beans, rinsed and drained

4 cups chicken broth

2 bay leaves

1/2 to 1 teaspoon salt

1/2 to 1 teaspoon Cajun seasoning

1/2 teaspoon pepper

1/4 to 1/2 teaspoon hot pepper sauce

■In a 5-qt. slow cooker, combine the peppers, celery, onions and beans. Stir in the remaining ingredients.

■Cover and cook on low for 6 hours or until vegetables are tender. Discard bay leaves before serving.

YIELD: 12 servings (3 quarts).

spicy slow-cooked chili

COOK TIME: 4 TO 6 HOURS

Sabrina Corrigan
Williamsburg, Pennsylvania

If you like your chili thick, you'll enjoy this simple, fuss-free version.

2 pounds ground beef

2 to 3 hot chili peppers of your choice

3 cans (16 ounces *each*) kidney beans, rinsed and drained

1 can (6 ounces) tomato paste

1 medium onion, chopped

1 medium green pepper, seeded and chopped

2 teaspoons chili powder

2 teaspoons cider vinegar

1 teaspoon garlic powder

1 teaspoon dried oregano

1/4 to 1/2 teaspoon ground cinnamon

1/4 teaspoon pepper

2 to 4 cups tomato juice

■In a large skillet, cook beef over medium heat until no longer pink; drain. Transfer to a 5-qt. slow cooker. Remove seeds from the chili peppers if desired; chop peppers. Add to the slow cooker. Stir in the beans, tomato paste, onion, green pepper, seasonings and 2 cups tomato juice.

■Cover and cook on low for 4-6 hours or until heated through, adding more tomato juice if needed to achieve desired thickness.

YIELD: 8 servings.

EDITOR'S NOTE: When cutting or seeding hot peppers, use rubber or plastic gloves to protect your hands. Avoid touching your face.

HEARTY ITALIAN SANDWICHES

SPICY SLOW-COOKED CHILI

mexican chicken soup

COOK TIME: 3 TO 4 HOURS

Marlene Kane
Lainesburg, Michigan

This zesty dish is loaded with chicken, corn and black beans in a mildly spicy red broth. I'm always looking for dinner recipes that can be prepared in the morning. The kids love the taco-like taste of this easy soup.

- **1-1/2 pounds boneless skinless chicken breasts, cubed**
- **2 teaspoons canola oil**
- **1/2 cup water**
- **1 envelope taco seasoning**
- **1 can (32 ounces) V8 juice**
- **1 jar (16 ounces) salsa**
- **1 can (15 ounces) black beans, rinsed and drained**
- **1 package (10 ounces) frozen corn, thawed**
- **6 tablespoons cheddar cheese**
- **6 tablespoons sour cream**
- **2 tablespoons chopped fresh cilantro**

- In a large nonstick skillet, saute chicken in oil until no longer pink. Add water and taco seasoning; simmer until chicken is well coated.

- Transfer to a 3-qt. slow cooker. Add the V8 juice, salsa, beans and corn; mix well. Cover and cook on low for 3-4 hours or until heated through. Serve with cheese, sour cream and cilantro.

YIELD: 6 servings.

spicy french dip

COOK TIME: 8 TO 10 HOURS

Ginny Koeppen
Winnfield, Louisiana

If I'm cooking for a party or family get-together, I can put this beef in the slow cooker in the morning and then concentrate on other preparations. It's a great time-saver and never fails to get rave reviews.

- **1 boneless beef sirloin tip roast (about 3 pounds), cut in half**
- **1/2 cup water**
- **1 can (4 ounces) diced jalapeno peppers, drained**
- **1 envelope Italian salad dressing mix**
- **12 crusty rolls (5 inches)**

- Place beef in a 5-qt. slow cooker. In a small bowl, combine the water, jalapenos and dressing mix; pour over beef.

- Cover and cook on low for 8-10 hours or until meat is tender. Remove beef and shred using two forks. Skim fat from cooking juices. Serve beef on buns with juice.

YIELD: 12 servings.

hearty pasta tomato soup

COOK TIME: 3-1/2 TO 4-1/2 HOURS

Lydia Kroese
Minnetonka, Minnesota

I adapted the original recipe for this flavorful soup so I could make it in the slow cooker. It's ideal when you don't have easy access to a stove or oven.

- **1 pound bulk Italian sausage**
- **6 cups beef broth**
- **1 can (28 ounces) stewed tomatoes**
- **1 can (15 ounces) tomato sauce**
- **2 cups sliced zucchini**
- **1 large onion, chopped**
- **1 cup sliced carrots**
- **1 cup sliced fresh mushrooms**
- **1 medium green pepper, chopped**
- **1/4 cup minced fresh parsley**
- **2 teaspoons sugar**
- **1 teaspoon dried oregano**
- **1 teaspoon dried basil**
- **1 garlic clove, minced**
- **2 cups frozen cheese tortellini**

Grated Parmesan cheese, optional

- In a skillet, cook the sausage over medium heat until no longer pink; drain. Transfer to a 5-qt. slow cooker; add the next 13 ingredients. Cover and cook on high for 3-4 hours or until the vegetables are tender.

- Cook tortellini according to package directions; drain. Stir into slow cooker; cover and cook 30 minutes longer. Serve with Parmesan cheese if desired.

YIELD: 14 servings (about 3-1/2 quarts).

MEXICAN CHICKEN SOUP

bandito chili dogs

COOK TIME: 4 TO 5 HOURS

Marion Lowery
Medford, Oregon

I've brought these beefy chili dogs to family functions for years. The ingredients cook while you're at a game or other activity, so the meal is ready when you get home.

- 1 package (1 pound) hot dogs
- 2 cans (15 ounces *each*) chili without beans
- 1 can (10-3/4 ounces) condensed cheddar cheese soup, undiluted
- 1 can (4 ounces) chopped green chilies
- 10 hot dog buns, split
- 1 medium onion, chopped
- 1 to 2 cups corn chips, coarsely crushed
- 1 cup (4 ounces) shredded cheddar cheese

- Place hot dogs in a 3-qt. slow cooker. In a bowl, combine the chili, soup and green chilies; pour over hot dogs.

- Cover and cook on low for 4-5 hours. Serve hot dogs in buns; top with the chili mixture, onion, corn chips and cheese.

YIELD: 10 servings.

meaty tomato soup

COOK TIME: 8 HOURS

Ann Bost
Elkhart, Texas

As an elementary school librarian and choir director, I rely on and enjoy slow-cooked meals.

- 1 can (28 ounces) diced tomatoes, undrained
- 2 cans (8 ounces *each*) tomato sauce
- 2 cups water
- 1/2 pound ground beef, cooked and drained
- 1/2 pound bulk pork sausage, cooked and drained
- 2 tablespoons dried minced onion
- 2 chicken bouillon cubes
- 3/4 teaspoon garlic salt
- 3/4 cup uncooked elbow macaroni

Shredded cheddar cheese, optional

- In a 3-qt. slow cooker, combine the first eight ingredients; mix well. Cover and cook on low for 8 hours.

- Add macaroni and mix well. Cover and cook 15 minutes longer or until macaroni is tender. Garnish with cheese if desired.

YIELD: 8-10 servings (2-1/4 quarts).

curried lentil soup

COOK TIME: 8 HOURS

Christina Till
South Haven, Michigan

Curry gives a different taste sensation to this chili-like soup. It's delicious with a dollop of sour cream. My family welcomes it with open arms and watering mouths.

- 4 cups hot water
- 1 can (28 ounces) crushed tomatoes
- 3 medium potatoes, peeled and diced
- 3 medium carrots, thinly sliced
- 1 large onion, chopped
- 1 celery rib, chopped
- 1 cup dried lentils, rinsed
- 2 garlic cloves, minced
- 2 bay leaves
- 4 teaspoons curry powder
- 1-1/2 teaspoons salt

- In a 5-qt. slow cooker, combine all of the ingredients; stir well. Cover and cook on low for 8 hours or until vegetables and lentils are tender. Discard bay leaves before serving.

YIELD: 10 servings (2-1/2 quarts).

BANDITO CHILI DOGS

italian beef hoagies

COOK TIME: 8 HOURS

Lori Piatt
Danville, Illinois

You'll need just five ingredients to feed a crowd these tender tangy sandwiches. On weekends, I start the roast the night before, so I can shred it in the morning.

- **1 boneless sirloin tip roast (about 4 pounds), halved**
- **2 envelopes Italian salad dressing mix**
- **2 cups water**
- **1 jar (16 ounces) mild pepper rings, undrained**
- **18 hoagie buns, split**

■ Place roast in a 5-qt. slow cooker. Combine the salad dressing mix and water; pour over roast. Cover and cook on low for 8 hours or until meat is tender.

■ Remove meat; shred with a fork and return to slow cooker. Add pepper rings; heat through. Spoon 1/2 cup meat mixture onto each bun.

YIELD: 18 servings.

veggie meatball soup

COOK TIME: 4 TO 5 HOURS

Charla Tinney
Tyrone, Oklahoma

It's a snap to put together this hearty soup before I leave for work. I just add cooked pasta when I get home, and I have a few minutes to relax before supper is ready.

- **3 cups beef broth**
- **2 cups frozen mixed vegetables, thawed**
- **1 can (14-1/2 ounces) stewed tomatoes**
- **15 frozen fully cooked meatballs, thawed**
- **3 bay leaves**
- **1/4 teaspoon pepper**
- **1 cup spiral pasta, cooked and drained**

■ In a 3-qt. slow cooker, combine the first six ingredients. Cover and cook on low for 4-5 hours. Discard the bay leaves. Just before serving, stir in pasta; heat through.

YIELD: 6 servings.

buffalo chicken wing soup

COOK TIME: 4 TO 5 HOURS

Pat Farmer
Falconer, New York

My husband and I love buffalo chicken wings, so we created a soup with the same zippy flavor. It's very popular with guests. Start with a small amount of hot sauce, then add more if needed to suit your family's tastes.

- **6 cups milk**
- **3 cans (10-3/4 ounces *each*) condensed cream of chicken soup, undiluted**
- **3 cups shredded cooked chicken (about 1 pound)**
- **1 cup (8 ounces) sour cream**
- **1/4 to 1/2 cup hot pepper sauce**

■ Combine all ingredients in a 3-qt. slow cooker. Cover and cook on low for 4-5 hours.

YIELD: 8 servings (2 quarts).

SLOW COOKER TIP: Frozen meat should be completely thawed before placing in a slow cooker. Whole roasts and poultry should be cut in half or into smaller pieces to ensure thorough cooking.

Off   Low   High

ITALIAN BEEF HOAGIES

chili sandwiches

COOK TIME: 5 TO 6 HOURS

Kerry Haglund
Wyoming, Minnesota

No one will be able to resist these special sandwiches stuffed with spicy chili.

- 1 pound dried navy beans
- 2 pounds beef stew meat
- 2 cups water
- 1 pound sliced bacon, diced
- 1 cup chopped onion
- 1 cup shredded carrots
- 1 cup chopped celery
- 1/3 cup chopped green pepper
- 1/3 cup chopped sweet red pepper
- 4 garlic cloves, minced
- 3 cans (14-1/2 ounces *each*) diced tomatoes, undrained
- 1 cup barbecue sauce
- 1 cup chili sauce
- 1/2 cup honey
- 1/4 cup hot pepper sauce
- 1 tablespoon chili powder
- 1 tablespoon baking cocoa
- 1 tablespoon Dijon mustard
- 1 tablespoon Worcestershire sauce
- 1 bay leaf
- 4 teaspoons beef bouillon granules
- 30 hamburger buns, split

■ Place beans and enough water to cover in a saucepan. Bring to a boil; boil for 2 minutes. Remove from the heat and let stand for 1 hour; drain and rinse.

■ In a large kettle, simmer beans and beef in water 2 hours or until very tender; drain. Shred beef; place it and the beans in a 5-qt. slow cooker.

■ In a large skillet, cook bacon until crisp. With a slotted spoon, remove bacon to the slow cooker. Discard all but 3 tablespoons drippings. Saute onion, carrots, celery, peppers and garlic in drippings until tender.

■ Transfer to the slow cooker. Add remaining ingredients except buns. Cover and cook on high for 3-4 hours, stirring often. Remove bay leaf. Spoon 1/2 cup onto each bun.

YIELD: 30 servings.

ham and lentil soup

COOK TIME: 4 HOURS

Connie Jones Pixley
Roxboro, North Carolina

This delicious soup is a great way to use up leftover cooked ham. Its hearty broth makes this dish perfect for a cold day. Just serve with fresh crusty bread and butter.

- 1 cup chopped celery
- 1 cup chopped carrots
- 1/2 cup chopped onion
- 1 tablespoon butter
- 8 cups water
- 2 cups dried lentils, rinsed
- 1 cup cubed fully cooked ham
- 2 teaspoons salt
- 1 teaspoon dried marjoram
- 1/2 teaspoon pepper

■ In a large skillet, saute the celery, carrots and onion in butter for 3-4 minutes or until crisp-tender.

■ In a 5-qt. slow cooker, combine the water, lentils, ham, salt, marjoram and pepper. Stir in the celery mixture. Cover and cook on low for 4 hours or until lentils are tender.

YIELD: 11 servings.

beefy vegetable soup

COOK TIME: 8 HOURS

Teresa King
Chambersburg, Pennsylvania

I adapted this recipe from one I saw in a cookbook in an effort to add more vegetables to our diet. Our two young sons eat this up without hesitation.

- 1 pound ground beef
- 1 medium onion, chopped
- 1 garlic clove, minced
- 2 cans (8 ounces *each*) tomato sauce
- 2 cans (16 ounces *each*) kidney beans, rinsed and drained, optional
- 1 package (10 ounces) frozen corn
- 1 cup shredded carrots
- 1 cup chopped green pepper
- 1 cup chopped sweet red pepper
- 1 cup chopped fresh tomato
- 1 tablespoon chili powder
- 1/2 teaspoon dried basil
- 1/2 teaspoon salt
- 1/4 teaspoon pepper

Shredded cheddar cheese, sour cream and tortilla chips, optional

■ In a skillet, cook beef, onion and the garlic over medium heat until the meat is no longer pink; drain. Transfer to a 5-qt. slow cooker. Add the tomato sauce, beans if desired, vegetables and seasonings; mix well.

■ Cover and cook on low for 8 hours or until thick and bubbly, stirring occasionally. Serve with cheese, sour cream and chips if desired.

YIELD: 8-10 servings (about 2-1/2 quarts).

BEEFY VEGETABLE SOUP

santa fe chili

COOK TIME: 4 HOURS

Laura Manning
Lilburn, Georgia
This colorful and hearty chili is perfect for heartwarming, holiday get-togethers. My family has been enjoying it for years.

- **2 pounds ground beef**
- **1 medium onion, chopped**
- **2 cans (16 ounces *each*) kidney beans, rinsed and drained**
- **2 cans (15 ounces *each*) black beans, rinsed and drained**
- **2 cans (15 ounces *each*) pinto beans, rinsed and drained**
- **2 cans (11 ounces *each*) shoepeg corn**
- **1 can (14-1/2 ounces) whole tomatoes, diced**
- **1 can (10 ounces) diced tomatoes and green chilies**
- **1 can (11-1/2 ounces) V8 juice**
- **2 envelopes ranch salad dressing mix**
- **2 envelopes taco seasoning**

Sour cream, shredded cheddar cheese and corn chips, optional

- In a skillet, cook beef and onion over medium heat until meat is no longer pink; drain. Transfer to a 5-qt. slow cooker. Stir in the beans, corn, tomatoes, juice, salad dressing mix and taco seasoning.

- Cover and cook on high for 4 hours or until heated through. Serve with sour cream, cheese and corn chips if desired.

YIELD: 4 quarts (16 servings).

navy bean vegetable soup

COOK TIME: 9 TO 10 HOURS

Eleanor Mielke
Mitchell, South Dakota
My family likes bean soup, so I came up with this hearty version. Leftovers freeze well for first-rate future meals.

- **4 medium carrots, thinly sliced**
- **2 celery ribs, chopped**
- **1 medium onion, chopped**
- **2 cups cubed fully cooked ham**
- **1-1/2 cups dried navy beans**
- **1 package (1.68 ounces) vegetable soup mix**
- **1 envelope onion soup mix**
- **1 bay leaf**
- **1/2 teaspoon pepper**
- **8 cups water**

- In a 5-qt. slow cooker, combine the first nine ingredients. Stir in water. Cover and cook on low for 9-10 hours or until beans are tender. Discard bay leaf.

YIELD: 12 servings.

sausage pepper sandwiches

COOK TIME: 8 HOURS

Suzette Gessel
Albuquerque, New Mexico
Peppers and onions add a fresh taste to this zippy sausage sandwich filling.

- **5 uncooked Italian sausage links (about 20 ounces)**
- **1 medium green pepper, cut into 1-inch pieces**
- **1 large onion, cut into 1-inch pieces**
- **1 can (8 ounces) tomato sauce**
- **1/8 teaspoon pepper**
- **6 hoagie *or* submarine sandwich buns, split**

- In a large skillet, brown sausage over medium heat. Cut into 1/2-in. slices; place in a 3-qt. slow cooker. Stir in green pepper, onion, tomato sauce and pepper. Cover; cook on low 8 hours or until sausage is no longer pink and vegetables are tender. Use a slotted spoon to serve on buns.

YIELD: 6 servings.

SANTA FE CHILI

SAUSAGE PEPPER SANDWICHES

pork and beef barbecue

COOK TIME: 6 TO 8 HOURS

Corbin Detgen
Buchanan, Michigan

It's the delectable combination of beef stew meat and pork tenderloin that keeps friends and family asking about these tangy sandwiches.

- 1 can (6 ounces) tomato paste
- 1/2 cup packed brown sugar
- 1/4 cup chili powder
- 1/4 cup cider vinegar
- 2 teaspoons Worcestershire sauce
- 1 teaspoon salt
- 1-1/2 pounds beef stew meat, cut into 3/4-inch cubes
- 1-1/2 pounds pork chop suey meat *or* pork tenderloin, cut into 3/4-inch cubes
- 3 medium green peppers, chopped
- 2 large onions, chopped
- 14 sandwich rolls, split

Lettuce and tomatoes, optional

- In a 5-qt. slow cooker, combine the first six ingredients. Stir in beef, pork, green peppers and onions. Cover and cook on high for 6-8 hours or until meat is tender.

- Remove meat; cool slightly. Shred meat with two forks. Return to the slow cooker. Serve on rolls with lettuce and tomatoes if desired.

YIELD: 14 servings.

SLOW COOKER TIP:
Before cooking in a slow cooker, trim excess fat from meats and remove the skin from poultry.

hearty bean soup

COOK TIME: 6 TO 7 HOURS

Alice Schnoor
Arion, Iowa

This is an easy-to-assemble soup that has old-fashioned goodness. I enjoy the thick broth and the tasty medley of ham, great northern beans and root vegetables.

- 3 cups chopped parsnips
- 2 cups chopped carrots
- 1 cup chopped onion
- 1-1/2 cups dried great northern beans
- 5 cups water
- 1-1/2 pounds smoked ham hocks *or* ham shanks
- 2 garlic cloves, minced
- 2 teaspoons salt
- 1/2 teaspoon pepper
- 1/8 to 1/4 teaspoon hot pepper sauce

- In a 5-qt. slow cooker, place the parsnips, carrots and onion. Top with beans. Add water, ham, garlic, salt, pepper and hot pepper sauce. Cover and cook on high for 6-7 hours or until beans are tender.

- Remove meat and bones when cool enough to handle. Cut meat into bite-size pieces and return to slow cooker; heat through.

YIELD: 6 servings.

easy minestrone

COOK TIME: 6 TO 8 HOURS

Yvonne Andrus
Highland, Utah

Put together this wonderful recipe in the morning and forget about it the rest of the day.

- 4 medium tomatoes, chopped
- 2 medium carrots, chopped
- 2 celery ribs, chopped
- 1 medium zucchini, halved and sliced
- 1-1/2 cups shredded cabbage
- 1 can (16 ounces) kidney beans, rinsed and drained
- 1 can (15 ounces) garbanzo beans *or* chickpeas, rinsed and drained
- 6 cups reduced-sodium chicken broth *or* vegetable broth
- 1-1/4 teaspoons Italian seasoning
- 1 teaspoon salt
- 1/4 teaspoon pepper
- 2 cups cooked elbow macaroni
- 5 tablespoons shredded Parmesan cheese

- In a 5-qt. slow cooker, combine the first 11 ingredients. Cover and cook on low for 6-8 hours or until vegetables are tender. Just before serving, stir in macaroni and heat through. Serve with Parmesan cheese.

YIELD: 10 servings (about 3-1/4 quarts).

HEARTY BEAN SOUP

EASY MINESTRONE

turkey enchiladas

COOK TIME: 6 TO 8 HOURS

Stella Schams
Tempe, Arizona

I simmer turkey thighs with tomato sauce, green chilies and seasonings until they're tender and flavorful. Then I shred the turkey and serve it in tortillas with other fresh fixings.

> 2 turkey thighs *or* drumsticks (about 2 pounds)
>
> 1 can (8 ounces) tomato sauce
>
> 1 can (4 ounces) chopped green chilies
>
> 1/3 cup chopped onion
>
> 2 tablespoons Worcestershire sauce
>
> 1 to 2 tablespoons chili powder
>
> 1/4 teaspoon garlic powder
>
> 8 flour tortillas (6 inches)

Optional toppings: chopped green onions, sliced ripe olives, chopped tomatoes, shredded cheddar cheese, sour cream *and/or* shredded lettuce

■ Remove skin from turkey. Place in a 5-qt. slow cooker. Combine tomato sauce, chilies, onion, Worcestershire sauce, chili powder and garlic powder; pour over turkey. Cover and cook on low for 6-8 hours or until turkey is tender.

■ Remove turkey; shred meat with a fork and return to the slow cooker. Heat through. Spoon about 1/2 cup of turkey mixture down the center of each tortilla. Fold bottom of tortilla over filling and roll up. Add toppings of your choice.

YIELD: 4 servings.

slow-cooked corn chowder

COOK TIME: 6 HOURS

Mary Hogue
Rochester, Pennsylvania

I combine and refrigerate the ingredients for this easy chowder the night before. In the morning, I pour the mixture into the slow cooker and turn it on before I leave for work. When I come home, a hot meal awaits.

> 2-1/2 cups milk
>
> 1 can (14-3/4 ounces) cream-style corn
>
> 1 can (10-3/4 ounces) condensed cream of mushroom soup, undiluted
>
> 1-3/4 cups frozen corn
>
> 1 cup frozen shredded hash brown potatoes
>
> 1 cup cubed fully cooked ham
>
> 1 large onion, chopped
>
> 2 tablespoons butter
>
> 2 teaspoons dried parsley flakes

Salt and pepper to taste

■ In a 3-qt. slow cooker, combine all ingredients. Cover and cook on low for 6 hours.

YIELD: 8 servings (2 quarts).

dilly beef sandwiches

COOK TIME: 8 TO 9 HOURS

Donna Blankenheim
Madison, Wisconsin

My younger sister shared this recipe, which puts a twist on the traditional barbecue sandwich. As a busy mother of four, I never have much time to cook, but I do like to entertain. This crowd-pleaser, made in a convenient slow cooker, is perfect for our large family gatherings.

> 1 boneless beef chuck roast (3 to 4 pounds)
>
> 1 jar (16 ounces) whole dill pickles, undrained
>
> 1/2 cup chili sauce
>
> 2 garlic cloves, minced
>
> 10 to 12 hamburger buns, split

■ Cut roast in half and place in a 3-qt. slow cooker. Add pickles with juice, chili sauce and garlic. Cover and cook on low for 8-9 hours or until beef is tender.

■ Discard pickles. Remove roast. When cool enough to handle, shred the meat. Return to the sauce and heat through. Using a slotted spoon, fill each bun with about 1/2 cup meat mixture.

YIELD: 10-12 servings.

TURKEY ENCHILADAS

texas black bean soup

COOK TIME: 4 TO 5 HOURS

Pamela Scott
Garland, Texas

This hearty stew made with convenient canned items is perfect for spicing up a family gathering on a cool day. It tastes great and requires so little time and attention.

- **2 cans (15 ounces *each*) black beans, rinsed and drained**
- **1 can (14-1/2 ounces) stewed tomatoes *or* Mexican stewed tomatoes, cut up**
- **1 can (14-1/2 ounces) diced tomatoes *or* diced tomatoes with green chilies**
- **1 can (14-1/2 ounces) chicken broth**
- **1 can (11 ounces) Mexicorn, drained**
- **2 cans (4 ounces *each*) chopped green chilies**
- **4 green onions, thinly sliced**
- **2 to 3 tablespoons chili powder**
- **1 teaspoon ground cumin**
- **1/2 teaspoon dried minced garlic**

- In a 5-qt. slow cooker, combine all of the ingredients. Cover and cook on high for 4-5 hours or until heated through.

YIELD: 8-10 servings (about 2-1/2 quarts).

pork tortillas

COOK TIME: 8 TO 9 HOURS

Rita Hahnbaum
Muscatine, Iowa

I season my pork roast with onions, garlic and spices, and then I cook it slowly until tender. It's delicious!

- **1 boneless pork shoulder roast (2-1/2 to 3 pounds), halved**
- **1 cup boiling water**
- **2 teaspoons beef bouillon granules**
- **3 garlic cloves, minced**
- **1 tablespoon dried basil**
- **1 tablespoon dried oregano**
- **1 teaspoon ground cumin**
- **1 teaspoon pepper**
- **1 teaspoon dried tarragon**
- **1 teaspoon white pepper**
- **2 medium onions, sliced**
- **1 *each* large green, sweet red and yellow pepper, sliced**
- **1 tablespoon butter**
- **12 to 14 flour tortillas (6 inches), warmed**

Shredded lettuce, chopped ripe olives and sour cream

- Place pork roast halves in a 5-qt. slow cooker. Combine water, bouillon, garlic and seasonings; pour over roast. Top with onions. Cover; cook on high 1 hour. Reduce heat to low. Cook 7-8 hours or until pork is tender. When cool enough to handle, remove meat from bone. Shred meat. Return to slow cooker; heat through.

- In a skillet, saute peppers in butter until tender. Using a slotted spoon, place 1/2 cup pork and onion mixture down the center of each tortilla; top with peppers. Serve with lettuce, olives and sour cream.

YIELD: 12-14 servings.

fresh pumpkin soup

COOK TIME: 8 TO 10 HOURS

Jane Shapton
Portland, Oregon

This appealing soup harvests the fall flavors of just-picked pumpkins and tart apples...and is sure to warm you up on a crisp autumn day. I top the creamy puree with a sprinkling of toasted pumpkin seeds.

- **8 cups chopped fresh pumpkin (about 3 pounds)**
- **4 cups chicken broth**
- **3 small tart apples, peeled and chopped**
- **1 medium onion, chopped**
- **2 tablespoons lemon juice**
- **2 teaspoons minced fresh gingerroot**
- **2 garlic cloves, minced**
- **1/2 teaspoon salt**

TOASTED PUMPKIN SEEDS:

- **1/2 cup pumpkin seeds**
- **1 teaspoon canola oil**
- **1/8 teaspoon salt**

- In a 3-qt. slow cooker, combine the first eight ingredients; mix well. Cover and cook on low for 8-10 hours or until pumpkin and apples are tender. Meanwhile, toss pumpkin seeds with oil and salt. Spread in an ungreased 15-in. x 10-in. x 1-in. baking pan. Bake at 250° for 50-60 minutes or until golden brown. Set aside.

- Cool the pumpkin mixture slightly; process in batches in a blender or food processor. Transfer to a large saucepan; heat through. Garnish with toasted pumpkin seeds.

YIELD: 9 servings.

TEXAS BLACK BEAN SOUP

side dishes

Scrumptious side dishes are made even more simple when you use your all-purpose slow cooker! Appealing partners, such delicious Creamy Red Potatoes, page 102, offer delicious new taste twists on old family favorites.

For potlucks, luncheons or large family parties, you'll appreciate the crowd-serving options in this chapter. Best of all, you can make and take your dish to pass in the same pot—and keep it warm throughout mealtime.

sweet 'n' sour beans

COOK TIME: 3 TO 4 HOURS

Barbara Short
Mena, Arkansas

This recipe is popular on both sides of the border. It came from a friend in Alaska, then traveled with me to old Mexico, where I lived for 5 years, and is now a potluck favorite in my Arkansas community. It's easy to keep warm and serve from a slow cooker.

- 8 bacon strips, diced
- 2 medium onions, halved and thinly sliced
- 1 cup packed brown sugar
- 1/2 cup cider vinegar
- 1 teaspoon salt
- 1 teaspoon ground mustard
- 1/2 teaspoon garlic powder
- 1 can (28 ounces) baked beans, undrained
- 1 can (16 ounces) kidney beans, rinsed and drained
- 1 can (15-1/2 ounces) pinto beans, rinsed and drained
- 1 can (15 ounces) lima beans, rinsed and drained
- 1 can (15-1/2 ounces) black-eyed peas, rinsed and drained

■ In a large skillet, cook bacon over medium heat until crisp. Remove with slotted spoon to paper towels. Drain, reserving 2 tablespoons drippings. Saute onions in the drippings until tender. Add brown sugar, vinegar, salt, mustard and garlic powder. Bring to a boil.

■ In a 5-qt. slow cooker, combine beans and peas. Add onion mixture and bacon; mix well. Cover and cook on high for 3-4 hours or until heated through.

YIELD: 15-20 servings.

marmalade-glazed carrots

COOK TIME: 5-1/2 TO 6-1/2 HOURS

Barb Rudyk
Vermilion, Alberta

This side dish is ideal when you'd like to serve your vegetables in a different way for a special dinner. Cinnamon and nutmeg season baby carrots that are simmered with orange marmalade and brown sugar.

- 1 package (2 pounds) fresh baby carrots
- 1/2 cup orange marmalade
- 3 tablespoons cold water, *divided*
- 2 tablespoons brown sugar
- 1 tablespoon butter, melted
- 1/2 teaspoon ground cinnamon
- 1/4 teaspoon salt
- 1/4 teaspoon ground nutmeg
- 1/8 teaspoon pepper
- 1 tablespoon cornstarch

■ In a 3-qt. slow cooker, combine the carrots, marmalade, 1 tablespoon water, brown sugar, butter and seasonings. Cover and cook on low for 5-6 hours or until carrots are tender.

■ Combine cornstarch and remaining water until smooth; stir into carrot mixture. Cover and cook on high for 30 minutes or until thickened. Serve with a slotted spoon.

YIELD: 6 servings.

au gratin garlic potatoes

COOK TIME: 6 TO 7 HOURS

Tonya Vowels
Vine Grove, Kentucky

Cream cheese and a can of cheese soup turn potatoes into a perfect side dish.

- 1/2 cup milk
- 1 can (10-3/4 ounces) condensed cheddar cheese soup, undiluted
- 1 package (8 ounces) cream cheese, cubed
- 1 garlic clove, minced
- 1/4 teaspoon ground nutmeg
- 1/8 teaspoon pepper
- 2 pounds potatoes, peeled and sliced
- 1 small onion, chopped

Paprika, optional

■ In a saucepan, heat milk over medium heat until bubbles form around side of saucepan. Remove from heat. Add soup, cream cheese, garlic, nutmeg and pepper; stir until smooth.

■ Place the potatoes and onion in a 3-qt. slow cooker. Pour the milk mixture over the potato mixture; mix well. Cover and cook on low for 6-7 hours or until potatoes are tender. Sprinkle with paprika if desired.

YIELD: 6-8 servings.

MARMALADE-GLAZED CARROTS

AU GRATIN GARLIC POTATOES

slow-cooked broccoli

COOK TIME: 2-1/2 TO 3 HOURS

Connie Slocum
St. Simons Island, Georgia

This casserole is quick to assemble and full of good flavor. Even those who don't usually like broccoli enjoy it prepared this way.

- 2 packages (10 ounces *each*) frozen chopped broccoli, partially thawed
- 1 can (10-3/4 ounces) condensed cream of celery soup, undiluted
- 1-1/2 cups (6 ounces) shredded sharp cheddar cheese, *divided*
- 1/4 cup chopped onion
- 1/2 teaspoon Worcestershire sauce
- 1/4 teaspoon pepper
- 1 cup crushed butter-flavored crackers (about 25)
- 2 tablespoons butter

- In a large bowl, combine broccoli, soup, 1 cup cheese, onion, Worcestershire sauce and pepper. Pour into a greased 3-qt. slow cooker. Sprinkle the crackers on top; dot with butter.

- Cover and cook on high for 2-1/2 to 3 hours. Sprinkle with remaining cheese. Cook 10 minutes longer or until the cheese is melted.

YIELD: 8-10 servings.

lemon red potatoes

COOK TIME: 2-1/2 TO 3 HOURS

Tara Branham
Cedar Park, Texas

Butter, lemon juice, parsley and chives enhance this simple side dish. I usually prepare these potatoes when I'm having company. Since they cook in the slow cooker, there's plenty of room on the stove for other dishes.

- 1-1/2 pounds medium red potatoes
- 1/4 cup water
- 1/4 cup butter, melted
- 1 tablespoon lemon juice
- 3 tablespoons snipped fresh parsley
- 1 tablespoon snipped fresh chives

Salt and pepper to taste

- Cut a strip of peel from around the middle of each potato. Place potatoes and water in a 3-qt. slow cooker.

- Cover and cook on high for 2-1/2 to 3 hours or until tender (do not overcook); drain. Combine butter, lemon juice, parsley and chives; mix well. Pour over the potatoes and toss to coat. Season with salt and pepper.

YIELD: 6 servings.

hearty pork 'n' beans

COOK TIME: 4 TO 5 HOURS

Janice Toms
Saline, Louisiana

This sweet chunky mixture tastes great as a main dish with French bread or corn bread. It's also a good side dish to serve at a barbecue or potluck.

- 1 pound ground beef
- 1 medium green pepper, chopped
- 1 small onion, chopped
- 1 package (16 ounces) smoked sausage, halved lengthwise and thinly sliced
- 1 can (16 ounces) pork and beans, undrained
- 1 can (15-1/4 ounces) lima beans, rinsed and drained
- 1 can (15 ounces) pinto beans, rinsed and drained
- 1 cup ketchup
- 1/2 cup packed brown sugar
- 1 teaspoon salt
- 1/2 teaspoon garlic powder
- 1/4 teaspoon pepper

- In a skillet, cook beef, green pepper and onion over medium heat until meat is no longer pink; drain.

- In a 3-qt. slow cooker, combine all of the remaining ingredients. Stir in beef mixture. Cover and cook on high for 4-5 hours or until heated through.

YIELD: 12 side-dish servings or 8 main-dish servings.

SLOW-COOKED BROCCOLI

creamy red potatoes

COOK TIME: 8 HOURS

Shelia Schmitt
Topeka, Kansas

I can please a crowd with this rich and creamy side dish. It's easy to double, and I always receive compliments when I take it to potlucks. With a slow cooker and just four ingredients, it couldn't be simpler to prepare. I know you'll find it goes with any entree.

- **2 pounds small red potatoes, quartered**
- **1 package (8 ounces) cream cheese, softened**
- **1 can (10-3/4 ounces) condensed cream of potato soup, undiluted**
- **1 envelope ranch salad dressing mix**

- Place potatoes in a 3-qt. slow cooker. In a small mixing bowl, beat cream cheese, soup and salad dressing mix until blended. Stir into potatoes. Cover and cook on low for 8 hours or until potatoes are tender.

YIELD: 4-6 servings.

SLOW COOKER TIP:

If in a rush, think of a slow cooker as a warmer instead of a cooker. Using convenient canned soups in a slow cooker can be a lifesaver on a busy weekday evening. Heat the soup on the stove, and just before leaving to pick up the kids from an after-school activity, put the soup in the slow cooker to keep warm. When you get home, all you need to do is fill bowls with steaming, flavorful soup.

pineapple baked beans

COOK TIME: 4 TO 8 HOURS

Gladys De Boer
Castleford, Idaho

Tangy pineapple dresses up these hearty baked beans. Cook the beef while you open cans and chop the vegetables, and it won't take long to get this ready for the slow cooker.

- **1 pound ground beef**
- **1 can (28 ounces) baked beans**
- **1 can (8 ounces) pineapple tidbits, drained**
- **1 jar (4-1/2 ounces) sliced mushrooms, drained**
- **1 large onion, chopped**
- **1 large green pepper, chopped**
- **1/2 cup barbecue sauce**
- **2 tablespoons soy sauce**
- **1 garlic clove, minced**
- **1/2 teaspoon salt**
- **1/4 teaspoon pepper**

- In a skillet, cook beef until no longer pink; drain. Transfer to a 5-qt. slow cooker. Add remaining ingredients and mix well. Cover and cook on low for 4-8 hours or until bubbly. Serve in bowls.

YIELD: 6-8 main-dish or 12-16 side-dish servings.

corn spoon bread

COOK TIME: 3 TO 4 HOURS

Tamara Ellefson
Frederic, Wisconsin

This comforting side dish is moister than corn pudding made in the oven.

- **1 package (8 ounces) cream cheese, softened**
- **1/3 cup sugar**
- **1 cup milk**
- **1/2 cup egg substitute**
- **2 tablespoons butter, melted**
- **1 teaspoon salt**
- **1/4 teaspoon ground nutmeg**

Dash pepper

2-1/3 cups frozen corn, thawed

- **1 can (14-3/4 ounces) cream-style corn**
- **1 package (8-1/2 ounces) corn bread/muffin mix**

- In a large mixing bowl, beat cream cheese and sugar until smooth. Gradually beat in milk. Beat in the egg substitute, butter, salt, nutmeg and pepper until blended. Stir in corn and cream-style corn. Stir in corn bread mix just until moistened.

- Pour into a greased 3-qt. slow cooker. Cover and cook on high for 3-4 hours or until center is almost set.

YIELD: 8 servings.

CREAMY RED POTATOES

CORN SPOON BREAD

sausage dressing

COOK TIME: 4 TO 5 HOURS

Mary Kendall
Appleton, Wisconsin

I relied on this slow cooker recipe at Thanksgiving when there was no room in my oven to bake stuffing. The results were fantastic—very moist and flavorful. Even family members who don't usually eat stuffing had some. There were no leftovers.

  1 pound bulk pork sausage

  1 large onion, chopped

  2 celery ribs, chopped

  1 package (14 ounces) seasoned stuffing croutons

  1 can (14-1/2 ounces) chicken broth

  1 large tart apple, chopped

  1 cup chopped walnuts *or* pecans

  1/2 cup egg substitute

  1/4 cup butter, melted

1-1/2 teaspoons rubbed sage

  1/2 teaspoon pepper

■ In a large skillet, cook the sausage, onion and celery over medium heat until meat is no longer pink; drain. Transfer to a greased 5-qt. slow cooker. Stir in the remaining ingredients. Cover and cook on low for 4-5 hours or until heated through.

YIELD: 12 servings.

mushroom potatoes

COOK TIME: 6 TO 8 HOURS

Linda Bernard
Golden Meadow, Louisiana

With its comforting flavor, these potatoes are a nice accompaniment to most meat entrees.

  7 medium potatoes, peeled and thinly sliced

  1 medium onion, sliced

  4 garlic cloves, minced

  2 green onions, chopped

  1 can (8 ounces) mushroom stems and pieces, drained

  1/4 cup all-purpose flour

  2 teaspoons salt

  1/2 teaspoon pepper

  1/4 cup butter, cubed

  1 can (10-3/4 ounces) condensed cream of mushroom soup, undiluted

  1 cup (4 ounces) shredded Colby-Monterey Jack cheese

■ In a 3-qt. slow cooker, layer half of the potatoes, onion, garlic, green onions, mushrooms, flour, salt, pepper and butter. Repeat layers. Pour soup over the top. Cover; cook on low 6-8 hours or until potatoes are tender; sprinkle with cheese during the last 30 minutes of cooking time.

YIELD: 8-10 servings.

four-bean medley

COOK TIME: 6 TO 7 HOURS

Susanne Wasson
Montgomery, New York

This bean side dish always draws compliments. Because it's easy to fix ahead and simmer in the slow cooker, it's convenient to take to potlucks, church meals and family gatherings.

  8 bacon strips, diced

  2 medium onions, quartered and sliced

  3/4 cup packed brown sugar

  1/2 cup cider vinegar

  1 teaspoon salt

  1 teaspoon ground mustard

  1/2 teaspoon garlic powder

  1 can (16 ounces) baked beans, undrained

  1 can (16 ounces) kidney beans, rinsed and drained

  1 can (15 ounces) butter beans, rinsed and drained

  1 can (14-1/2 ounces) cut green beans, drained

■ In a large skillet, cook bacon until crisp. Drain, reserving 2 tablespoons drippings; set bacon aside. Saute onions in drippings until tender. Stir in brown sugar, vinegar, salt, mustard and garlic powder.

■ Simmer, uncovered, for 15 minutes or until onions are golden brown. Place the beans in a 3-qt. slow cooker. Add onion mixture and bacon; stir to combine. Cover and cook on low 6-7 hours or until heated through. Serve with a slotted spoon.

YIELD: 8-10 servings.

SAUSAGE DRESSING

FOUR-BEAN MEDLEY

scalloped taters

COOK TIME: 4-1/2 TO 5 HOURS

Lucinda Wolker
Somerset, Pennsylvania

This creamy and comforting side dish is a snap to assemble with convenient frozen hash browns.

> 1 package (2 pounds) frozen cubed hash brown potatoes
>
> 1 can (10-3/4 ounces) condensed cream of chicken soup, undiluted
>
> 1-1/2 cups milk
>
> 1 cup (4 ounces) shredded cheddar cheese
>
> 1/2 cup plus 1 tablespoon butter, melted, *divided*
>
> 1/4 cup dried minced onion
>
> 1/2 teaspoon salt
>
> 1/8 teaspoon pepper
>
> 3/4 cup crushed cornflakes

- In a large bowl, combine the hash browns, soup, milk, cheese, 1/2 cup butter, onion, salt and pepper. Pour into a greased 5-qt. slow cooker. Cover and cook on low for 4-1/2 to 5 hours or until potatoes are tender.

- Just before serving, combine the cornflake crumbs and remaining butter in a pie plate. Bake at 350° for 4-6 minutes or until golden brown. Stir the potatoes; sprinkle with crumb topping.

YIELD: 12 servings.

pineapple sweet potatoes

COOK TIME: 4 TO 5 HOURS

Bette Fulcher
Lexington, Texas

Pineapple and pecans make a pretty topping for this no-fuss fall side dish. It's light, tasty and not too sweet. Making it in the slow cooker leaves extra space in the oven when preparing a holiday turkey and other dishes.

> 4 eggs
>
> 1 cup milk
>
> 1/2 cup butter, softened
>
> 6 to 6-1/2 cups mashed sweet potatoes (without added milk *or* butter)
>
> 1 teaspoon vanilla extract
>
> 1 teaspoon salt
>
> 1 teaspoon ground cinnamon
>
> 1/2 teaspoon ground nutmeg
>
> 1/2 teaspoon lemon extract
>
> 1 can (8 ounces) sliced pineapple, drained
>
> 1/4 cup chopped pecans

- In a large mixing bowl, combine the first nine ingredients. Transfer to a 3-qt. slow cooker. Top with pineapple slices and pecans. Cover and cook on low for 4-5 hours or until a thermometer reads 160°.

YIELD: 12-14 servings.

stuffing from the slow cooker

COOK TIME: 3 TO 4 HOURS

Mrs. Donald Seiler
Macon, Mississippi

If you're hosting a big Thanksgiving dinner, add this simple, slow-cooked stuffing to your menu to ease entertaining. This recipe comes in handy when you run out of oven space at large family gatherings. I use it often.

> 1 cup chopped onion
>
> 1 cup chopped celery
>
> 1/4 cup butter
>
> 6 cups cubed day-old white bread
>
> 6 cups cubed day-old whole wheat bread
>
> 1 teaspoon salt
>
> 1 teaspoon poultry seasoning
>
> 1 teaspoon rubbed sage
>
> 1/2 teaspoon pepper
>
> 1 can (14-1/2 ounces) reduced-sodium chicken broth *or* vegetable broth
>
> 1/2 cup egg substitute

- In a small nonstick skillet over medium heat, cook onion and celery in butter until tender. In a large bowl, combine the bread cubes, salt, poultry seasoning, sage and pepper. Stir in onion mixture. Combine broth and egg substitute; add to bread mixture and toss to coat.

- Transfer to a 3-qt. slow cooker coated with nonstick cooking spray. Cover and cook on low for 3-4 hours or until heated through.

YIELD: 12 servings.

SCALLOPED TATERS

STUFFING FROM THE SLOW COOKER

bacon hash browns

COOK TIME: 4 TO 5 HOURS

Donna Downes
Las Vegas, Nevada

My mother often took this comforting side dish to social dinners because it was such a hit. Now I get the same compliments when I make it. Bacon and onion jazz up a creamy mixture that takes advantage of convenient frozen hash browns and canned soups.

> **1 package (2 pounds) frozen cubed hash brown potatoes**
>
> **2 cups (8 ounces) cubed process cheese (Velveeta)**
>
> **2 cups (16 ounces) sour cream**
>
> **1 can (10-3/4 ounces) condensed cream of celery soup, undiluted**
>
> **1 can (10-3/4 ounces) condensed cream of chicken soup, undiluted**
>
> **1 pound sliced bacon, cooked and crumbled**
>
> **1 large onion, chopped**
>
> **1/4 cup butter, melted**
>
> **1/4 teaspoon pepper**

■ Place potatoes in an ungreased 5-qt. slow cooker. In a bowl, combine the remaining ingredients. Pour over potatoes and mix well.

■ Cover and cook on low for 4-5 hours or until potatoes are tender and heated through.

YIELD: 14 servings.

moist poultry dressing

COOK TIME: 4 TO 5 HOURS

Ruth Ann Stelfox
Raymond, Alberta

Tasty mushrooms and onions complement the big herb flavor in this stuffing. This dressing stays so moist when cooked this way.

> **2 jars (4-1/2 ounces *each*) sliced mushrooms, drained**
>
> **4 celery ribs, chopped**
>
> **2 medium onions, chopped**
>
> **1/4 cup minced fresh parsley**
>
> **3/4 cup butter**
>
> **1-1/2 pounds day-old bread, crusts removed and cubed (about 13 cups)**
>
> **1-1/2 teaspoons salt**
>
> **1-1/2 teaspoons rubbed sage**
>
> **1 teaspoon poultry seasoning**
>
> **1 teaspoon dried thyme**
>
> **1/2 teaspoon pepper**
>
> **2 eggs**
>
> **1 can (14-1/2 ounces) chicken broth**

■ In a large skillet, saute the mushrooms, celery, onions and parsley in butter until the vegetables are tender. In a large bowl, toss the bread cubes with salt, sage, poultry seasoning, thyme and pepper. Add the mushroom mixture. Combine eggs and broth; add to the bread mixture and toss.

■ Transfer to a 3-qt. slow cooker. Cover and cook on low for 4-5 hours or until a meat thermometer reads 160°.

YIELD: 12-16 servings.

vegetable medley

COOK TIME: 5 TO 6 HOURS

Terry Maly
Olathe, Kansas

This is a wonderful side dish to make when garden vegetables are plentiful. The colorful combination is a great accompaniment to any entree.

> **4 cups diced peeled potatoes**
>
> **1-1/2 cups frozen whole kernel corn *or* 1 can (15-1/4 ounces) whole kernel corn, drained**
>
> **4 medium tomatoes, seeded and diced**
>
> **1 cup sliced carrots**
>
> **1/2 cup chopped onion**
>
> **3/4 teaspoon salt**
>
> **1/2 teaspoon sugar**
>
> **1/2 teaspoon dill weed**
>
> **1/8 teaspoon pepper**

■ In a 3-qt. slow cooker, combine all ingredients. Cover and cook on low for 5-6 hours or until vegetables are tender.

YIELD: 8 servings.

BACON HASH BROWNS

spanish hominy

COOK TIME: 6 TO 8 HOURS

Donna Brockett
Kingfisher, Oklahoma

I received this recipe from a good friend who is a fabulous cook. The colorful side dish gets its zesty flavor from spicy canned tomatoes with green chilies.

- **4 cans (15-1/2 ounces *each*) hominy, drained**
- **1 can (14-1/2 ounces) diced tomatoes, undrained**
- **1 can (10 ounces) diced tomatoes and green chilies, undrained**
- **1 can (8 ounces) tomato sauce**
- **3/4 pound sliced bacon, diced**
- **1 large onion, chopped**
- **1 medium green pepper, chopped**

■ In a 3-qt. slow cooker, combine the hom-iny, tomatoes and tomato sauce. In a skillet, cook bacon until crisp; remove with a slotted spoon to paper towels. Drain, reserving 1 tablespoon drippings.

■ Saute onion and green pepper in drippings until tender. Stir onion mixture and bacon into hominy mixture. Cover and cook on low for 6-8 hours or until heated through.

YIELD: 12 servings.

cheesy spinach

COOK TIME: 5 TO 6 HOURS

Frances Moore
Decatur, Illinois

My daughter often serves this cheese and spinach blend at church suppers. Even people who don't usually eat spinach like this flavorful treatment once they try it. There is never any left.

- **2 packages (10 ounces *each*) frozen chopped spinach, thawed and well drained**
- **2 cups (16 ounces) small-curd cottage cheese**
- **1-1/2 cups cubed process cheese (Velveeta)**
- **3 eggs, lightly beaten**
- **1/4 cup butter, cubed**
- **1/4 cup all-purpose flour**
- **1 teaspoon salt**

■ In a large bowl, combine all of the ingredients. Pour into a greased 3-qt. slow cooker. Cover and cook on high for 1 hour. Reduce heat to low; cook 4-5 hours longer or until a knife inserted near the center comes out clean.

YIELD: 6-8 servings.

barbecued beans

COOK TIME: 10 TO 12 HOURS

Diane Hixon
Niceville, Florida

Most members of my family would agree that no picnic is complete until these delicious beans have made their appearance. Preparing them in a slow cooker makes them easy to transport to any gathering.

- **1 pound dried navy beans**
- **1 pound sliced bacon, cooked and crumbled**
- **1 bottle (32 ounces) tomato juice**
- **1 can (8 ounces) tomato sauce**
- **2 cups chopped onion**
- **2/3 cup packed brown sugar**
- **1 tablespoon soy sauce**
- **2 teaspoons garlic salt**
- **1 teaspoon Worcestershire sauce**
- **1 teaspoon ground mustard**

■ Place beans in a 3-qt. saucepan; cover with water. Bring to a boil; boil for 2 minutes. Remove from the heat; let stand for 1 hour. Drain beans and discard liquid.

■ In a 5-qt. slow cooker, combine all of the remaining ingredients; mix well. Add the beans. Cover and cook on high for 2 hours. Reduce heat to low and cook 8-10 hours longer or until beans are tender.

YIELD: 12-15 servings.

SPANISH HOMINY

hot german potato salad

COOK TIME: 4 TO 5 HOURS

Marlene Muckenhirn
Delano, Minnesota

I make this zesty salad with potatoes, celery and onion. It's a terrific side dish when served warm with crumbled bacon and fresh parsley sprinkled on top.

- **8 medium potatoes, peeled and cut into 1/4-inch slices**
- **2 celery ribs, chopped**
- **1 large onion, chopped**
- **1 cup water**
- **2/3 cup cider vinegar**
- **1/3 cup sugar**
- **2 tablespoons quick-cooking tapioca**
- **1 teaspoon salt**
- **3/4 teaspoon celery seed**
- **1/4 teaspoon pepper**
- **6 bacon strips, cooked and crumbled**
- **1/4 cup minced fresh parsley**

■ In a 3-qt. slow cooker, combine potatoes, celery and onion. In a bowl, combine water, vinegar, sugar, tapioca, salt, celery seed and pepper. Pour over potatoes; stir gently to coat.

■ Cover and cook on high for 4-5 hours or until potatoes are tender. Just before serving, sprinkle with bacon and parsley.

YIELD: 8-10 servings.

hearty wild rice

COOK TIME: 5 HOURS

Mrs. Garnet Pettigrew
Columbia City, Indiana

My father-in-law used to make this casserole in the oven. I switched to the slow cooker so I wouldn't need to keep an eye on it. This side dish complements many meals.

- **1 pound ground beef**
- **1/2 pound bulk pork sausage**
- **6 celery ribs, diced**
- **2 cans (10-1/2 ounces *each*) condensed beef broth, undiluted**
- **1-1/4 cups water**
- **1 medium onion, chopped**
- **1 cup uncooked wild rice**
- **1 can (4 ounces) mushroom stems and pieces, drained**
- **1/4 cup soy sauce**

■ In a skillet, cook beef and sausage over medium heat until no longer pink; drain. Transfer to a 5-qt. slow cooker. Add the celery, broth, water, onion, rice, mushrooms and soy sauce; mix well.

■ Cover and cook on high for 1 hour. Reduce heat to low; cover and cook for 4 hours or until the rice is tender.

YIELD: 10-12 servings.

zippy bean stew

COOK TIME: 4 TO 5 HOURS

Debbie Matthews
Bluefield, West Virginia

This bean stew is a staple for my coworkers and me once the weather turns cool.

- **1 can (14-1/2 ounces) vegetable *or* chicken broth**
- **1 can (16 ounces) kidney beans, rinsed and drained**
- **1 can (15 ounces) pinto beans, rinsed and drained**
- **1 can (14-1/2 ounces) diced tomatoes and green chilies**
- **1 can (4 ounces) chopped green chilies, undrained**
- **1 package (10 ounces) frozen corn, thawed**
- **3 cups water**
- **1 large onion, chopped**
- **2 medium carrots, sliced**
- **2 garlic cloves, minced**
- **2 teaspoons chili powder**

■ Combine all ingredients in a 3-qt. slow cooker. Cover and cook on high for 4-5 hours or until heated through and flavors are blended.

YIELD: 6 servings.

SLOW COOKER TIP: Since vegetables cook slower than meat and poultry in a slow cooker, place them in first. Then add meat or cover the food with liquid such as broth, water or barbecue sauce. Keep the lid in place, removing only to stir the food or check for doneness.

HOT GERMAN POTATO SALAD

side dishes

cheesy creamed corn

COOK TIME: 4 HOURS

Mary Ann Truitt
Wichita, Kansas

My family really likes this cheesy side dish—and it's so easy to make. Even those who usually don't eat much corn will ask for a second helping.

> **3 packages (16 ounces *each*) frozen corn**
>
> **2 packages (one 8 ounces, one 3 ounces) cream cheese, cubed**
>
> **1/4 cup butter, cubed**
>
> **3 tablespoons water**
>
> **3 tablespoons milk**
>
> **2 tablespoons sugar**
>
> **6 slices process American cheese, cut into small pieces**

■ Combine all ingredients in a 3-qt. slow cooker; mix well. Cover and cook on low for 4 hours or until heated through and the cheese is melted. Stir well before serving.

YIELD: 12 servings.

slow-cooked vegetables

COOK TIME: 7 TO 8 HOURS

Kathy Westendorf
Westgate, Iowa

I simmer an assortment of garden-fresh vegetables into this satisfying side dish. My sister-in-law shared this recipe with me. It's a favorite at holiday gatherings and potlucks.

> **4 celery ribs, cut into 1-inch pieces**
>
> **4 small carrots, cut into 1-inch pieces**
>
> **2 medium tomatoes, cut into chunks**
>
> **2 medium onions, thinly sliced**
>
> **2 cups cut fresh green beans (1-inch pieces)**
>
> **1 medium green pepper, cut into 1-inch pieces**
>
> **1/4 cup butter, melted**
>
> **3 tablespoons quick-cooking tapioca**
>
> **1 tablespoon sugar**
>
> **2 teaspoons salt**
>
> **1/8 teaspoon pepper**

■ Place the vegetables in a 3-qt. slow cooker. Combine butter, tapioca, sugar, salt and pepper; pour over vegetables and stir well.

■ Cover and cook on low for 7-8 hours or until vegetables are tender. Serve with a slotted spoon.

YIELD: 8 servings.

simple saucy potatoes

COOK TIME: 4 TO 5 HOURS

Gloria Schroeder
Ottawa Lake, Michigan

These rich and creamy potatoes are simple to prepare for potlucks. And this saucy dish always gets rave reviews wherever I take it.

> **4 cans (15 ounces *each*) sliced white potatoes, drained**
>
> **2 cans (10-3/4 ounces *each*) condensed cream of celery soup, undiluted**
>
> **2 cups (16 ounces) sour cream**
>
> **10 bacon strips, cooked and crumbled**
>
> **6 green onions, thinly sliced**

■ Place the potatoes in a 3-qt. slow cooker. Combine the remaining ingredients; pour over potatoes and mix well. Cover and cook on high for 4-5 hours.

YIELD: 12 servings.

CHEESY CREAMED CORN

cheesy potatoes

COOK TIME: 8 TO 10 HOURS

Melissa Marzof
Maysville, Michigan

For a comforting side dish that feeds a crowd, try these saucy slow-cooked potatoes. A topping of buttered croutons covers the creamy combination.

- **6 medium potatoes, peeled and cut into 1/4-inch strips**
- **2 cups (8 ounces) shredded cheddar cheese**
- **1 can (10-3/4 ounces) condensed cream of chicken soup, undiluted**
- **1 small onion, chopped *or* 1 tablespoon dried minced onion**
- **7 tablespoons butter, melted, *divided***
- **1 teaspoon salt**
- **1 teaspoon pepper**
- **1 cup (8 ounces) sour cream**
- **2 cups seasoned stuffing cubes**

■ Toss the potatoes and cheese; place in a 5-qt. slow cooker. Combine the soup, onion, 4 tablespoons butter, salt and pepper; pour over potato mixture.

■ Cover and cook on low for 8-10 hours or until the potatoes are tender. Stir in sour cream. Toss the stuffing cubes and remaining butter; sprinkle over potatoes.

YIELD: 10-12 servings.

slow-cooked sage dressing

COOK TIME: 4 TO 5 HOURS

Ellen Benninger
Stoneboro, Pennsylvania

This recipe is such a help when I fix a large meal. It leaves room in the oven for other dishes since it's made in a slow cooker.

- **14 to 15 cups day-old bread cubes**
- **3 cups chopped celery**
- **1-1/2 cups chopped onion**
- **1-1/2 teaspoons rubbed sage**
- **1 teaspoon salt**
- **1/2 teaspoon pepper**
- **1-1/4 cups butter, melted**

■ Combine bread, celery, onion, sage, salt and pepper; mix well. Add butter and toss. Spoon into a 5-qt. slow cooker. Cover and cook on low for 4-5 hours, stirring once.

YIELD: about 12 servings.

squash stuffing casserole

COOK TIME: 4 TO 5 HOURS

Pamela Thorson
Hot Springs, Arkansas

My friends just rave about this creamy side dish. It's a snap to jazz up summer squash, zucchini and carrots with canned soup and stuffing mix.

- **1/4 cup all-purpose flour**
- **1 can (10-3/4 ounces) condensed cream of chicken soup, undiluted**
- **1 cup (8 ounces) sour cream**
- **2 medium yellow summer squash, cut into 1/2-inch slices**
- **2 medium zucchini, cut into 1/2-inch slices**
- **1 small onion, chopped**
- **1 cup shredded carrots**
- **1 package (8 ounces) stuffing mix**
- **1/2 cup butter, melted**

■ In a bowl, combine the flour, soup and sour cream until blended. Add the vegetables and gently stir to coat.

■ Combine the stuffing mix and butter; sprinkle half into a 5-qt. slow cooker. Top with vegetable mixture and remaining stuffing mixture. Cover and cook on low for 4-5 hours or until vegetables are tender.

YIELD: 8 servings.

SLOW COOKER TIP: To speed up the cooking time for most slow cooker recipes, follow the general rule that 1 hour on high is equal to 2 hours on low.

CHEESY POTATOES

creamy corn

COOK TIME: 4 HOURS

Judy McCarthy
Derby, Kansas

A handful of ingredients and a slow cooker are all you'll need for this rich side dish. I first tasted it at a potluck with our camping club. I knew I had to have the recipe since corn is always a favorite with our friends. It's easy to assemble and frees up time to prepare the main course.

- 2 packages (16 ounces *each*) frozen corn
- 1 package (8 ounces) cream cheese, cubed
- 1/3 cup butter, cubed
- 1/2 teaspoon garlic powder
- 1/2 teaspoon salt
- 1/4 teaspoon pepper

■ In a 3-qt. slow cooker, combine all ingredients. Cover and cook on low for 4 hours or until heated through and cheese is melted. Stir well before serving.

YIELD: 6 servings.

SLOW COOKER TIPS:

When a slow cooker recipe calls for rice, use long-grain converted rice. It tends to give the best results.

High altitudes make a difference in slow cooker times. Add an additional 30 minutes for each hour of cooking time called for in a recipe. Legumes take twice as long to cook at high altitudes than at sea level.

---

sausage spanish rice

COOK TIME: 5 TO 6 HOURS

Michelle McKay
Garden City, Michigan

My husband and I both work the midnight shift, so I'm always on the lookout for slow cooker recipes. This one couldn't be easier. It's good as a side dish, but we often enjoy it as the main course because it's so hearty.

- 1 pound fully cooked kielbasa *or* Polish sausage, cut into 1/4-inch slices
- 2 cans (14-1/2 ounces *each*) diced tomatoes, undrained
- 2 cup water
- 1-1/2 cups uncooked converted rice
- 1 cup salsa
- 1 medium onion
- 1/2 cup chopped green pepper
- 1/2 cup chopped sweet red pepper
- 1 can (4 ounces) chopped green chilies
- 1 envelope taco seasoning

■ In a 3-qt. slow cooker, combine all ingredients; stir to blend. Cover and cook on low for 5-6 hours or until rice is tender.

YIELD: 9 servings.

SAUSAGE SPANISH RICE

---

spiced acorn squash

COOK TIME: 4 HOURS

Carol Greco
Centereach, New York

This cinnamony treatment for squash is a recipe I converted especially for the slow cooker.

- 3/4 cup packed brown sugar
- 1 teaspoon ground cinnamon
- 1 teaspoon ground nutmeg
- 2 small acorn squash, halved and seeded
- 3/4 cup raisins
- 4 tablespoons butter
- 1/2 cup water

■ In a small bowl, combine the brown sugar, cinnamon and nutmeg; spoon into squash halves. Sprinkle with raisins. Top each with 1 tablespoon of butter. Wrap each squash half individually in heavy-duty foil; seal tightly.

■ Pour water into a 5-qt. slow cooker. Place the squash, cut side up, in slow cooker (packets may be stacked). Cover and cook on high for 4 hours or until the squash is tender. Open foil packets carefully to allow steam to escape.

YIELD: 4 servings.

SPICED ACORN SQUASH

smoky beef 'n' beans

COOK TIME: 6 TO 7 HOURS

Anita Curtis
Camarillo, California

Liquid Smoke gives a unique taste to this thick and hearty combination of beef and beans. I serve it with a crisp salad to make a complete meal.

- 1 pound ground beef
- 1 cup chopped onion
- 12 bacon strips, cooked and crumbled
- 2 cans (16 ounces *each*) pork and beans
- 1 can (16 ounces) kidney beans, rinsed and drained
- 1 can (16 ounces) butter beans, drained
- 1 cup ketchup
- 1/4 cup packed brown sugar
- 3 tablespoons white vinegar
- 1 teaspoon Liquid Smoke, optional
- 1/2 teaspoon salt
- 1/4 teaspoon pepper

■ In a skillet, cook the beef and onion over medium heat until meat is no longer pink; drain. Transfer to a 3-qt. slow cooker. Stir in the remaining ingredients. Cover and cook on low for 6-7 hours or until heated through.

YIELD: 8 servings.

SLOW COOKER TIP:

When using pasta in slow cooker recipes, it's best to cook the pasta first—just until tender—in boiling water and drain, then add the cooked pasta to the slow cooker toward the end of the cooking process.

cheddar spirals

COOK TIME: 2-1/2 HOURS

Heidi Ferkovich
Park Falls, Wisconsin

Our kids just love this and will sample a spoonful right from the slow cooker when they walk by. Sometimes I add cocktail sausages, sliced Polish sausage or cubed ham to the cheesy pasta for a hearty all-in-one dinner.

- 1 package (16 ounces) spiral pasta
- 2 cups half-and-half cream
- 1 can (10-3/4 ounces) condensed cheddar cheese soup
- 1/2 cup butter, melted
- 4 cups (16 ounces) shredded cheddar cheese

■ Cook pasta according to package directions; drain. In a 5-qt. slow cooker, combine the cream, soup and butter until smooth; stir in the cheese and pasta.

■ Cover and cook on low for 2-1/2 hours or until cheese is melted.

YIELD: 12-15 servings.

CHEDDAR SPIRALS

vegetable-stuffed peppers

COOK TIME: 8 HOURS

Sandra Allen
Austin, Texas

This recipe came with my slow cooker. Green peppers are filled with a flavorful combination of cooked rice, kidney beans, corn and onions. These satisfying peppers can even be a meatless main dish for a change of pace. This recipe has become a mainstay for my family.

- 2 cans (14-1/2 ounces *each*) diced tomatoes, undrained
- 1 can (16 ounces) kidney beans, rinsed and drained
- 1-1/2 cups cooked rice
- 2 cups (8 ounces) shredded cheddar cheese, *divided*
- 1 package (10 ounces) frozen corn, thawed
- 1/4 cup chopped onion
- 1 teaspoon Worcestershire sauce
- 3/4 teaspoon chili powder
- 1/2 teaspoon pepper
- 1/4 teaspoon salt
- 6 medium green peppers

■ In a large bowl, combine the tomatoes, beans, rice, 1-1/2 cups cheese, corn, onion, Worcestershire sauce, chili powder, pepper and salt.

■ Remove and discard tops and seeds of green peppers. Fill each pepper with about 1 cup vegetable mixture. Place in a 5-qt. slow cooker. Cover and cook on low for 8 hours.

■ Sprinkle with remaining cheese. Cover and cook 15 minutes longer or until peppers are tender and cheese is melted.

YIELD: 6 servings.

VEGETABLE-STUFFED PEPPERS

sweet potato stuffing

COOK TIME: 4 HOURS

Kelly Pollock
London, Ontario

Mom likes to make sure there will be enough stuffing to satisfy our large family. For our holiday gatherings, she slow-cooks this tasty sweet potato dressing in addition to the traditional stuffing cooked inside the turkey.

- 1/2 cup chopped celery
- 1/2 cup chopped onion
- 1/4 cup butter
- 6 cups dry bread cubes
- 1 large sweet potato, cooked, peeled and finely chopped
- 1/2 cup chicken broth
- 1/4 cup chopped pecans
- 1/2 teaspoon poultry seasoning
- 1/2 teaspoon rubbed sage
- 1/2 teaspoon salt
- 1/2 teaspoon pepper

■ In a skillet, saute celery and onion in butter until tender. Add remaining ingredients; toss gently. Transfer to a greased 3-qt. slow cooker.

■ Cover and cook on low for 4 hours or until bread and vegetables are soft.

YIELD: 10 servings.

slow-cooked mac 'n' cheese

COOK TIME: 4-1/2 HOURS

Bernice Glascoe
Roxboro, North Carolina

This classic casserole is so rich, you can serve it as meatless main dish.

- 1 package (16 ounces) elbow macaroni
- 1/2 cup butter, melted
- 2 eggs, beaten
- 1 can (12 ounces) evaporated milk
- 1 can (10-3/4 ounces) condensed cheddar cheese soup, undiluted
- 1 cup milk
- 4 cups (16 ounces) shredded cheddar cheese, *divided*
- 1/8 teaspoon paprika

■ Cook macaroni according to package directions; drain. Place in a 5-qt. slow cooker; add butter. In a bowl, combine the eggs, evaporated milk, soup, milk and 3 cups cheese. Pour over macaroni mixture; stir to combine. Cover and cook on low for 4 hours.

■ Sprinkle with the remaining cheese. Cook 15 minutes longer or until cheese is melted. Sprinkle with paprika.

YIELD: 10 servings.

cheesy hash brown potatoes

COOK TIME: 4 TO 4-1/2 HOURS

Becky Weseman
Becker, Minnesota

I adapted this recipe for my slow cooker so I could bring these cheesy potatoes to a potluck picnic. Canned soup and frozen hash browns make this dish easy to assemble.

- 2 cans (10-3/4 ounces *each*) condensed cheddar cheese soup, undiluted
- 1-1/3 cups buttermilk
- 2 tablespoons butter, melted
- 1/2 teaspoon seasoned salt
- 1/4 teaspoon garlic powder
- 1/4 teaspoon pepper
- 1 package (32 ounces) frozen cubed hash brown potatoes
- 1/4 cup grated Parmesan cheese
- 1 teaspoon paprika

■ In a 3-qt. slow cooker, combine first six ingredients; stir in hash browns.

■ Sprinkle with Parmesan cheese and paprika. Cover and cook on low for 4 to 4-1/2 hours or until potatoes are tender.

YIELD: 6-8 servings.

SLOW COOKER TIP: Whenever possible, leave the peel on vegetables to help retain their shape and nutrients. Simply scrub the skins of potatoes or carrots until clean before chopping and adding to the slow cooker.

SWEET POTATO STUFFING

slow-cooked beans

COOK TIME: 2 HOURS

Joy Beck
Cincinnati, Ohio

This flavorful bean dish adds nice variety to any buffet—it's a bit different than traditional baked beans. It's a snap to prepare, too, since it uses convenient canned beans and prepared barbecue sauce and salsa.

- 4 cans (15-1/2 ounces *each*) great northern beans, rinsed and drained
- 4 cans (15 ounces *each*) black beans, rinsed and drained
- 2 cans (15 ounces *each*) butter beans, rinsed and drained
- 2-1/4 cups barbecue sauce
- 2-1/4 cups salsa
- 3/4 cup packed brown sugar
- 1/2 to 1 teaspoon hot pepper sauce

■ In a 5-qt. slow cooker, gently combine all ingredients. Cover and cook on low for 2 hours or until heated through.

YIELD: 16 servings.

rich spinach casserole

COOK TIME: 2-1/2 HOURS

Vioda Geyer
Uhrichsville, Ohio

I found this recipe in an old slow cooker cookbook. When I took it to our church sewing circle, it was a big hit. The two kinds of cheese make a rich sauce that ensures this spinach is a comforting side dish for any meal.

- 2 packages (10 ounces *each*) frozen chopped spinach, thawed and well drained
- 2 cups (16 ounces) small-curd cottage cheese
- 1 cup cubed process cheese (Velveeta)
- 3/4 cup egg substitute
- 2 tablespoons butter, cubed
- 1/4 cup all-purpose flour
- 1/2 teaspoon salt

■ In a 3-qt. slow cooker, combine all ingredients; mix well. Cover and cook on low for 2-1/2 hours or until the cheese is melted.

YIELD: 8 servings.

roasted red pepper sauce

COOK TIME: 4 HOURS

Mrs. Timothy Tosh
Lumberton, New Jersey

I often use Greek olives with the artichoke hearts to add zing to this pasta sauce. Roast the peppers yourself if you have the time.

- 4 pounds plum tomatoes (about 17), coarsely chopped
- 1 large sweet onion, chopped
- 1 can (29 ounces) tomato puree
- 3 jars (7 ounces *each*) roasted sweet red peppers, drained and chopped
- 2 jars (6-1/2 ounces *each*) marinated artichoke hearts, drained and chopped
- 1/2 pound fresh mushrooms, quartered
- 2 cans (2-1/4 ounces *each*) sliced ripe olives, drained
- 1/4 cup sugar
- 1/4 cup balsamic vinegar
- 1/4 cup olive oil
- 3 garlic cloves, minced
- 1 tablespoon dried basil
- 1 tablespoon dried oregano
- 1 teaspoon salt

Hot cooked pasta

■ In a 5-qt. slow cooker, combine the first 14 ingredients. Cover and cook on high for 4 hours or until flavors are blended. Serve over pasta.

YIELD: about 15 cups.

SLOW-COOKED BEANS

ROASTED RED PEPPER SAUCE

slow-simmered kidney beans
COOK TIME: 6 TO 8 HOURS

Sheila Vail
Long Beach, California
We often take this side dish to potlucks and family gatherings.

- **6 bacon strips, diced**
- **1/2 pound fully cooked Polish sausage, chopped**
- **4 cans (16 ounces _each_) kidney beans, rinsed and drained**
- **1 can (28 ounces) diced tomatoes, drained**
- **2 medium sweet red peppers, chopped**
- **1 large onion, chopped**
- **1 cup ketchup**
- **1/2 cup packed brown sugar**
- **1/4 cup honey**
- **1/4 cup molasses**
- **1 tablespoon Worcestershire sauce**
- **1 teaspoon salt**
- **1 teaspoon ground mustard**
- **2 medium unpeeled red apples, cored and cut into 1/2-inch pieces**

■ In a skillet, cook bacon until crisp. Remove with a slotted spoon to paper towels. Add sausage to drippings; cook and stir for 5 minutes. Drain and set aside.

■ In an ungreased 5-qt. slow cooker, combine the beans, tomatoes, red peppers, onion, ketchup, brown sugar, honey, molasses, Worcestershire sauce, salt and mustard. Stir in the bacon and sausage. Cover and cook on low for 4-6 hours. Stir in apples. Cover and cook 2 hours longer or until bubbly.

YIELD: 16 servings.

mushroom wild rice
COOK TIME: 7 TO 8 HOURS

Bob Malchow
Monon, Indiana
This is one of my favorite recipes from my mother. With only seven ingredients, it's quick to assemble in the morning before I leave for work. By the time I get home, mouth-watering aromas have filled the house.

- **2-1/4 cups water**
- **1 can (10-1/2 ounces) condensed beef consomme, undiluted**
- **1 can (10-1/2 ounces) condensed French onion soup, undiluted**
- **3 cans (4 ounces _each_) mushroom stems and pieces, drained**
- **1/2 cup butter, melted**
- **1 cup uncooked brown rice**
- **1 cup uncooked wild rice**

■ In a 5-qt. slow cooker, combine all ingredients; stir well. Cover and cook on low for 7-8 hours or until the rice is tender.

YIELD: 12-16 servings.

mashed potatoes
COOK TIME: 2 TO 4 HOURS

Trudy Vincent
Valles Mines, Missouri
Sour cream and cream cheese give richness to these smooth, make-ahead potatoes. They are wonderful for Thanksgiving or Christmas dinner since there's no last-minute mashing required.

- **1 package (3 ounces) cream cheese, softened**
- **1/2 cup sour cream**
- **1/4 cup butter, softened**
- **1 envelope ranch salad dressing mix**
- **1 teaspoon dried parsley flakes**
- **6 cups warm mashed potatoes (prepared without milk or butter)**

■ In a bowl, combine the cream cheese, sour cream, butter, salad dressing mix and parsley; stir in potatoes. Transfer to a 3-qt. slow cooker. Cover and cook on low for 2-4 hours.

YIELD: 8-10 servings.

EDITOR'S NOTE: This recipe was tested with fresh potatoes (not instant) in a slow cooker with heating elements surrounding the unit, not only in the base.

SLOW-SIMMERED KIDNEY BEANS

■■■beef & ground beef

Beef up your next dinner menu with exceptional entrees from your slow cooker! Longer cook times in the handy appliance produce tasty, tender meats like Creamy Swiss Steak. You'll find that recipe on page 184.

Whether you crave a comforting casserole, prefer a succulent roast or are searching for the perfect one-pot meal the whole family will love, turn the work over to the slow cooker when you choose from this delicious batch of recipes.

cranberry meatballs

COOK TIME: 6 HOURS

Nina Hall
Spokane, Washington

These tasty meatballs are sure to be popular. Cranberry and chili sauces give them extra sweetness. They taste great over noodles.

> 2 eggs, beaten
>
> 1 cup dry bread crumbs
>
> 1/3 cup minced fresh parsley
>
> 2 tablespoons finely chopped onion
>
> 1-1/2 pounds ground beef
>
> 1 can (16 ounces) jellied cranberry sauce
>
> 1 bottle (12 ounces) chili sauce
>
> 1/3 cup ketchup
>
> 2 tablespoons brown sugar
>
> 1 tablespoon lemon juice

- In a large bowl, combine the eggs, bread crumbs, parsley and onion. Crumble beef over mixture and mix well. Shape into 1-1/2-in. balls. Place in a 3-qt. slow cooker.

- In a small bowl, combine remaining ingredients; mix well. Pour over meatballs. Cover and cook on low for 6 hours or until meat is no longer pink.

YIELD: 6 servings.

slow-cooked swiss steak

COOK TIME: 8 TO 9 HOURS

Kathie Morris
Redmond, Oregon

Here's an easy way to make a traditional favorite. Your family will love it!

> 3/4 cup all-purpose flour
>
> 1 teaspoon pepper
>
> 1/4 teaspoon salt
>
> 2 to 2-1/2 pounds boneless beef top round steak
>
> 1 to 2 tablespoons butter
>
> 1 can (10-3/4 ounces) condensed cream of mushroom soup, undiluted
>
> 1-1/3 cups water
>
> 1 cup sliced celery, optional
>
> 1/2 cup chopped onion
>
> 1 to 3 teaspoons beef bouillon granules
>
> 1/2 teaspoon minced garlic

- In a shallow bowl, combine flour, pepper and salt. Cut steak into six pieces; dredge in flour mixture.

- In a large skillet, brown steak in butter. Transfer to a 3-qt. slow cooker. Combine the remaining ingredients; pour over steak. Cover; cook on low 8-9 hours or until meat is tender.

YIELD: 6 servings.

green chili beef burritos

COOK TIME: 8 TO 9 HOURS

Shirley Davidson
Thornton, Colorado

The meat is so tender, you'll love these tasty burritos.

> 2 boneless beef top sirloin roasts (3 pounds *each*)
>
> 4 cans (4 ounces *each*) chopped green chilies
>
> 1 medium onion, chopped
>
> 3 medium jalapeno peppers, seeded and chopped
>
> 3 garlic cloves, sliced
>
> 3 teaspoons chili powder
>
> 1-1/2 teaspoons ground cumin
>
> 1 teaspoon salt-free seasoning blend, optional
>
> 1 cup beef broth
>
> 24 flour tortillas (8 inches), warmed

Chopped tomatoes, shredded lettuce and shredded cheddar cheese, optional

- Trim fat from roasts; cut meat into large chunks. Place in a 5-qt. slow cooker. Top with next 7 ingredients. Pour broth over all. Cover; cook on low 8-9 hours.

- Remove beef; shred with two forks. Cool cooking liquid slightly; skim fat. In a blender, cover and process cooking liquid in small batches until smooth. Return liquid and beef to slow cooker; heat through. Place 1/3 cup beef on each tortilla. Top with tomatoes, lettuce and cheese if desired. Fold in ends and sides.

YIELD: 2 dozen.

EDITOR'S NOTE: When cutting or seeding hot peppers, use rubber or plastic gloves to protect your hands. Avoid touching your face.

SLOW-COOKED SWISS STEAK

GREEN CHILI BEEF BURRITOS

barbecued beef brisket

COOK TIME: 4 TO 5 HOURS

Anita Keppinger
Philomath, Oregon

I enjoy fixing a sit-down meal for my husband and myself every evening, so this entree is often on the menu. It's fairly inexpensive and takes little effort to prepare. The tender beef tastes wonderful.

    1 teaspoon salt
    1 teaspoon chili powder
    1/2 teaspoon garlic powder
    1/4 teaspoon onion powder
    1/4 teaspoon celery seed
    1/4 teaspoon pepper
    1 fresh beef brisket (2-1/2
      pounds), trimmed

SAUCE:

    1/2 cup ketchup
    1/2 cup chili sauce
    1/4 cup packed brown sugar
    2 tablespoons cider vinegar
    2 tablespoons Worcestershire
      sauce
    1 to 1-1/2 teaspoons Liquid
      Smoke, optional
    1/2 teaspoon ground mustard

■ Combine the first six ingredients; rub over brisket. Place in a 3-qt. slow cooker. In a bowl, combine the sauce ingredients. Pour half over the brisket; set the remaining sauce aside.

■ Cover and cook on high for 4-5 hours or until meat is tender. Serve with the reserved sauce.

YIELD: 8 servings.

creamy beef and pasta

COOK TIME: 6 HOURS

Carol Losier
Baldwinsville, New York

A friend shared the recipe for this fix-it-and-forget-it meal. I often make it for our children when my husband and I go out. Even the baby-sitters have said how much they like it.

    2 cans (10-3/4 ounces *each*)
      condensed cream of
      mushroom soup, undiluted
    2 cups (8 ounces) shredded
      cheddar *or* mozzarella
      cheese
    1 pound ground beef, cooked
      and drained
    2 cups uncooked small pasta
    2 cups milk
    1/2 to 1 teaspoon onion powder
    1/2 to 1 teaspoon salt
    1/4 to 1/2 teaspoon pepper

■ In a 3-qt. slow cooker, combine all ingredients; mix well. Cover and cook on low for 6 hours or until pasta is tender.

YIELD: 4-6 servings.

ground beef stew

COOK TIME: 6 TO 8 HOURS

Mary Jo Walker
Jasper, Tennessee

Since I work all day, it's great to come home knowing I have a very delicious meal simmering in the slow cooker. I like to serve generous helpings of this stew with corn bread muffins.

    2 large potatoes, sliced
    2 medium carrots, sliced
    1 can (15 ounces) peas,
      drained
    3 medium onions, sliced
    2 celery ribs, sliced
    1-1/2 pounds ground beef, cooked
      and drained
    1 can (10-3/4 ounces)
      condensed tomato soup,
      undiluted
    1-1/3 cups water

■ In a 3-qt. slow cooker, layer the first six ingredients in the order listed. Combine soup and water; mix well. Pour over beef.

■ Cover and cook on low for 6-8 hours or until vegetables are tender.

YIELD: 6 servings.

BARBECUED BEEF BRISKET

easy chow mein

COOK TIME: 4 HOURS

Kay Bade
Mitchell, South Dakota

Our daughter welcomed me home from a hospital stay some years ago with this Oriental dish and a copy of the recipe. Now that I'm a widow, I freeze leftovers for fast future meals.

- 1 pound ground beef
- 1 medium onion, chopped
- 1 bunch celery, sliced
- 2 cans (14 ounces *each*) Chinese vegetables, drained
- 2 envelopes brown gravy mix
- 2 tablespoons soy sauce

Hot cooked rice

- In a skillet, cook beef and onion over medium heat until meat is no longer pink; drain. Transfer to a 3-qt. slow cooker. Stir in the celery, Chinese vegetables, gravy mixes and soy sauce.

- Cover and cook on low for 4 hours or until celery is tender, stirring occasionally. Serve over rice.

YIELD: 8 servings.

autumn beef stew

COOK TIME: 8 TO 9 HOURS

Margaret Shauers
Great Bend, Kansas

Let the aroma of this savory supper welcome you home after work. Chock-full of tender beef, hearty potatoes and colorful carrots, this down-home dinner is a staple in my kitchen.

- 12 small red potatoes, halved
- 1 pound carrots, cut into 1-inch pieces
- 1 large onion, cut into wedges
- 2 pounds beef stew meat, cut into 1-inch cubes
- 1/3 cup butter
- 1 tablespoon all-purpose flour
- 1 cup water
- 1 teaspoon salt
- 1 teaspoon dried parsley flakes
- 1/2 teaspoon celery seed
- 1/2 teaspoon dried thyme
- 1/8 teaspoon pepper

- Place potatoes, carrots and onion in a 5-qt. slow cooker. In a large skillet, brown beef in butter. Transfer beef to slow cooker with a slotted spoon.

- Stir flour into the pan drippings until blended; cook and stir until browned. Gradually add water. Bring to a boil; cook and stir for 2 minutes or until thickened. Add salt, parsley, celery seed, thyme and pepper; pour over beef. Cover and cook on low for 8-9 hours or until meat and vegetables are tender.

YIELD: 8 servings.

spaghetti and meatballs

COOK TIME: 8 TO 10 HOURS

Jackie Grant
Vanderhoof, British Columbia

I first sampled this spaghetti sauce at my sister-in-law's and had to have the recipe. After all these years, I still think it's about the best I've ever tasted.

- 3 pounds ground beef
- 1 cup finely chopped onion, *divided*
- 1 teaspoon salt
- 1/2 teaspoon pepper
- 1 can (46 ounces) tomato juice
- 1 can (28 ounces) diced tomatoes, drained
- 1 can (15 ounces) tomato sauce
- 2 celery ribs, chopped
- 3 bay leaves
- 2 garlic cloves, minced

- In a bowl, combine the beef, 1/2 cup onion, salt and pepper; mix well. Shape into 1-in. balls. In a large skillet over medium heat, brown meatballs with remaining onion.

- Transfer to a 5-qt. slow cooker; add the remaining ingredients. Cover and cook on low for 8-10 hours or until heated through, stirring occasionally. Discard bay leaves before serving.

YIELD: 20 servings (about 4-1/2 quarts).

SLOW COOKER TIP: One of the nice things about using a slow cooker is that it can help you make meats more tender. But condensation from the cooking process can create more liquid. So you may want to reduce the liquid or thicken it with flour or cornstarch to make sauce or gravy.

EASY CHOW MEIN

slow-cooker pizza casserole

COOK TIME: 2 TO 3 HOURS

Virginia Krites
Cridersville, Ohio

A comforting casserole with mass appeal is just what you need when cooking for a crowd. For added convenience, it stays warm in a slow cooker.

1 package (16 ounces) rigatoni *or* large tube pasta

1-1/2 pounds ground beef

1 small onion, chopped

4 cups (16 ounces) shredded part-skim mozzarella cheese

2 cans (15 ounces *each*) pizza sauce

1 can (10-3/4 ounces) condensed cream of mushroom soup, undiluted

1 package (8 ounces) sliced pepperoni

■ Cook pasta according to package directions. Meanwhile, in a skillet, cook beef and onion over medium heat until meat is no longer pink; drain.

■ Drain pasta; place in a 5-qt. slow cooker. Stir in the beef mixture, cheese, pizza sauce, soup and pepperoni. Cover and cook on low for 2-3 hours or until heated through and the cheese is melted.

YIELD: 12-14 servings.

peppery beef roast

COOK TIME: 8 TO 9 HOURS

Kelly Lindsay
Longmont, Colorado

As a stay-at-home mom, slow cooker recipes are a lifesaver for me, especially on special days!

1 boneless beef rump roast (3-1/2 to 4 pounds)

1/2 cup ketchup

3 tablespoons brown sugar

1 tablespoon ground mustard

1 tablespoon lemon juice

2 teaspoons celery salt

2 teaspoons pepper

2 teaspoons Worcestershire sauce

1 teaspoon garlic powder

1 teaspoon onion powder

1 teaspoon Liquid Smoke, optional

1/2 to 1 teaspoon salt

1/8 teaspoon hot pepper sauce

■ Cut roast in half; place in a 5-qt. slow cooker. Combine the remaining ingredients; pour over roast. Cover and cook on low for 8-9 hours or until meat is tender. Thicken cooking juices if desired.

YIELD: 10-12 servings.

melt-in-your-mouth meat loaf

COOK TIME: 5 TO 6 HOURS

Suzanne Codner
Starbuck, Minnesota

When my husband and I were first married, he refused to eat meat loaf because he said it was bland and dry. Then I prepared this version, and it became his favorite meal.

2 eggs

3/4 cup milk

2/3 cup seasoned bread crumbs

2 teaspoons dried minced onion

1 teaspoon salt

1/2 teaspoon rubbed sage

1-1/2 pounds ground beef

1/4 cup ketchup

2 tablespoons brown sugar

1 teaspoon ground mustard

1/2 teaspoon Worcestershire sauce

■ In a large bowl, combine the first six ingredients. Crumble beef over mixture and mix well (mixture will be moist).

■ Shape into a round loaf; place in a 5-qt. slow cooker. Cover and cook on low for 5-6 hours or until a meat thermometer reads 160°.

■ In a small bowl, whisk the ketchup, brown sugar, mustard and Worcestershire sauce. Spoon over the meat loaf. Cook 15 minutes longer or until heated through. Let stand for 10-15 minutes before cutting.

YIELD: 6 servings.

SLOW-COOKER PIZZA CASSEROLE

MELT-IN-YOUR-MOUTH MEAT LOAF

beef in mushroom gravy

COOK TIME: 7 TO 8 HOURS

Margery Bryan
Royal City, Washington

This is one of the best and easiest meals I've ever made. It has only four ingredients, and they all go into the pot at once. The meat is nicely seasoned and makes its own gravy—it tastes wonderful when you serve it over mashed potatoes.

- 2 to 2-1/2 pounds boneless round steak
- 1 to 2 envelopes dry onion soup mix
- 1 can (10-3/4 ounces) condensed cream of mushroom soup, undiluted
- 1/2 cup water

Mashed potatoes, optional

- Cut steak into six serving-size pieces; place in a 3-qt. slow cooker. Combine soup mix, soup and water; pour over beef.

- Cover and cook on low for 7-8 hours or until meat is tender. Serve with mashed potatoes if desired.

YIELD: 6 servings.

beef and beans

COOK TIME 6-1/2 TO 8-1/2 HOURS

Marie Leadmon
Bethesda, Maryland

This deliciously spicy steak and beans over rice will have family and friends asking for more. It's a favorite in my recipe collection.

- 1-1/2 pounds boneless round steak
- 1 tablespoon prepared mustard
- 1 tablespoon chili powder
- 1/2 teaspoon salt, optional
- 1/4 teaspoon pepper
- 1 garlic clove, minced
- 2 cans (14-1/2 ounces *each*) diced tomatoes, undrained
- 1 medium onion, chopped
- 1 beef bouillon cube, crushed
- 1 can (16 ounces) kidney beans, rinsed and drained

Hot cooked rice

- Cut steak into thin strips. Combine mustard, chili powder, salt if desired, pepper and garlic in a bowl; add steak and toss to coat.

- Transfer to a 3-qt. slow cooker; add tomatoes, onion and bouillon. Cover and cook on low for 6-8 hours. Stir in beans; cook 30 minutes longer. Serve over rice.

YIELD: 8 servings.

stuffed cabbage casserole

COOK TIME: 4 TO 5 HOURS

Joann Alexander
Center, Texas

I love the taste of cabbage rolls but don't always have the time to prepare them. My version uses the same ingredients in a simpler manner for hearty results everyone enjoys!

- 1 pound ground beef
- 1 small onion, chopped
- 4 cups chopped cabbage
- 1 medium green pepper, chopped
- 1 cup uncooked instant rice
- 1 cup water
- 1 can (6 ounces) tomato paste
- 1 can (14-1/2 ounces) diced tomatoes, undrained
- 1/2 cup ketchup
- 2 tablespoons cider vinegar
- 1 to 2 tablespoons sugar, optional
- 1 tablespoon Worcestershire sauce
- 1-1/2 teaspoons salt
- 1/2 teaspoon pepper
- 1/4 teaspoon garlic powder

- In a skillet, cook beef and onion over medium heat until meat is no longer pink; drain. Transfer to a 3-qt. slow cooker; add the cabbage, green pepper and rice.

- In a bowl, combine the water and tomato paste. Stir in the remaining ingredients. Pour over beef mixture; mix well. Cover and cook on low for 4-5 hours or until rice and vegetables are tender.

YIELD: 4-6 servings.

BEEF IN MUSHROOM GRAVY

slow-cooked sirloin

COOK TIME: 3-1/2 TO 4-1/2 HOURS

Vicki Tormaschy
Dickinson, North Dakota
My family of five likes to eat beef, so this recipe is a favorite. I usually serve it with homemade bread or rolls to soak up the tasty gravy.

- 1 boneless beef sirloin steak (1-1/2 pounds)
- 1 medium onion, cut into 1-inch chunks
- 1 medium green pepper, cut into 1-inch chunks
- 1 can (14-1/2 ounces) reduced-sodium beef broth
- 1/4 cup Worcestershire sauce
- 1/4 teaspoon dill weed
- 1/4 teaspoon dried thyme
- 1/4 teaspoon pepper
- Dash crushed red pepper flakes
- 2 tablespoons cornstarch
- 2 tablespoons water

■ In a large nonstick skillet coated with nonstick cooking spray, brown beef on both sides. Place onion and green pepper in a 3-qt. slow cooker. Top with beef. Combine the broth, Worcestershire sauce, dill weed, thyme, pepper and pepper flakes; pour over beef. Cover and cook on high for 3-4 hours or until meat reaches desired doneness and vegetables are crisp-tender.

■ Remove beef and keep warm. Combine cornstarch and water until smooth; gradually stir into cooking juices. Cover and cook about 30 minutes longer or until slightly thickened. Return beef to the slow cooker; heat through.

YIELD: 6 servings.

minestrone stew

COOK TIME: 4 TO 6 HOURS

Janie Hoskins
Red Bluff, California
I add green chilies to this slow-cooked stew made from convenient pantry ingredients. You're sure to like the beef, beans and veggies.

- 1 pound ground beef
- 1 small onion, chopped
- 1 can (19 ounces) ready-to-serve minestrone soup
- 1 can (15 ounces) pinto beans, rinsed and drained
- 1 can (14-1/2 ounces) stewed tomatoes
- 1 can (11 ounces) whole kernel corn, drained
- 1 can (4 ounces) chopped green chilies
- 1 teaspoon salt
- 1/2 teaspoon garlic powder
- 1/2 teaspoon onion powder

■ In a skillet, cook beef and onion over medium heat until meat is no longer pink; drain. Transfer to a 3-qt. slow cooker. Add the remaining ingredients; mix well. Cover and cook on low for 4-6 hours or until heated through.

YIELD: 8 servings.

braised beef short ribs

COOK TIME: 6 TO 7 HOURS

Cheryl Martinetto
Grand Rapids, Minnesota
The sweetness of the brown sugar coupled with the uniqueness of the curry powder give these tender ribs a boost of flavor!

- 4 pounds bone-in beef short ribs
- 2 tablespoons vegetable oil
- 2-1/2 cups sliced onions
- 1-1/2 cups beef broth
- 1-1/2 cups chili sauce
- 2/3 cup cider vinegar
- 1 tablespoon brown sugar
- 2 teaspoons paprika
- 1-1/2 teaspoons curry powder
- 1 teaspoon minced garlic
- 1 teaspoon salt
- 1/2 teaspoon ground mustard
- 1/2 teaspoon pepper

■ In a large skillet, brown ribs in oil in batches. Transfer to a 5-qt. slow cooker; add onions. Combine the remaining ingredients; pour over ribs. Cover and cook on low for 6-7 hours or until meat is tender.

YIELD: 8 servings.

MINESTRONE STEW

BRAISED BEEF SHORT RIBS

slow-cooker pizza

COOK TIME: 3 TO 4 HOURS

Julie Sterchi
Harrisburg, Illinois
Always a hit at our church dinners, this hearty casserole keeps folks coming back for more.

> 1 package (16 ounces) wide egg noodles
>
> 1-1/2 pounds ground beef *or* turkey
>
> 1/4 cup chopped onion
>
> 1 jar (26 ounces) spaghetti sauce
>
> 1 jar (4-1/2 ounces) sliced mushrooms, drained
>
> 1-1/2 teaspoons Italian seasoning
>
> 1 package (3-1/2 ounces) sliced pepperoni, halved
>
> 3 cups (12 ounces) shredded mozzarella cheese
>
> 3 cups (12 ounces) shredded cheddar cheese

- Cook noodles according to package directions. Meanwhile, in a large skillet, cook beef and onion over medium heat until meat is no longer pink; drain. Stir in the spaghetti sauce, mushrooms and Italian seasoning. Drain noodles.

- In a 5-qt. slow cooker coated with nonstick cooking spray, spread a third of the meat sauce. Cover with a third of the noodles and pepperoni. Sprinkle with a third of the cheeses. Repeat layers twice. Cover and cook on low for 3-4 hours or until heated through and cheese is melted.

YIELD: 6-8 servings.

flavorful beef in gravy

COOK TIME: 7 TO 8 HOURS

Cheryl Sindergard
Plover, Iowa
Served over noodles, this fantastic supper showcases tender chunks of savory beef stew meat. I use canned soups and onion soup mix to make the mouth-watering gravy. With a green salad and crusty bread, dinner is complete.

> 1/3 cup all-purpose flour
>
> 3 pounds beef stew meat, cut into 1-inch cubes
>
> 3 tablespoons vegetable oil
>
> 2 cans (10-3/4 ounces *each*) condensed cream of mushroom soup, undiluted
>
> 1 can (10-3/4 ounces) condensed golden mushroom soup, undiluted
>
> 1 can (10-3/4 ounces) condensed cream of celery soup, undiluted
>
> 1-1/3 cups milk
>
> 1 envelope onion soup mix

Hot cooked noodles *or* mashed potatoes

- Place flour in a large resealable plastic bag; add beef and toss to coat. In a skillet, brown beef in oil. Transfer beef to a 5-qt. slow cooker. Stir in the soups, milk and soup mix.

- Cover and cook on low for 7-8 hours or until the meat is tender. Serve over noodles or potatoes.

YIELD: 10-12 servings.

hamburger supper

COOK TIME: 4 TO 6 HOURS

Dolores Hickenbottom
Greensburg, Pennsylvania
My mother-in-law shared this recipe with me when my husband and I were first married. Over the past 50 years, I've relied on this meal-in-one more times than I can count.

> 1 pound ground beef
>
> 1/4 cup hot water
>
> 3 small potatoes, peeled and diced
>
> 1 medium onion, chopped
>
> 1 can (15 ounces) peas and carrots, drained
>
> 1 can (14-1/2 ounces) diced tomatoes, undrained
>
> 1 tablespoon sugar
>
> 1/2 teaspoon salt
>
> 1/4 teaspoon pepper

- Shape beef into four patties. In a skillet, cook patties over medium heat until no longer pink. Transfer to a 3-qt. slow cooker. Add water to skillet and stir to loosen browned bits from pan. Pour into slow cooker. Add the remaining ingredients.

- Cover and cook on low for 4-6 hours or until potatoes are tender.

YIELD: 4 servings.

SLOW-COOKER PIZZA

old-world sauerbraten

COOK TIME: 6 TO 8 HOURS

Susan Garoutte
Georgetown, Texas

I serve this with potato pancakes and vegetables. Crushed gingersnaps, lemon and vinegar give the marinated slow-cooked beef and gravy their appetizing sweet-sour flavor.

1-1/2 cups water, *divided*

1-1/4 cups cider vinegar, *divided*

2 large onions, sliced, *divided*

1 medium lemon, sliced

15 whole cloves, *divided*

6 bay leaves, *divided*

6 whole peppercorns

2 tablespoons sugar

2 teaspoons salt

1 beef sirloin tip roast (3 pounds), cut in half

1/4 teaspoon pepper

12 gingersnap cookies, crumbled

■ In a large resealable plastic bag, combine 1 cup water, 1 cup vinegar, half of the onions, lemon, 10 cloves, four bay leaves, peppercorns, sugar and salt; mix well. Add roast. Seal bag and turn to coat; refrigerate overnight, turning occasionally.

■ Drain and discard marinade. Place roast in a 3-qt. slow cooker; add pepper and remaining water, vinegar, onions, cloves and bay leaves. Cover and cook on low for 6-8 hours or until meat is tender. Remove roast and keep warm. Discard bay leaves. Stir in gingersnaps. Cover and cook on high for 10-15 minutes or until gravy is thickened. Slice roast; serve with gravy.

YIELD: 12 servings.

hobo stew

COOK TIME: 6 HOURS

Mrs. Dick Brazeal
Carlin, Nevada

I got this recipe from my husband's family in Missouri. I've yet to meet anyone who doesn't rave about this easy stew.

1-1/2 pounds ground beef

1 medium onion, diced

3 cans (10-3/4 ounces *each*) condensed minestrone soup, undiluted

2 cans (15 ounces *each*) ranch-style beans, undrained

1 can (10 ounces) diced tomatoes and green chilies, undrained

■ In a large skillet, cook beef and onion over medium heat until the meat is no longer pink; drain.

■ Transfer to a 3-qt. slow cooker. Add the remaining ingredients. Cover and cook on low for 6 hours or until heated through.

YIELD: 8 servings.

confetti casserole

COOK TIME: 8 TO 10 HOURS

Joy Vincent
Newport, North Carolina

To create this comforting casserole, I adapted a recipe from the cookbook that came with my first slow cooker. I love to serve this with fresh bread from my bread maker.

1 pound ground beef

1 medium onion, finely chopped

1 teaspoon garlic powder

4 medium potatoes, peeled and quartered

3 medium carrots, cut into 1-inch chunks

1 package (10 ounces) frozen cut green beans

1 package (10 ounces) frozen corn

1 can (14-1/2 ounces) Italian diced tomatoes, undrained

■ In a skillet, cook beef, onion and garlic powder over medium heat until meat is no longer pink; drain. In a 3-qt. slow cooker, layer potatoes, carrots, beans and corn. Top with beef mixture. Pour tomatoes over the top.

■ Cover and cook on low for 8-10 hours or until the potatoes are tender.

YIELD: 8 servings.

OLD-WORLD SAUERBRATEN

green chili stew

COOK TIME: 7 TO 8 HOURS

Jacqueline Thompson Graves
Lawrenceville, Georgia

This stew is much heartier than most. Men especially enjoy the zippy broth and the generous amounts of tender beef. They frequently request second helpings.

- 2 pounds beef stew meat, cut into 1-inch cubes
- 2 medium onions, chopped
- 2 tablespoons vegetable oil
- 1 can (15 ounces) pinto beans, rinsed and drained
- 1 can (14-1/2 ounces) diced tomatoes, undrained
- 2 cans (4 ounces *each*) chopped green chilies
- 1 cup water
- 3 beef bouillon cubes
- 1 garlic clove, minced
- 1 teaspoon sugar
- 1/2 teaspoon salt
- 1/4 teaspoon pepper

Shredded cheddar *or* Monterey Jack cheese, optional

- In a skillet, brown beef and onions in oil; drain. Transfer to a 5-qt. slow cooker. Combine the beans, tomatoes, chilies, water, bouillon, garlic, sugar, salt and pepper; pour over beef.

- Cover and cook on low for 7-8 hours or until beef is tender. Sprinkle with cheese if desired.

YIELD: 8 servings.

flank steak roll-up

COOK TIME: 8 TO 10 HOURS

Sheryl Johnson
Las Vegas, Nevada

As a working mother of five hungry boys, I rely on my slow cooker to give me a head start on meals. I roll stuffing mix and mushrooms into flank steak before simmering it in an easy gravy.

- 1 can (4 ounces) mushroom stems and pieces, undrained
- 2 tablespoons butter, melted
- 1 package (6 ounces) seasoned stuffing mix
- 1 beef flank steak (1-3/4 pounds)
- 1 envelope brown gravy mix
- 1/4 cup chopped green onions
- 1/4 cup dry red wine *or* beef broth

- In a bowl, toss the mushrooms, butter and dry stuffing mix. Spread over steak to within 1 in. of edges. Roll up jelly-roll style, starting with a long side; tie with kitchen string. Place in a 3-qt. slow cooker.

- Prepare gravy mix according to package directions; add onions and wine or broth. Pour over meat. Cover and cook on low for 8-10 hours. Remove meat to a serving platter and keep warm. Strain cooking juices and thicken if desired. Remove string from roll-up; slice and serve with gravy.

YIELD: 6 servings.

all-day meatballs

COOK TIME: 6 TO 8 HOURS

Cathy Ryan
Red Wing, Minnesota

Folks who work outside the home can pop these meatballs into the slow cooker in the morning. By the time they get home, dinner's ready!

- 1 cup milk
- 3/4 cup quick-cooking oats
- 3 tablespoons finely chopped onion
- 1-1/2 teaspoons salt
- 1-1/2 pounds ground beef
- 1 cup ketchup
- 1/2 cup water
- 3 tablespoons vinegar
- 2 tablespoons sugar

- In a bowl, combine the first four ingredients. Crumble beef over the mixture and mix well. Shape into 1-in. balls. Place in a 3-qt. slow cooker. In a bowl, combine the ketchup, water, vinegar and sugar; mix well. Pour over meatballs.

- Cover and cook on low for 6-8 hours or until the meat is no longer pink.

YIELD: 6 servings.

SLOW COOKER TIP: A timer will allow you to cook a dish for 6 hours even though you're away for 8 hours. For food safety, make sure all ingredients are chilled before cooking. Program the cooking to start no longer than 2 hours after you leave. Cooked food should not stand for longer than 2 hours after the cooking time ends.

GREEN CHILI STEW

onion meat loaf

COOK TIME: 5 TO 6 HOURS

Rhonda Cowden
Quincy, Illinois

My husband and I really enjoy this delicious meat loaf. Only five ingredients are needed to assemble this easy entree before popping it in the slow cooker.

> 2 eggs
>
> 1/2 cup ketchup
>
> 3/4 cup quick-cooking oats
>
> 1 envelope onion soup mix
>
> 2 pounds ground beef

- In a large bowl, combine the eggs, ketchup, oats and soup mix. Crumble beef over mixture; mix well. Shape into a round loaf.

- Cut three 20-in. x 3-in. strips of heavy-duty aluminum foil. Crisscross the strips so they resemble the spokes of a wheel. Place meat loaf in the center of the strips; pull the strips up and bend the edges to form handles. Grasp the foil handles to transfer loaf to a 3-qt. slow cooker. (Leave the foil in while meat loaf cooks.)

- Cover and cook on low for 5-6 hours or until a meat thermometer reads 160°. Using foil strips, lift meat loaf out of slow cooker.

YIELD: 8 servings.

slow-cooked tamale casserole

COOK TIME: 4 HOURS

Diana Briggs
Veneta, Oregon

I've been making this recipe for years because my family really likes it.

> 1 pound ground beef
>
> 1 egg
>
> 1-1/2 cups milk
>
> 3/4 cup cornmeal
>
> 1 can (15-1/4 ounces) whole kernel corn, drained
>
> 1 can (14-1/2 ounces) diced tomatoes, undrained
>
> 1 can (2-1/4 ounces) sliced ripe olives, drained
>
> 1 envelope chili seasoning
>
> 1 teaspoon seasoned salt
>
> 1 cup (4 ounces) shredded cheddar cheese

- In a skillet, cook beef over medium heat until no longer pink; drain. In a bowl, combine the egg, milk and cornmeal until smooth. Add corn, tomatoes, olives, chili seasoning, seasoned salt and beef.

- Transfer to a greased 3-qt. slow cooker. Cover and cook on high for 3 hours and 45 minutes. Sprinkle with cheese; cover and cook 15 minutes longer or until cheese is melted.

YIELD: 6 servings.

SLOW-COOKED TAMALE CASSEROLE

beer-braised beef

COOK TIME: 6 TO 6-1/2 HOURS

Geri Faustich
Appleton, Wisconsin

I put together this recipe in the morning, and in the evening, all we do is cook noodles and eat!

> 3 bacon strips, diced
>
> 2 pounds beef stew meat, cut into 1-inch cubes
>
> 1/2 teaspoon pepper
>
> 1/4 teaspoon salt
>
> 1 teaspoon vegetable oil
>
> 1 onion, cut into wedges
>
> 1 teaspoon minced garlic
>
> 1 bay leaf
>
> 1 can (12 ounces) beer *or* nonalcoholic beer
>
> 1 tablespoon soy sauce
>
> 1 tablespoon Worcestershire sauce
>
> 1 teaspoon dried thyme
>
> 2 tablespoons all-purpose flour
>
> 1/4 cup water

Hot cooked noodles

- In a large skillet, cook bacon over medium heat until crisp. Remove to paper towels; drain, discarding drippings. Sprinkle beef with pepper and salt. In the same skillet, brown beef in oil. Transfer to a 5-qt. slow cooker.

- Add the bacon, onion, garlic and bay leaf. In a small bowl, combine beer, soy sauce, Worcestershire sauce and thyme. Pour over beef mixture. Cover; cook on low 5-1/2 to 6 hours or until tender.

- In a small bowl, combine flour and water until smooth. Gradually stir into slow cooker. Cover; cook on high 30 minutes or until thickened. Discard bay leaf. Serve over noodles.

YIELD: 8 servings.

BEER-BRAISED BEEF

meatball stew

COOK TIME: 9 TO 10 HOURS

Iris Schultz
Miamisburg, Ohio

I came up with this hearty meal-in-one as another way to use frozen meatballs. It's quick to put together in the morning and ready when my husband gets home in the evening.

- 3 medium potatoes, peeled and cut into 1/2-inch cubes
- 1 package (16 ounces) fresh baby carrots, quartered
- 1 large onion, chopped
- 3 celery ribs, sliced
- 1 package (12 ounces) frozen cooked meatballs
- 1 can (10-3/4 ounces) condensed tomato soup, undiluted
- 1 can (10-1/2 ounces) beef gravy
- 1 cup water
- 1 envelope onion soup mix
- 2 teaspoons beef bouillon granules

■ Place the potatoes, carrots, onion, celery and meatballs in a 5-qt. slow cooker. In a bowl, combine the remaining ingredients. Pour over meatball mixture.

■ Cover and cook on low for 9-10 hours or until the vegetables are crisp-tender.

YIELD: 6 servings.

roast beef with gravy

COOK TIME: 6 TO 8 HOURS

Tracy Ashbeck
Wisconsin Rapids, Wisconsin

Start this simple roast in the morning, and you'll have savory slices of meat and gravy ready at suppertime. The tender beef is loaded with homemade taste and leaves plenty for main dishes later in the week.

- 1 boneless beef sirloin tip roast (about 4 pounds)
- 1/2 cup all-purpose flour, *divided*
- 1 envelope onion soup mix
- 1 envelope brown gravy mix
- 2 cups cold water

Hot mashed potatoes

■ Cut roast in half; rub with 1/4 cup flour. Place in a 5-qt. slow cooker. In a bowl, combine soup and gravy mixes and remaining flour; stir in water until blended. Pour over roast.

■ Cover and cook on low for 6-8 hours or until meat is tender. Slice roast; serve with mashed potatoes and gravy.

YIELD: 16 servings.

slow-cooked short ribs

COOK TIME: 9 TO 10 HOURS

Pam Halfhill
Medina, Ohio

Smothered in a mouth-watering barbecue sauce, these meaty ribs are a popular entree wherever I serve them.

- 2/3 cup all-purpose flour
- 2 teaspoons salt
- 1/2 teaspoon pepper
- 4 to 4-1/2 pounds boneless beef short ribs
- 1/4 to 1/3 cup butter
- 1 large onion, chopped
- 1-1/2 cups beef broth
- 3/4 cup red wine vinegar
- 3/4 cup packed brown sugar
- 1/2 cup chili sauce
- 1/3 cup ketchup
- 1/3 cup Worcestershire sauce
- 5 garlic cloves, minced
- 1-1/2 teaspoons chili powder

■ In a large resealable plastic bag, combine the flour, salt and pepper. Add ribs in batches and shake to coat. In a large skillet, brown ribs in butter.

■ Transfer to a 5-qt. slow cooker. In the same skillet, combine the remaining ingredients. Cook and stir until mixture comes to a boil; pour over ribs (slow cooker will be full). Cover and cook on low for 9-10 hours or until meat is tender.

YIELD: 12-15 servings.

MEATBALL STEW

thai-style brisket
COOK TIME: 8-1/2 TO 9-1/2 HOURS

Teri Rasey-Bolf
Cadillac, Michigan

I let my slow cooker do the work when preparing this brisket flavored with peanuts, soy and zesty seasonings.

> 1 fresh beef brisket
> (3 to 4 pounds), cut in half
>
> 3 tablespoons olive oil, *divided*
>
> 1 cup chunky peanut butter
>
> 2/3 cup soy sauce
>
> 4 teaspoons sesame oil
>
> 1 tablespoon minced fresh cilantro
>
> 1 tablespoon lemon juice
>
> 1 teaspoon garlic powder
>
> 1 teaspoon crushed red pepper flakes
>
> 1 teaspoon pepper
>
> 1 tablespoon cornstarch
>
> 1 cup water
>
> 1-1/4 cups julienned carrots
>
> 1 medium sweet red pepper, sliced
>
> 1 medium green pepper, sliced
>
> 1/2 cup chopped green onions
>
> 1 cup unsalted peanuts, optional

Hot cooked rice

■ In a skillet over medium-high heat, brown brisket in 2 tablespoons olive oil. Transfer meat and drippings to a 5-qt. slow cooker. Combine the next eight ingredients; pour over brisket. Cover and cook on low for 8-9 hours or until meat is tender.

■ Remove brisket and keep warm. Combine cornstarch and water until smooth; stir into cooking juices. Cover and cook on high for 30 minutes or until thickened.

■ Meanwhile, in a large skillet or wok, stir-fry the carrots, peppers and onions in remaining olive oil until crisp-tender. Add peanuts if desired. Stir cooking juices and stir into vegetable mixture.

■ Thinly slice meat across the grain. Place rice on a large serving platter; top with meat and vegetables.

YIELD: 6-8 servings.

EDITOR'S NOTE: This is a fresh beef brisket, not corned beef. The meat comes from the first cut of the brisket.

gone-all-day casserole
COOK TIME: 6 TO 8 HOURS

Janet Haak Aarness
Pelican Rapids, Minnesota

Even less expensive cuts of meat become deliciously tender when cooked slowly in this savory casserole.

> 1 cup uncooked wild rice, rinsed and drained
>
> 1 cup chopped celery
>
> 1 cup chopped carrots
>
> 2 cans (4 ounces *each*) mushroom stems and pieces, drained
>
> 1 large onion, chopped
>
> 1 garlic clove, minced
>
> 1/2 cup slivered almonds
>
> 3 beef bouillon cubes
>
> 2-1/2 teaspoons seasoned salt
>
> 2 pounds boneless round steak, cut into 1-inch cubes
>
> 3 cups water

■ Place ingredients in order listed in a 5-qt. slow cooker (do not stir). Cover and cook on low for 6-8 hours or until rice is tender. Stir before serving.

YIELD: 12 servings.

sirloin roast with gravy
COOK TIME: 5-1/2 TO 6 HOURS

Rita Clark
Monument, Colorado

This recipe is perfect for my husband, who is a meat-and-potatoes kind of guy. The peppery roast combined with the rich gravy creates a tasty centerpiece for any meal.

> 1 boneless beef sirloin tip roast (about 3 pounds)
>
> 1 to 2 tablespoons coarsely ground pepper
>
> 1-1/2 teaspoons minced garlic
>
> 1/4 cup reduced-sodium soy sauce
>
> 3 tablespoons balsamic vinegar
>
> 1 tablespoon Worcestershire sauce
>
> 2 teaspoons ground mustard
>
> 2 tablespoons cornstarch
>
> 1/4 cup cold water

■ Rub roast with pepper and garlic; cut in half and place in a 3-qt. slow cooker. Combine the soy sauce, vinegar, Worcestershire sauce and mustard; pour over beef. Cover and cook on low for 5-1/2 to 6 hours or until the meat is tender.

■ Remove roast and keep warm. Strain cooking juices into a small saucepan; skim fat. Combine cornstarch and water until smooth; gradually stir into cooking juices. Bring to a boil; cook and stir for 2 minutes or until thickened. Serve with beef.

YIELD: 10 servings.

SIRLOIN ROAST WITH GRAVY

round steak roll-ups

COOK TIME: 6 HOURS

Kimberly Alonge
Westfield, New York

Since I'm a working mom, I assemble these steak rolls at night and pop them in the slow cooker the next morning before we're all out the door.

2 pounds boneless beef round steak

1/2 cup grated carrot

1/3 cup chopped zucchini

1/4 cup chopped sweet red pepper

1/4 cup chopped green pepper

1/4 cup sliced green onions

2 tablespoons grated Parmesan cheese

1 tablespoon minced fresh parsley

1 garlic clove, minced

1/4 teaspoon salt

1/4 teaspoon pepper

2 tablespoons canola oil

1 jar (14 ounces) meatless spaghetti sauce

Hot cooked spaghetti

Additional Parmesan cheese

- Cut meat into six pieces; pound to 1/4-in. thickness. Combine the vegetables, Parmesan cheese and seasonings; place 1/3 cup in the center of each piece. Roll meat up around filling; secure with toothpicks.

- In a large skillet, brown roll-ups in oil over medium-high heat. Transfer to a 5-qt. slow cooker; top with spaghetti sauce. Cover; cook on low for 6 hours or until meat is tender. Discard toothpicks. Serve roll-ups and sauce over spaghetti. Sprinkle with cheese.

YIELD: 6 servings.

beefy au gratin potatoes

COOK TIME: 4 HOURS

Eileen Majerus
Pine Island, Minnesota

Vary the flavor of this family-favorite casserole by using different kinds of soup and potato mixes. I usually dish out hearty helpings with a salad and garlic bread.

1 package (5-1/4 ounces) au gratin *or* cheddar and bacon potatoes

1 can (15-1/4 ounces) whole kernel corn, drained

1 can (10-3/4 ounces) condensed cream of potato soup, undiluted

1 cup water

1 can (4 ounces) chopped green chilies, drained

1 can (4 ounces) mushroom stems and pieces, drained

1 jar (4 ounces) diced pimientos, drained

1 pound ground beef

1 medium onion, chopped

- Set potato sauce mix aside. Place potatoes in a 3-qt. slow cooker; top with corn. In a bowl, combine soup, water, chilies, mushrooms, pimientos and reserved sauce mix; mix well. Pour a third of the mixture over corn. In a skillet, cook beef and onion over medium heat until the meat is no longer pink; drain.

- Transfer to a 3-qt. slow cooker. Top with remaining sauce mixture. Do not stir. Cover and cook on low for 4 hours or until potatoes are tender.

YIELD: 4-6 servings.

skier's stew

COOK TIME: 5 TO 6 HOURS

Traci Gangwer
Denver, Colorado

This recipe got its name because you put it in the slow cooker...and head for the slopes! I like to prepare it two or three times a month in the fall and winter. When I come home after a busy day and get in out of the cold, a good, hot dinner is waiting for me.

5 large potatoes, peeled and cut into 1-inch cubes

8 medium carrots, cut into 1/4-inch slices

1-1/2 pounds beef stew meat, cut into 1-inch cubes

1 can (15 ounces) tomato sauce

1/2 cup water

1 envelope onion soup mix

- In a 5-qt. slow cooker, layer potatoes, carrots and beef. In a bowl, combine the tomato sauce, water and soup mix; pour over meat.

- Cover and cook on high for 5-6 hours or until the vegetables and meat are tender.

YIELD: 6 servings.

ROUND STEAK ROLL-UPS

corny chili

COOK TIME: 3 TO 4 HOURS

Marlene Olson
Hoople, North Dakota

This is so delicious and simple that I had to share it. I'm sure busy moms will be just as happy as I am with the taste and time-saving convenience of this pleasant chili.

- 1 pound ground beef
- 1 small onion, chopped
- 1 can (16 ounces) kidney beans, rinsed and drained
- 2 cans (14-1/2 ounces *each*) diced tomatoes, undrained
- 1 can (11 ounces) whole kernel corn, drained
- 3/4 cup picante sauce
- 1 tablespoon chili powder
- 1/4 to 1/2 teaspoon garlic powder

Corn chips, sour cream and shredded cheddar cheese, optional

- In a skillet, cook beef and onion over medium heat until meat is no longer pink; drain. Transfer to a 3-qt. slow cooker. Stir in the beans, tomatoes, corn, picante sauce, chili powder and garlic powder.

- Cover and cook on low for 3-4 hours or until heated through. Serve with corn chips, sour cream and cheese if desired.

YIELD: 4-6 servings.

meal-in-one casserole

COOK TIME: 4 HOURS

Dorothy Pritchett
Wills Point, Texas

Salsa gives zip to this hearty fix-and-forget-it meal. This recipe makes more than my husband and I can eat, so I freeze half of it. We think it tastes even better the second time.

- 1 pound ground beef
- 1 medium onion, chopped
- 1 medium green pepper, chopped
- 1 can (15-1/4 ounces) whole kernel corn, drained
- 1 can (4 ounces) mushroom stems and pieces, drained
- 1 teaspoon salt
- 1/4 teaspoon pepper
- 1 jar (11 ounces) salsa
- 5 cups cooked medium egg noodles
- 1 can (28 ounces) diced tomatoes, undrained
- 1 cup (4 ounces) shredded cheddar cheese *or* blend of cheddar, Monterey Jack and American cheeses

- In a skillet, cook beef and onion over medium heat until meat is no longer pink; drain. Transfer to a 3-qt. slow cooker.

- Top with the green pepper, corn and mushrooms. Sprinkle with salt and pepper. Pour salsa over mushrooms. Top with noodles. Pour tomatoes over all. Sprinkle with cheese. Cover and cook on low for 4 hours or until heated through.

YIELD: 4-6 servings.

flank steak 'n' stuffing

COOK TIME: 6 TO 8 HOURS

Diane Hixon
Niceville, Florida

I like to make this meal on special occasions. The tender steak cuts easily into appetizing spirals for serving, and extra stuffing cooks in a foil packet on top of the steak.

- 1 package (8 ounces) crushed corn bread stuffing
- 1 cup chopped onion
- 1 cup chopped celery
- 1/4 cup minced fresh parsley
- 2 eggs
- 1-1/4 cups beef broth
- 1/3 cup butter, melted
- 1/2 teaspoon seasoned salt
- 1/2 teaspoon pepper
- 1-1/2 pounds beef flank steak

- In a large bowl, combine stuffing, onion, celery and parsley. In a small bowl, beat eggs; stir in broth and butter. Pour over stuffing mixture. Sprinkle with seasoned salt and pepper; stir well. Pound steak to 1/2-in. thickness. Spread 1-1/2 cups stuffing mixture over steak. Roll up, starting with a short side; tie with string.

- Place in a 5-qt. slow cooker. Remaining stuffing can be wrapped tightly in foil and placed over the rolled steak. Cover and cook on low for 6-8 hours or until a meat thermometer inserted in stuffing reads 165°. Remove string before slicing.

YIELD: 6 servings.

EDITOR'S NOTE: No liquid is added to the slow cooker. The moisture comes from the meat.

CORNY CHILI

cube steaks with gravy

COOK TIME: 8-1/2 HOURS

Judy Long
Limestone, Tennessee

This is slow cooker comfort food at its best! Three different gravy mixes provide loads of flavor.

- 1/3 cup all-purpose flour
- 6 beef cube steaks (1-1/2 pounds)
- 1 tablespoon vegetable oil
- 1 large onion, sliced and separated into rings
- 3 cups water, *divided*
- 1 envelope brown gravy mix
- 1 envelope mushroom gravy mix
- 1 envelope onion gravy mix

Hot mashed potatoes *or* **cooked noodles**

- Place flour in a large resealable plastic bag. Add steaks, a few at a time, and shake until completely coated. In a skillet, cook steaks in oil until lightly browned on each side. Transfer to a 3-qt. slow cooker. Add the onion and 2 cups water. Cover and cook on low for 8 hours or until meat is tender.

- In a bowl, whisk together gravy mixes with remaining water. Add to slow cooker; cook 30 minutes more. Serve over mashed potatoes or noodles.

YIELD: 6 servings.

slow-cooked flank steak

COOK TIME: 7 TO 8 HOURS

Michelle Armistead
Keyport, New Jersey

My slow cooker gets lots of use, especially during the hectic summer months. I can fix this flank steak in the morning and forget about it until dinnertime. I serve it with noodles and a tossed salad.

- 1 flank steak (about 1-1/2 pounds), cut in half
- 1 tablespoon vegetable oil
- 1 large onion, sliced
- 1/3 cup water
- 1 can (4 ounces) chopped green chilies
- 2 tablespoons white vinegar
- 1-1/4 teaspoons chili powder
- 1 teaspoon garlic powder
- 1/2 teaspoon sugar
- 1/2 teaspoon salt
- 1/8 teaspoon pepper

- In a skillet, brown steak in oil; transfer to a 3-qt. slow cooker. In the same skillet, saute onion for 1 minute. Gradually add water, stirring to loosen browned bits from pan. Add remaining ingredients; bring to a boil. Pour over the flank steak. Cover and cook on low for 7-8 hours or until the meat is tender. Slice the meat; serve with onion and pan juices.

YIELD: 4-6 servings.

tangy beef and vegetable stew

COOK TIME: 6 HOURS

Amberleah Homlberg
Calgary, Alberta

This meal-in-one is sure to satisfy even the biggest of appetites. Mustard and horseradish add great kick.

- 6 cups cubed peeled potatoes (1/2-inch pieces)
- 8 medium carrots, cut into 1/2-inch pieces
- 2 medium onions, cubed
- 4 pounds beef stew meat, cut into 1-inch pieces
- 1/3 cup vegetable oil
- 1/3 cup all-purpose flour
- 4 beef bouillon cubes
- 3 cups boiling water
- 1/3 cup white vinegar
- 1/3 cup ketchup
- 3 tablespoons *each* prepared horseradish and prepared mustard
- 2 tablespoons sugar
- 2 cups *each* frozen peas and corn
- 2 cups sliced fresh mushrooms

- Place the potatoes, carrots and onions in a 6-qt. slow cooker.

- In a large skillet, brown beef in oil, a single layer at a time; place over the vegetables. Sprinkle with flour.

- Dissolve bouillon cubes in boiling water. Stir in vinegar, ketchup, horseradish, mustard and sugar; pour over meat and vegetables. Cover and cook on high for 5 hours. Add peas, corn and mushrooms. Cover and cook on high for 45 minutes.

YIELD: 12-16 servings.

CUBE STEAKS WITH GRAVY

TANGY BEEF AND VEGETABLE STEW

meat loaf burgers

COOK TIME: 7 TO 9 HOURS

Peggy Burdick
Burlington, Michigan

These hearty sandwiches are great for potluck dinners. Served on hamburger buns, the beefy patties get extra flavor when topped with the seasoned tomato sauce.

- 1 large onion, sliced
- 1 celery rib, chopped
- 2 pounds lean ground beef
- 1-1/2 teaspoons salt, *divided*
- 1/4 teaspoon pepper
- 2 cups tomato juice
- 4 garlic cloves, minced
- 1 tablespoon ketchup
- 1 bay leaf
- 1 teaspoon Italian seasoning
- 6 hamburger buns, split

- ■ Place onion and celery in a 3-qt. slow cooker. Combine beef, 1 teaspoon salt and pepper; shape into six patties. Place over onion mixture. Combine tomato juice, garlic, ketchup, bay leaf, Italian seasoning and remaining salt. Pour over the patties.

- ■ Cover and cook on low for 7-9 hours or until meat is tender. Discard bay leaf. Separate patties with a spatula if necessary; serve on buns.

YIELD: 6 servings.

chili mac

COOK TIME: 6 HOURS

Marie Posavec
Berwyn, Illinois

This recipe has appeared on my menus once a month for more than 40 years. It's never failed to please. I've also turned it into a soup by adding a can of beef broth.

- 1 pound ground beef, cooked and drained
- 2 cans (15 ounces *each*) hot chili beans, undrained
- 2 large green peppers, chopped
- 1 large onion, chopped
- 4 celery ribs, chopped
- 1 can (8 ounces) tomato sauce
- 1 envelope chili seasoning
- 2 garlic cloves, minced
- 1 package (7 ounces) elbow macaroni, cooked and drained

Salt and pepper to taste

- ■ In a 5-qt. slow cooker, combine the first eight ingredients; mix well. Cover and cook on low for 6 hours or until heated through.

- ■ Stir in macaroni; mix well. Season with salt and pepper.

YIELD: 12 servings.

beef burgundy

COOK TIME: 7-1/2 TO 8-1/2 HOURS

Sherri Mott
New Carlisle, Indiana

Tender beef, a burgundy wine sauce and savory vegetables star in this entree.

- 6 bacon strips, diced
- 1 boneless beef chuck roast (3 pounds), cut into 1-1/2-inch cubes
- 1 can (10-1/2 ounces) condensed beef broth, undiluted
- 1 small onion, sliced
- 1 medium carrot, sliced
- 2 tablespoons butter
- 1 tablespoon tomato paste
- 2 garlic cloves, minced
- 3/4 teaspoon dried thyme
- 1/2 teaspoon salt
- 1/2 teaspoon pepper
- 1 bay leaf
- 1/2 pound fresh mushrooms, sliced
- 1/2 cup burgundy wine *or* beef broth
- 5 tablespoons all-purpose flour
- 2/3 cup cold water

Hot cooked noodles

- ■ In a skillet, cook bacon over medium heat until crisp. Use a slotted spoon to remove to paper towels. In drippings, brown beef; drain. Place beef and bacon in a 5-qt. slow cooker. Add next 10 ingredients. Cover; cook on low 7-8 hours or until meat is tender.

- ■ Add mushrooms and wine. Combine flour and water until smooth; stir into slow cooker. Cover; cook on high 30-45 minutes or until thickened. Discard bay leaf. Serve over noodles.

YIELD: 8 servings.

MEAT LOAF BURGERS

potato 'n' beef stew

COOK TIME: 9 TO 10 HOURS

Randee Eckstein
Commack, New York
Here's a great beef stew that simmers in a wonderful gravy. Served with crusty bread and a salad, it's a tasty meal for grown-ups and kids alike.

> 5 medium red potatoes, peeled and cut into 1/2-inch chunks
>
> 2-1/2 cups sliced fresh mushrooms
>
> 4 medium carrots, sliced
>
> 2 celery ribs, thinly sliced
>
> 3 bacon strips, diced
>
> 1/4 cup all-purpose flour
>
> 3/4 teaspoon pepper, *divided*
>
> 1/2 teaspoon salt, *divided*
>
> 2 pounds beef stew meat, cut into 3/4-inch cubes
>
> 1 large onion, chopped
>
> 2 garlic cloves, minced
>
> 1 tablespoon vegetable oil
>
> 1 can (14-1/2 ounces) beef broth
>
> 1/2 cup dry red wine *or* additional beef broth
>
> 1 bay leaf
>
> 1/8 teaspoon dried thyme
>
> 1 can (10-3/4 ounces) condensed tomato soup, undiluted
>
> 1/3 cup water
>
> 2 tablespoons cornstarch
>
> 3 tablespoons cold water

- Place the first four ingredients in a 5-qt. slow cooker. In a large skillet, cook bacon over medium heat until crisp. Drain on paper towels. Reserve drippings.

- In a large resealable plastic bag, combine the flour, 1/4 teaspoon pepper and 1/4 teaspoon salt. Add meat; seal and shake to coat. Brown the beef, onion and garlic in drippings and oil. Transfer to slow cooker.

- Stir in broth, wine or additional broth, bay leaf, thyme, reserved bacon and remaining salt and pepper. Cover and cook on low for 8-9 hours or until tender. Discard bay leaf.

- Combine soup and water; add to slow cooker. Cover and cook on high for 30 minutes. Combine cornstarch and cold water; stir into slow cooker. Cover and cook for 30-40 minutes or until slightly thickened.

YIELD: 7-8 servings.

round steak supper

COOK TIME: 6 TO 8 HOURS

Sandra Castillo
Janesville, Wisconsin
Inexpensive round steak and potatoes are simmered for hours in an onion-flavored gravy to create this satisfying supper.

> 4 large potatoes, peeled and cut into 1/2-inch cubes
>
> 1-1/2 pounds boneless beef round steak
>
> 1 can (10-3/4 ounces) condensed cream of mushroom soup, undiluted
>
> 1/2 cup water
>
> 1 envelope onion soup mix
>
> Pepper and garlic powder to taste

- Place the potatoes in a 3-qt. slow cooker. Cut beef into four pieces; place over potatoes. In a bowl, combine the soup, water, soup mix, pepper and garlic powder. Pour over the beef. Cover and cook on low for 6-8 hours or until meat and potatoes are tender.

YIELD: 4 servings.

dilled pot roast

COOK TIME: 7-1/2 TO 8-1/2 HOURS

Amy Lingren
Jacksonville, Florida
It is hard to believe that this mouth-watering pot roast comes together so easily. I rely on dill weed, cider vinegar and a simple sour cream sauce to flavor the entree.

> 2 teaspoons dill weed, *divided*
>
> 1 teaspoon salt
>
> 1/4 teaspoon pepper
>
> 1 boneless chuck roast (2-1/2 pounds)
>
> 1/4 cup water
>
> 1 tablespoon cider vinegar
>
> 3 tablespoons all-purpose flour
>
> 1/4 cup cold water
>
> 1 cup (8 ounces) sour cream
>
> 1/2 teaspoon browning sauce, optional
>
> Hot cooked rice

- In a small bowl, combine 1 teaspoon dill, salt and pepper. Sprinkle over both sides of roast. Place in a 3-qt. slow cooker. Add water and vinegar. Cover and cook on low for 7-8 hours or until the meat is tender. Remove meat and keep warm.

- In a small bowl, combine flour and remaining dill; stir in cold water until smooth. Gradually stir into slow cooker. Cover and cook on high for 30 minutes or until thickened.

- Stir in sour cream and browning sauce if desired; heat through. Slice meat. Serve with sour cream sauce and rice.

YIELD: 6-8 servings.

DILLED POT ROAST

beef tips

COOK TIME: 6 TO 7 HOURS

Diane Benskin
Lewisville, Texas

This simple recipe showcases tender beef sirloin. Serve over pasta for a simple, filling meal.

> 1 pound beef sirloin tips, cut into 1-inch cubes
>
> 2 to 3 celery ribs, chopped
>
> 2 to 3 medium carrots, chopped
>
> 1 medium onion, chopped
>
> 1 can (10-3/4 ounces) condensed golden mushroom soup, undiluted
>
> 1/2 to 1 cup white wine *or* beef broth
>
> 2 teaspoons cornstarch
>
> 1/4 cup cold water

Hot cooked pasta

■ In a 3-qt. slow cooker, combine first six ingredients. Cover; cook on low for 6-7 hours or until meat is tender.

■ Combine cornstarch and water until smooth. Gradually stir into pan juices. Cover; cook on high 15 minutes or until thickened. Serve over pasta.

YIELD: 4 servings.

beef in onion gravy

COOK TIME: 6 TO 8 HOURS

Denise Albers
Freeburg, Illinois

I double this super recipe to feed our family of four so I'm sure to have leftovers to send with my husband to work for lunch. His co-workers tell him he's lucky to have someone who fixes him such special meals. It's our secret that it's an easy slow cooker dinner!

> 1 can (10-3/4 ounces) condensed cream of mushroom soup, undiluted
>
> 2 tablespoons onion soup mix
>
> 2 tablespoons beef broth
>
> 1 tablespoon quick-cooking tapioca
>
> 1 pound beef stew meat, cut into 1-inch cubes

Hot cooked noodles *or* mashed potatoes

■ In a 3-qt. slow cooker, combine the soup, soup mix, broth and tapioca; let stand for 15 minutes. Stir in the beef. Cover and cook on low for 6-8 hours or until meat is tender. Serve over noodles or mashed potatoes.

YIELD: 3 servings.

BEEF IN ONION GRAVY

slow-cooked cabbage rolls

COOK TIME: 6 TO 7 HOURS

Rosemary Jarvis
Sparta, Tennessee

I've worked full-time for more than 30 years, and this convenient recipe has been a lifesaver. It cooks while I'm away and smells heavenly when I walk in the door in the evening.

> 1 large head cabbage
>
> 1 egg, beaten
>
> 1 can (8 ounces) tomato sauce
>
> 3/4 cup quick-cooking rice
>
> 1/2 cup chopped green pepper
>
> 1/2 cup crushed saltines (about 15 crackers)
>
> 1 envelope onion soup mix
>
> 1-1/2 pounds ground beef
>
> 1 can (46 ounces) V8 juice

Salt to taste

Grated Parmesan cheese, optional

■ Remove core from cabbage. Steam 12 large outer leaves until limp; drain well. In a bowl, combine the egg, tomato sauce, rice, green pepper, cracker crumbs and soup mix. Crumble beef over mixture and mix well.

■ Place about 1/3 cup meat mixture on each cabbage leaf. Fold in sides, starting at an unfolded edge, and roll up completely to enclose the filling. Secure with toothpicks if desired.

■ Place cabbage rolls in a 3-qt. slow cooker. Pour V8 juice over rolls. Cover and cook on low for 6-7 hours or until filling reaches 160°. Just before serving, sprinkle with salt and cheese if desired.

YIELD: 6 servings.

SLOW-COOKED CABBAGE ROLLS

slow-cooker beef stew

COOK TIME: 8-1/2 TO 9-1/2 HOURS

Earnestine Wilson
Waco, Texas

Seasoned with thyme and dry mustard, the hearty, slow-cooked stew is chock-full of veggies and beef.

- 1-1/2 pounds potatoes, peeled and cubed
- 6 medium carrots, cut into 1-inch slices
- 1 medium onion, coarsely chopped
- 3 celery ribs, coarsely chopped
- 3 tablespoons all-purpose flour
- 1-1/2 pounds beef stew meat, cut into 1-inch cubes
- 3 tablespoons vegetable oil
- 1 can (14-1/2 ounces) diced tomatoes, undrained
- 1 cup beef broth
- 1 teaspoon ground mustard
- 1/2 teaspoon salt
- 1/2 teaspoon pepper
- 1/2 teaspoon dried thyme
- 1/2 teaspoon browning sauce

■ Layer the vegetables in a 5-qt. slow cooker. Place flour in a large resealable plastic bag. Add stew meat; seal and toss to coat evenly. In a large skillet, brown meat in oil in batches. Place over vegetables.

■ In a large bowl, combine the tomatoes, broth, mustard, salt, pepper, thyme and browning sauce. Pour over beef. Cover and cook on high for 1-1/2 hours. Reduce heat to low; cook 7-8 hours longer or until the meat and vegetables are tender.

YIELD: 8 servings.

garlic beef stroganoff

COOK TIME: 7 TO 8 HOURS

Erika Anderson
Wausau, Wisconsin

I'm a mom and work full time, so I try to use my slow cooker whenever possible. This Stroganoff is perfect because I can get it ready in the morning before the kids get up.

- 2 teaspoons beef bouillon granules
- 1 cup boiling water
- 1 can (10-3/4 ounces) condensed cream of mushroom soup, undiluted
- 2 jars (4-1/2 ounces *each*) sliced mushrooms, drained
- 1 large onion, chopped
- 3 garlic cloves, minced
- 1 tablespoon Worcestershire sauce
- 1-1/2 to 2 pounds boneless round steak, trimmed and cut into thin strips
- 2 tablespoons vegetable oil
- 1 package (8 ounces) cream cheese, cubed

Hot cooked noodles

■ In a 3-qt. slow cooker, dissolve bouillon in water. Add soup, mushrooms, onion, garlic and Worcestershire sauce. In a skillet, brown beef in oil. Transfer to the slow cooker.

■ Cover and cook on low for 7-8 hours or until the meat is tender. Stir in cream cheese until smooth. Serve over noodles.

YIELD: 6-8 servings.

no-fuss swiss steak

COOK TIME: 6 TO 8 HOURS

Sharon Morrell
Parker, South Dakota

I received the recipe for this dish from my cousin. I make it regularly because our children love the savory steak, tangy gravy and fork-tender veggies.

- 3 pounds boneless beef round steak, cut into serving-size pieces
- 2 tablespoons vegetable oil
- 2 medium carrots, cut into 1/2-inch slices
- 2 celery ribs, cut into 1/2-inch slices
- 1-3/4 cups water
- 1 can (11 ounces) condensed tomato rice soup, undiluted
- 1 can (10-1/2 ounces) condensed French onion soup, undiluted
- 1/2 teaspoon pepper
- 1 bay leaf

■ In a large skillet, brown beef in oil over medium-high heat; drain. Transfer to a 5-qt. slow cooker. Add carrots and celery. Combine the remaining ingredients; pour over meat and vegetables. Cover and cook on low for 6-8 hours or until meat is tender.

■ Discard the bay leaf before serving. Thicken cooking juices if desired.

YIELD: 8-10 servings.

SLOW-COOKER BEEF STEW

pepper beef goulash

COOK TIME: 4 TO 5 HOURS

Peggy Key
Grant, Alabama

A couple of common ingredients turns beef stew meat into a hearty entree. No one ever guesses the secret behind my great goulash—an envelope of sloppy joe seasoning.

- 1/2 cup water
- 1 can (6 ounces) tomato paste
- 2 tablespoons cider vinegar
- 1 envelope sloppy joe seasoning
- 2 to 2-1/4 pounds beef stew meat (3/4-inch cubes)
- 1 celery rib, cut into 1/2-inch slices
- 1 medium green pepper, cut into 1/2-inch chunks

Hot cooked noodles

- In a 3-qt. slow cooker, combine the water, tomato paste, vinegar and sloppy joe seasoning. Stir in the beef, celery and green pepper.

- Cover and cook on high for 4-5 hours. Serve over noodles.

YIELD: 4-5 servings.

easy-does-it spaghetti

COOK TIME: 5 HOURS

Genevieve Hrabe
Plainville, Kansas

This savory spaghetti sauce is a nice change from some of the sweeter store-bought varieties. With fresh bread and a green salad, you have a complete meal.

- 2 pounds ground beef, cooked and drained
- 1 can (46 ounces) tomato juice
- 1 can (15 ounces) tomato sauce
- 1 can (8 ounces) mushroom stems and pieces, drained
- 2 tablespoons dried minced onion
- 2 teaspoons salt
- 1 teaspoon garlic powder
- 1 teaspoon ground mustard
- 1/2 teaspoon *each* ground allspice, mace and pepper
- 1 package (7 ounces) spaghetti, broken in half

- In a 5-qt. slow cooker, combine beef, tomato juice, tomato sauce, mushrooms and seasonings; mix well.

- Cover and cook on high for 4 hours. Stir in spaghetti. Cover and cook 1 hour longer or until the spaghetti is tender.

YIELD: 8-10 servings.

italian ground beef stew

COOK TIME: 5 TO 6 HOURS

Sandra Castillo
Janesville, Wisconsin

I created this chunky soup when looking for something inexpensive and easy to make. The thick and hearty mixture is chock-full of ground beef, potatoes and baby carrots.

- 1 pound ground beef
- 6 medium potatoes, peeled and cubed
- 1 package (16 ounces) baby carrots
- 3 cups water
- 2 tablespoons dry onion soup mix
- 1 garlic clove, minced
- 1 teaspoon Italian seasoning
- 1 to 1-1/2 teaspoons salt
- 1/4 teaspoon garlic powder
- 1/4 teaspoon pepper
- 1 can (10-3/4 ounces) condensed tomato soup, undiluted
- 1 can (6 ounces) Italian tomato paste

- In a skillet, cook beef over medium heat until no longer pink; drain. In a 5-qt. slow cooker, combine the next nine ingredients. Stir in the beef.

- Cover and cook on high for 4-5 hours. Stir in soup and tomato paste; cover and cook for 1 hour or until heated through.

YIELD: 12 servings.

SLOW COOKER TIP: Pasta and rice can be cooked in the slow cooker. Pasta needs a large amount of liquid to cook properly and should be added during the last hour of cooking time. Converted rice can be cooked just like vegetables or meat. Make sure the recipe has enough liquid so the rice becomes tender.

PEPPER BEEF GOULASH

two-step stroganoff

COOK TIME: 7 HOURS

Roberta Menefee
Walcott, New York

I especially like to use my slow cooker on hot summer days when I want to keep my kitchen cool. I'm always trying new recipes for different occasions.

> 2 pounds ground beef, cooked and drained
>
> 2 medium onions, chopped
>
> 1 cup beef consomme
>
> 1 can (4 ounces) mushroom stems and pieces, drained
>
> 3 tablespoons tomato paste
>
> 2 garlic cloves, minced

1-1/2 teaspoons salt

1/4 teaspoon pepper

> 2 tablespoons all-purpose flour

3/4 cup sour cream

1/4 cup minced fresh parsley, optional

Hot cooked noodles

- In a 3-qt. slow cooker, combine the first eight ingredients; mix well. Cover and cook on low for 6 hours.

- In a small bowl, combine flour and sour cream until smooth; stir into beef mixture. Cover and cook 1 hour longer or until thickened. Garnish with parsley if desired. Serve over noodles.

YIELD: 6 servings.

beef and barley

COOK TIME: 4 HOURS

Linda Ronk
Melbourne, Florida

I double this country-style dish to serve company. I'm not sure where the recipe originated, but I've had it for years.

> 2 pounds ground beef, cooked and drained
>
> 1 can (15 ounces) diced carrots, undrained
>
> 1 can (14-1/2 ounces) diced tomatoes, undrained
>
> 1 can (10-3/4 ounces) condensed tomato soup, undiluted
>
> 2 celery ribs, finely chopped

1/2 cup water

1-1/2 to 2 teaspoons salt

1/2 teaspoon pepper

1/2 teaspoon chili powder

> 1 teaspoon Worcestershire sauce
>
> 1 bay leaf
>
> 1 cup quick-cooking barley
>
> 2 tablespoons butter
>
> 1 cup soft bread crumbs
>
> 1 cup (4 ounces) shredded cheddar cheese

- In a 3-qt. slow cooker, combine the first 11 ingredients. In a skillet, lightly brown barley in butter. Add to the slow cooker; mix well. Sprinkle with bread crumbs and cheese.

- Cover and cook on high for 4 hours or until heated through. Discard bay leaf before serving.

YIELD: 8 servings.

spiced chili

COOK TIME: 4 TO 5 HOURS

Julie Brendt
Antelope, California

My father was a cook in the Army and taught me the kitchen basics.

1-1/2 pounds ground beef

1/2 cup chopped onion

4 garlic cloves, minced

> 2 cans (16 ounces *each*) kidney beans, rinsed and drained
>
> 2 cans (15 ounces *each*) tomato sauce
>
> 2 cans (14-1/2 ounces *each*) stewed tomatoes, cut up

1 cup water

2 bay leaves

1/4 cup chili powder

1 tablespoon salt

1 tablespoon brown sugar

1 tablespoon dried basil

> 1 tablespoon Italian seasoning

1 tablespoon dried thyme

1 tablespoon pepper

1 teaspoon dried oregano

1 teaspoon dried marjoram

Shredded cheddar cheese and additional chopped onions, optional

- In a large skillet, cook beef, onion and garlic over medium heat until meat is no longer pink; drain. Transfer to a 5-qt. slow cooker. Stir in the beans, tomato sauce, tomatoes, water and seasonings.

- Cover and cook on low for 4-5 hours. Discard the bay leaves. If desired, garnish with cheese and onions.

YIELD: 12 servings (about 3 quarts).

TWO-STEP STROGANOFF

tender beef 'n' bean stew

COOK TIME: 8-1/2 TO 9-1/2 HOURS

Juline Goelzer
Arroyo Grande, California

I often whip up this easy stew on days when I am juggling a lot of the kids' sports schedules. Add a green salad and some corn bread or homemade rolls for a perfect meal.

- 1 pound beef stew meat, cut into 1-inch cubes
- 2 cans (16 ounces *each*) kidney beans, rinsed and drained
- 1 can (14-1/2 ounces) diced tomatoes, undrained
- 1-1/2 cups frozen corn
- 1 cup hot water
- 1 cup chopped onion
- 2 celery ribs, chopped
- 1 can (4 ounces) chopped green chilies
- 1 can (2-1/4 ounces) sliced ripe olives, drained
- 2 tablespoons uncooked long grain rice
- 1 to 2 tablespoons chili powder
- 2 teaspoons beef bouillon granules
- 1/4 teaspoon salt
- 1 can (8 ounces) tomato sauce

Shredded cheddar cheese and sour cream, optional

- In a 5-qt. slow cooker, combine the first 13 ingredients. Cover and cook on low for 8-9 hours or until the beef is tender. Stir in the tomato sauce; cover and cook for 30 minutes or until heated through. Garnish with the cheese and sour cream if desired.

YIELD: 10 servings.

tender beef brisket

COOK TIME: 6 HOURS

Sondra Morrow
Mesa, Arizona

A bit of sugar mellows the flavorful sauce that's drizzled over this brisket.

- 1 fresh beef brisket (3 to 4 pounds), trimmed and cut in half
- 1 cup ketchup
- 1 small onion, chopped
- 2 tablespoons cider vinegar
- 1 tablespoon prepared horseradish
- 1 tablespoon prepared mustard
- 1 teaspoon sugar
- 1/2 teaspoon pepper

- Place brisket in a 3-qt. slow cooker. In a bowl, combine remaining ingredients. Pour over brisket. Cover; cook on low 6 hours or until tender.

- Remove the beef; set aside. Pour the sauce into a saucepan; cook, uncovered, over low heat for 13-15 minutes or until reduced and thickened, stirring occasionally. Slice the meat across the grain; serve with sauce.

YIELD: 6-8 servings.

EDITOR'S NOTE: This is a fresh beef brisket, not corned beef.

saucy italian roast

COOK TIME: 8 TO 9 HOURS

Jan Roat
Red Lodge, Montana

This tender roast is one of my favorite fix-and-forget meals. I thicken the juices with a little flour and add ketchup, then serve the sauce and beef slices over pasta.

- 1 boneless beef rump roast (3 to 3-1/2 pounds)
- 1/2 to 1 teaspoon salt
- 1/2 teaspoon garlic powder
- 1/4 teaspoon pepper
- 1 jar (4-1/2 ounces) sliced mushrooms, drained
- 1 medium onion, diced
- 1 jar (14 ounces) spaghetti sauce
- 1/4 to 1/2 cup red wine *or* beef broth

Hot cooked pasta

- Cut the roast in half. Combine the salt, garlic powder and pepper; rub over roast. Place in a 5-qt. slow cooker. Top with mushrooms and onion. Combine the spaghetti sauce and wine or broth; pour over meat and vegetables. Cover and cook on low for 8-9 hours or until meat is tender. Slice roast; serve over pasta with pan juices.

YIELD: 10 servings.

TENDER BEEF BRISKET

SAUCY ITALIAN ROAST

hobo meatball stew

COOK TIME: 5 HOURS

Margery Bryan
Moses Lake, Washington
I usually have everything on hand for this recipe, so it's simple to start at noon. When I get home, dinner's waiting.

1 pound ground beef

1-1/2 teaspoons salt *or* salt-free seasoning blend, *divided*

1/2 teaspoon pepper, *divided*

4 medium potatoes, peeled and cut into chunks

4 medium carrots, cut into chunks

1 large onion, cut into chunks

1/2 cup *each* water and ketchup

1-1/2 teaspoons cider vinegar

1/2 teaspoon dried basil

3/4 cup frozen peas

- In a bowl, combine beef, 1 teaspoon salt and 1/4 teaspoon pepper. Shape into 1-in. balls. In a skillet over medium heat, brown meatballs; drain.

- Place the potatoes, carrots and onion in a 3-qt. slow cooker; top with meatballs. Combine the water, ketchup, vinegar, basil, and remaining salt and pepper; pour over meatballs. Cover; cook on high for 4-3/4 hours. Stir in peas; cook 15 minutes longer or until the vegetables are tender.

YIELD: 4 servings.

HOBO MEATBALL STEW

slow-cooked stroganoff

COOK TIME: 8 TO 10 HOURS

Karen Herbert
Placerville, California
I've been preparing Stroganoff in the slow cooker for more than 20 years.

3 pounds boneless beef round steak

1/2 cup all-purpose flour

1-1/2 teaspoons salt

1/2 teaspoon ground mustard

1/8 teaspoon pepper

1 medium onion, sliced and separated into rings

2 cans (4 ounces *each*) mushroom stems and pieces, drained

1 can (10-1/2 ounces) condensed beef broth, undiluted

1-1/2 cups (12 ounces) sour cream

Hot cooked noodles

- Cut steak into 3-in. x 1/2-in. strips. In a large resealable plastic bag, combine flour, salt, mustard and pepper. Add beef in batches; toss to coat.

- In a 5-qt. slow cooker, layer the onion, mushrooms and beef. Pour broth over all. Cover and cook on low for 8-10 hours or until meat is tender. Just before serving, stir in the sour cream. Serve over noodles.

YIELD: 8-10 servings.

flank steak fajitas

COOK TIME: 8 TO 9 HOURS

Twila Burkholder
Middleburg, Pennsylvania
The slow cooker tenderizes the flank steak for these filling, zippy fajitas.

1-1/2 to 2 pounds beef flank steak, cut into thin strips

1 can (10 ounces) diced tomatoes and green chilies, undrained

2 garlic cloves, minced

1 jalapeno pepper, seeded and chopped

1 tablespoon minced fresh cilantro

1 teaspoon chili powder

1/2 teaspoon ground cumin

1/4 teaspoon salt

1 *each* medium green and sweet red pepper, julienned

8 to 10 flour tortillas (7 to 8 inches)

Sour cream, salsa and shredded cheddar cheese, optional

- Place beef in a 3-qt. slow cooker. In a bowl, combine the tomatoes, garlic, jalapeno, cilantro, chili powder, cumin and salt; pour over beef. Cover and cook on low for 7-8 hours. Stir in green and red peppers. Cook 1 hour longer or until meat and peppers are tender. Thicken juices if desired.

- Using a slotted spoon, place about 1/2 cup beef mixture down the center of each tortilla; fold sides over filling. Serve with sour cream, salsa and cheese if desired.

YIELD: 8-10 servings.

EDITOR'S NOTE: When cutting or seeding hot peppers, use rubber or plastic gloves to protect your hands. Avoid touching your face.

FLANK STEAK FAJITAS

slow-cooker beef au jus

COOK TIME: 6 TO 7 HOURS

Carol Hille
Grand Junction, Colorado

It's easy to fix this roast, which has lots of onion flavor. Sometimes I also add cubed potatoes and baby carrots.

1 boneless beef rump roast (3 pounds)

1 large onion, sliced

3/4 cup reduced-sodium beef broth

1 envelope (1 ounce) au jus gravy mix

2 garlic cloves, halved

1/4 teaspoon pepper

■ Cut roast in half. In a large nonstick skillet coated with nonstick cooking spray, brown meat on all sides over medium-high heat. Place onion in a 5-qt. slow cooker. Top with meat. Combine the broth, gravy mix, garlic and pepper; pour over meat. Cover and cook on low for 6-7 hours or until meat and onion are tender.

■ Remove meat to a cutting board. Let stand for 10 minutes. Thinly slice meat and return to the slow cooker; serve with pan juices and onion.

YIELD: 10 servings.

SLOW-COOKER BEEF AU JUS

hearty hash brown dinner

COOK TIME: 4-1/2 TO 5 HOURS

Marge Berg
Gibbon, Minnesota

This meal-in-one with veggies and ground beef is frequent fare in my home.

3 cups frozen shredded hash brown potatoes, thawed

1/2 teaspoon salt

1/4 teaspoon pepper

1 pound ground beef

1/2 cup chopped onion

1 package (16 ounces) frozen California-blend vegetables

1 can (10-3/4 ounces) condensed cream of chicken soup, undiluted

1 cup milk

12 ounces process cheese (Velveeta), cubed

1 can (2.8 ounces) french-fried onions

■ Place potatoes in a lightly greased 5-qt. slow cooker; sprinkle with salt and pepper. In a large skillet, cook beef and onion over medium heat until meat is no longer pink; drain. Spoon over potatoes. Top with vegetables. Combine soup and milk; pour over vegetables. Cover and cook on low for 4 to 4-1/2 hours.

■ Top with cheese; cover and cook 30 minutes longer or until cheese is melted. Just before serving, sprinkle with french-fried onions.

YIELD: 4 servings.

apple cider beef stew

COOK TIME: 6 TO 7 HOURS

Margaret Wilson
Hemet, California

I created this slow cooker recipe using frozen vegetables to save time. Apple cider and cinnamon give a down-home flavor to this easy, economical beef stew.

4 cups frozen vegetables for stew (about 24 ounces), thawed

1 can (8 ounces) sliced water chestnuts, drained

1 jar (4-1/2 ounces) sliced mushrooms, drained

1 tablespoon dried minced onion

2 envelopes brown gravy mix

2 tablespoons onion soup mix

2 teaspoons steak seasoning

1/8 teaspoon ground cinnamon

2 pounds beef stew meat, cut into 1-inch cubes

1 can (14-1/2 ounces) beef broth

1-1/4 cups apple cider *or* unsweetened apple juice

1 can (8 ounces) tomato sauce

1 bay leaf

3 tablespoons cornstarch

1/3 cup cold water

■ Place the vegetables, water chestnuts, mushrooms and onion in a 5-qt. slow cooker. In a large resealable plastic bag, combine the gravy mix, soup mix, steak seasoning and cinnamon; add beef, a few pieces at a time. Shake to coat. Add to slow cooker.

■ Combine the broth, cider and tomato sauce; pour over beef. Add bay leaf. Cover and cook on low for 6-7 hours or until meat is tender.

■ Combine cornstarch and water until smooth; stir into stew. Cover and cook on high for 15 minutes or until thickened. Discard bay leaf.

YIELD: 12 servings.

APPLE CIDER BEEF STEW

mushroom round steak

COOK TIME: 8 HOURS

Linda Krivanek
Oak Creek, Wisconsin

I think our family would starve if I didn't have a slow cooker—I use it twice a week. This tender beef entree is perfect with mashed potatoes.

- 1/2 cup all-purpose flour
- 1 teaspoon salt
- 1/4 teaspoon pepper
- 2 to 2-1/2 pounds boneless beef round steak (1/2 inch thick), cut into serving-size pieces
- 2 tablespoons vegetable oil
- 1 can (10-1/2 ounces) condensed French onion soup, undiluted
- 1 can (8 ounces) mushroom stems and pieces, drained
- 3/4 cup water
- 1/4 cup ketchup
- 1 tablespoon Worcestershire sauce
- 2 tablespoons cornstarch
- 1/4 cup cold water
- 1 cup (8 ounces) sour cream

■ In a large resealable plastic bag, combine the flour, salt and pepper. Add beef, a few pieces at a time, and shake to coat. In a large skillet, brown the beef in batches in oil. Transfer meat to a 3-qt. slow cooker with a slotted spoon.

■ In a bowl, combine the soup, mushrooms, water, ketchup and Worcestershire sauce. Pour over meat. Cover and cook on low for 8 hours or until meat is tender.

■ Remove beef with a slotted spoon; keep warm. Transfer cooking liquid to a saucepan. Combine cornstarch and cold water until smooth; gradually stir into cooking liquid. Bring to a boil; cook and stir for 1-2 minutes or until thickened.

■ Stir a small amount of hot liquid into sour cream. Return all to the pan; cook on low until heated through. Serve over meat.

YIELD: 6 servings.

southern pot roast

COOK TIME: 5 TO 6 HOURS

Amber Zurbrugg
Alliance, Ohio

Cajun seasoning adds kick to this tender beef roast that's served with a corn and tomato mixture. It is an unusual dish, but it's bursting with flavor.

- 1 boneless beef chuck roast (2-1/2 pounds)
- 1 tablespoon Cajun seasoning
- 1 package (9 ounces) frozen corn, thawed
- 1/2 cup chopped onion
- 1/2 cup chopped green pepper
- 1 can (14-1/2 ounces) diced tomatoes, undrained
- 1/2 teaspoon pepper
- 1/2 teaspoon hot pepper sauce

■ Cut roast in half; place in a 5-qt. slow cooker. Sprinkle with Cajun seasoning. Top with corn, onion and green pepper. Combine the tomatoes, pepper and hot pepper sauce; pour over vegetables.

■ Cover and cook on low for 5-6 hours or until meat is tender. Serve corn mixture with slotted spoon.

YIELD: 5 servings.

cabbage patch stew

COOK TIME: 6 TO 8 HOURS

Karen Ann Bland
Gove, Kansas

For those who have a surplus of garden cabbage or just enjoy the tangy flavor of those hearty leaves, this tasty recipe is for you. It's a robust and easy fix-it-and-forget-it meal.

- 1 pound ground beef
- 1 cup chopped onion
- 2 celery ribs, chopped
- 11 cups chopped cabbage (about 2 pounds)
- 2 cans (14-1/2 ounces *each*) stewed tomatoes
- 1 can (15 ounces) pinto beans, rinsed and drained
- 1 can (10 ounces) diced tomatoes with green chilies
- 1/2 cup ketchup
- 1 to 1-1/2 teaspoons chili powder
- 1/2 teaspoon dried oregano
- 1/2 teaspoon pepper
- 1/4 teaspoon salt
- Shredded cheddar cheese and sour cream, optional

■ In a large skillet, cook the beef, onion and celery over medium heat until meat is no longer pink and vegetables are tender; drain.

■ Transfer to a 5-qt. slow cooker. Stir in the cabbage, stewed tomatoes, beans, diced tomatoes, ketchup, chili powder, oregano, pepper and salt.

■ Cover and cook on low for 6-8 hours or until cabbage is tender. Serve with the cheese and sour cream if desired.

YIELD: 8 servings.

CABBAGE PATCH STEW

beef 'n' bean torta

COOK TIME: 4 TO 5 HOURS

Joan Hallford
North Richland Hills, Texas

This zesty dish is a favorite of mine because it has a wonderful Southwestern taste and is easy to prepare. I serve it on nights when we have only a few minutes to eat before running off to meetings or sports events.

- **1 pound ground beef**
- **1 small onion, chopped**
- **1 can (15 ounces) pinto *or* black beans, rinsed and drained**
- **1 can (10 ounces) diced tomatoes and green chilies, undrained**
- **1 can (2-1/4 ounces) sliced ripe olives, drained**
- **1-1/2 teaspoons chili powder**
- **1/2 teaspoon salt**
- **1/8 teaspoon pepper**
- **3 drops hot pepper sauce**
- **4 flour tortillas (8 inches)**
- **1 cup (4 ounces) shredded cheddar cheese**

Minced fresh cilantro, optional

Salsa, sour cream, shredded lettuce and chopped tomatoes, optional

- Cut four 20-in. x 3-in. strips of heavy-duty foil; crisscross so they resemble spokes of a wheel. Place strips on the bottom and up the sides of a 5-qt. slow cooker. Coat strips with nonstick cooking spray.

- In a large skillet, cook beef and onion over medium heat until meat is no longer pink; drain. Stir in the beans, tomatoes, olives, chili powder, salt, pepper and hot pepper sauce. Spoon about 1-2/3 cups into prepared slow cooker; top with one tortilla and 1/4 cup cheese. Repeat layers three times.

- Cover and cook on low for 4-5 hours or until heated through. Using foil strips as handles, remove the tortilla stack to a platter. Sprinkle with cilantro. Serve with the salsa, sour cream, lettuce and tomatoes if desired.

YIELD: 4 servings.

coffee pot roast

COOK TIME: 9-1/2 TO 10-1/2 HOURS

Janet Dominick
Bagley, Minnesota

Use a cup of leftover coffee from your morning pot to make this flavorful roast! It's tender, tasty and uses just five main ingredients.

- **2 medium onions, thinly sliced**
- **2 garlic cloves, minced**
- **1 boneless beef chuck roast (3-1/2 to 4 pounds), quartered**
- **1 cup brewed coffee**
- **1/4 cup soy sauce**
- **1/4 cup cornstarch**
- **6 tablespoons cold water**

- Place half of the onions in a 5-qt. slow cooker. Top with garlic and half of the beef. Top with remaining onion and beef. Combine coffee and soy sauce; pour over beef. Cover and cook on low for 9-10 hours or until meat is tender.

- Combine cornstarch and water until smooth; stir into cooking juices. Cover and cook on high for 30 minutes or until gravy is thickened.

YIELD: 10-12 servings.

bavarian pot roast

COOK TIME: 6 TO 8 HOURS

Patricia Gasmund
Rockford, Illinois

I grew up eating pot roast but disliked it until I got this recipe at a church social and changed a few ingredients. My 7-year-old especially enjoys the seasoned apple gravy.

- **1 boneless beef top round roast (about 4 pounds), halved**
- **1-1/2 cups apple juice**
- **1 can (8 ounces) tomato sauce**
- **1 small onion, chopped**
- **2 tablespoons white vinegar**
- **1 tablespoon salt**
- **2 to 3 teaspoons ground cinnamon**
- **1 tablespoon minced fresh gingerroot**
- **1/4 cup cornstarch**
- **1/2 cup water**

- In a Dutch oven coated with non-stick cooking spray, brown the roast on all sides over medium-high heat; drain. Transfer to a 5-qt. slow cooker.

- In a bowl, combine the apple juice, tomato sauce, onion, vinegar, salt, cinnamon and gingerroot; pour over roast. Cover and cook on high for 5-7 hours.

- In a small bowl, combine cornstarch and water until smooth; stir into cooking juices until well combined. Cover and cook 1 hour longer or until the meat is tender and gravy begins to thicken.

YIELD: 12 servings.

BAVARIAN POT ROAST

artichoke beef stew

COOK TIME: 7-1/2 TO 8-1/2 HOURS

Janell Schmidt
Athelstane, Wisconsin

The recipe for this stew is from a dear friend. She served it with dumplings, but my husband prefers noodles.

- 1/3 cup all-purpose flour
- 1 teaspoon salt
- 1/2 teaspoon pepper
- 2-1/2 pounds lean beef stew meat, cut into 1-inch cubes
- 3 tablespoons vegetable oil
- 1 can (10-1/2 ounces) condensed beef consomme, undiluted
- 2 medium onions, halved and sliced
- 1 cup red wine *or* beef broth
- 1 garlic clove, minced
- 1/2 teaspoon dill weed
- 2 jars (6-1/2 ounces *each*) marinated artichoke hearts, drained and chopped
- 20 small fresh mushrooms, halved

Hot cooked noodles

■ In a shallow bowl or large resealable plastic bag, combine the flour, salt and pepper. Add beef and toss to coat. In a skillet, brown beef in oil. Transfer to a 3-qt. slow cooker with a slotted spoon. Gradually add consomme to the skillet. Bring to a boil; stir to loosen browned bits from pan. Stir in onions, wine or broth, garlic and dill. Pour over beef.

■ Cover and cook on low for 7-8 hours or until the meat is nearly tender. Stir in the artichokes and mushrooms; cook 30 minutes longer or until heated through. Serve over noodles.

YIELD: 6-8 servings.

two-pot dinner

COOK TIME: 4 HOURS

Jean Roper
Palermo, California

My daughter received this recipe from an acquaintance a while ago. Bacon gives this dish a wonderfully rich flavor, making it a favorite dish to pass at potlucks.

- 1 pound sliced bacon, cut into 2-inch pieces
- 1 large onion, chopped
- 1 pound ground beef
- 1 can (31 ounces) pork and beans
- 1 can (30 ounces) kidney beans, rinsed and drained
- 1 can (15 ounces) great northern beans, rinsed and drained
- 1 cup ketchup
- 1/3 cup packed brown sugar
- 3 tablespoons vinegar
- 1 tablespoon Liquid Smoke, optional

■ In a skillet, cook bacon over medium heat until crisp; remove with a slotted spoon to a 5-qt. slow cooker. Reserve 2 tablespoons drippings in the pan. Saute onion in drippings until browned; remove with a slotted spoon to slow cooker.

■ In the same skillet, cook beef until no longer pink; drain and transfer to slow cooker. Add the remaining ingredients; mix well. Cover and cook on low for 4 hours or until heated through.

YIELD: 10 servings.

colorful veggie medley

COOK TIME: 4 HOURS

Kerry Johnson
Decorah, Iowa

When my freezer or garden is bulging with vegetables, I bring out the slow cooker to make this dish. My mother found the recipe in an area newspaper.

- 1-1/2 pounds ground beef, cooked and drained
- 1 package (10 ounces) frozen cut green beans, thawed
- 1 package (10 ounces) frozen peas, thawed
- 1 package (6 ounces) frozen pea pods, thawed
- 1 can (14-1/2 ounces) diced tomatoes, undrained
- 1-1/2 cups thinly sliced carrots
- 2 celery ribs, sliced
- 1 can (8 ounces) sliced water chestnuts, drained
- 1/2 cup chopped green pepper
- 3 tablespoons butter
- 3 tablespoons sugar
- 3 tablespoons quick-cooking tapioca
- 1-1/2 teaspoons salt
- 1/2 teaspoon pepper

■ In a 5-qt. slow cooker, combine all of the ingredients and mix well. Cover and cook on low for 4 hours or until heated through.

YIELD: 6-8 servings.

ARTICHOKE BEEF STEW

creamy swiss steak

COOK TIME: 8 TO 9 HOURS

Gloria Carpenter
Bancroft, Michigan

When I was working, I'd put this Swiss steak in the slow cooker before I left for the day. A creamy mushroom sauce made with canned soup nicely flavors the tender round steak.

- 3/4 cup all-purpose flour
- 1 teaspoon salt
- 1/2 teaspoon pepper
- 2 pounds boneless beef round steak, cut into serving-size portions
- 2 tablespoons butter
- 1/2 cup chopped onion
- 2 cans (10-3/4 ounces *each*) condensed cream of mushroom soup, undiluted
- 1 cup water

Hot cooked noodles

■ In a shallow bowl, combine the flour, salt and pepper; dredge beef. In a large skillet, brown beef in butter on both sides. Transfer to a 3-qt. slow cooker; top with onion. Combine soup and water; pour over onion. Cover; cook on low 8-9 hours or until meat is tender. Serve with noodles.

YIELD: 8 servings.

CREAMY SWISS STEAK

apple and onion beef pot roast

COOK TIME: 5 TO 6 HOURS

Rachel Koistinen
Hayti, South Dakota

Rely on your slow cooker to help prepare this moist, tasty pot roast.

- 1 boneless beef sirloin tip roast (3 pounds), cut in half
- 1 cup water
- 1 teaspoon seasoned salt
- 1/2 teaspoon reduced-sodium soy sauce
- 1/2 teaspoon Worcestershire sauce
- 1/4 teaspoon garlic powder
- 1 large tart apple, quartered
- 1 large onion, sliced
- 2 tablespoons cornstarch
- 2 tablespoons cold water
- 1/8 teaspoon browning sauce

■ In a large nonstick skillet coated with nonstick cooking spray, brown roast on all sides. Transfer to a 5-qt. slow cooker. Add water to the skillet, stirring to loosen any browned bits; pour over roast. Sprinkle with seasoned salt, soy sauce, Worcestershire sauce and garlic powder. Top with apple and onion. Cover and cook on low for 5-6 hours or until the meat is tender.

■ Remove roast and onion; let stand for 15 minutes before slicing. Strain cooking liquid into a saucepan, discarding apple. Bring liquid to a boil; cook until reduced to 2 cups, about 15 minutes. Combine cornstarch and cold water until smooth; stir in browning sauce. Stir into cooking liquid. Bring to a boil; cook and stir for 2 minutes or until thickened. Serve over beef and onion.

YIELD: 8 servings with leftovers.

mushroom salsa chili

COOK TIME: 8 TO 9 HOURS

Richard Rundels
Waverly, Ohio

Green, sweet red and yellow peppers give this hearty chili a splash of color. I often fix it for my grandsons. Because they don't like spicy chili, I use mild salsa, but try it with a hotter variety if you prefer it zestier.

- 1 pound ground beef
- 1 pound bulk pork sausage
- 2 cans (16 ounces *each*) kidney beans, rinsed and drained
- 1 jar (24 ounces) chunky salsa
- 1 can (14-1/2 ounces) diced tomatoes, undrained
- 1 large onion, chopped
- 1 can (8 ounces) tomato sauce
- 1 can (4 ounces) mushroom stems and pieces, drained
- 1/2 cup *each* chopped green pepper, sweet red and yellow pepper
- 1/2 teaspoon dried oregano
- 1/4 teaspoon garlic powder
- 1/8 teaspoon dried thyme
- 1/8 teaspoon dried marjoram

■ In a large skillet, cook beef and sausage over medium heat until meat is no longer pink; drain. Transfer meat to a 5-qt. slow cooker.

■ Stir in the remaining ingredients. Cover and cook on low for 8-9 hours or until vegetables are tender.

YIELD: 8 servings.

MUSHROOM SALSA CHILI

lots-a-veggies stew

COOK TIME: 5 HOURS

Judy Page
Edenville, Michigan
When I needed a no-fuss meal, I went through my pantry and refrigerator and created this catchall dish.

- 1 pound ground beef
- 1 medium onion, diced
- 2 garlic cloves, minced
- 1 can (16 ounces) baked beans, undrained
- 1 can (16 ounces) kidney beans, rinsed and drained
- 1 can (15 ounces) butter beans, rinsed and drained
- 1 can (14-1/2 ounces) beef broth
- 1 can (11 ounces) whole kernel corn, undrained
- 1 can (10-1/2 ounces) condensed vegetable soup, undiluted
- 1 can (6 ounces) tomato paste
- 1 medium green pepper, diced
- 1 cup sliced carrots
- 1 cup sliced celery
- 2 tablespoons chili powder
- 1 teaspoon dried oregano
- 1 teaspoon dried thyme
- 1 teaspoon salt, optional
- 1/2 teaspoon dried marjoram
- 1/2 teaspoon pepper

■ In a skillet, cook beef, onion and garlic over medium heat until meat is no longer pink; drain. Transfer to a 5-qt. slow cooker. Add the remaining ingredients and mix well. Cover and cook on low for 5 hours or until vegetables are tender.

YIELD: 10 servings.

stuffed flank steak

COOK TIME: 8 TO 10 HOURS

Kathy Clark
Byron, Minnesota
This recipe came with my first slow cooker. Now I'm on my fourth slow cooker and still use the recipe.

- 1 beef flank steak (2 pounds)
- 1 medium onion, chopped
- 1 garlic clove, minced
- 1 tablespoon butter
- 1-1/2 cups soft bread crumbs (about 3 slices)
- 1/2 cup chopped fresh mushrooms
- 1/4 cup minced fresh parsley
- 1/4 cup egg substitute
- 3/4 teaspoon poultry seasoning
- 1/2 teaspoon salt
- 1/8 teaspoon pepper
- 1/2 cup beef broth
- 2 teaspoons cornstarch
- 4 teaspoons water

■ Flatten steak to 1/2-in. thickness. In a nonstick skillet, saute onion and garlic in butter until tender. Add bread crumbs, mushrooms, parsley, egg substitute, poultry seasoning, salt and pepper; mix well. Spread over steak to within 1 in. of edge. Roll up jelly-roll style, starting with a long side; tie with kitchen string. Place in a 5-qt. slow cooker; add broth. Cover; cook on low 8-10 hours.

■ Remove meat to a serving platter and keep warm. Skim fat from cooking juices; pour into a small saucepan. Combine cornstarch and water until smooth; stir into juices. Bring to a boil; cook and stir for 1-2 minutes or until thickened. Remove string before slicing steak; serve with gravy.

YIELD: 8 servings.

brisket with cranberry gravy

COOK TIME: 8 TO 10 HOURS

Nina Hall
Spokane, Washington
Cranberry sauce adds a pleasant sweetness to this slow-cooked version. Use jellied sauce instead of whole-berry sauce if you like.

- 1 fresh beef brisket (2-1/2 pounds)
- 1/2 teaspoon salt
- 1/4 teaspoon pepper
- 1 can (16 ounces) whole-berry cranberry sauce
- 1 can (8 ounces) tomato sauce
- 1/2 cup chopped onion
- 1 tablespoon prepared mustard

■ Rub brisket with salt and pepper; place in a 5-qt. slow cooker. Combine the cranberry sauce, tomato sauce, onion and mustard; pour over the brisket.

■ Cover and cook on low for 8-10 hours or until meat is tender. Remove brisket; thinly slice across the grain. Skim fat from cooking juices; serve with brisket.

YIELD: 6-8 servings.

EDITOR'S NOTE: This is a fresh beef brisket, not corned beef. The meat comes from the first cut of the brisket.

> **SLOW COOKER TIP:**
> Hearty vegetables, like carrots and potatoes, cook more slowly than meat. Be sure to place those vegetables in the bottom of the pot (under the meat) for quicker cooking.

BRISKET WITH CRANBERRY GRAVY

sweet-sour beef

COOK TIME: 7 TO 8 HOURS

Beth Husband
Billings, Montana

Pasta lovers will savor this sweet and sour specialty over noodles. Chock-full of tender beef, sliced carrots, green pepper and onion, this stew-like sauce is also a hit over rice.

- 2 pounds boneless beef round *or* chuck steak, cut into 1-inch cubes
- 2 tablespoons vegetable oil
- 2 cans (8 ounces *each*) tomato sauce
- 2 cups sliced carrots
- 2 cups pearl onions
- 1 large green pepper, cut into 1-inch pieces
- 1/2 cup molasses
- 1/3 cup cider vinegar
- 1/4 cup sugar
- 2 teaspoons chili powder
- 2 teaspoons paprika
- 1 teaspoon salt

Hot cooked macaroni

- In a skillet, brown steak in oil; transfer to a 5-qt. slow cooker. Add the next 10 ingredients; stir well.

- Cover and cook on low for 7-8 hours or until meat is tender. Thicken if desired. Serve over macaroni.

YIELD: 10-12 servings.

marinated pot roast

COOK TIME: 8 TO 10 HOURS

Marijane Rea
Milwaukie, Oregon

I've long used whole or ground cloves as my secret ingredient in cooking and baking. Added to an overnight marinade, they provide the gravy in this meaty main dish with great flavor.

- 1 cup dry white wine *or* beef broth
- 1/3 cup soy sauce
- 1 tablespoon olive oil
- 4 garlic cloves, minced
- 2 green onions, thinly sliced
- 1-1/2 teaspoons ground ginger
- 1/4 teaspoon pepper
- 4 whole cloves
- 1 boneless beef top round roast (4 pounds)
- 5 teaspoons cornstarch
- 5 teaspoons cold water

- In a gallon-size resealable plastic bag, combine the first eight ingredients. Cut roast in half; add to marinade. Seal bag and turn to coat; refrigerate overnight. Place roast and marinade in a 5-qt. slow cooker.

- Cover and cook on low for 8-10 hours or until meat is tender. Remove roast to a serving platter and keep warm. Pour cooking juices into a 2-cup measuring cup; discard whole cloves.

- In a saucepan, combine cornstarch and cold water until smooth; stir in 1-1/2 cups cooking juices. Bring to a boil; cook and stir for 2 minutes or until thickened. Serve with roast.

YIELD: 12 servings.

mushroom beef and noodles

COOK TIME: 8 HOURS

Virgil Killman
Mascoutah, Illinois

I've prepared this flavorful beef dish many times for family and friends. I've also shared the easy six-ingredient recipe with lots of cooks, and everyone thinks it's great.

- 1 can (10-3/4 ounces) condensed golden mushroom soup, undiluted
- 1 can (10-3/4 ounces) condensed beefy mushroom soup, undiluted
- 1 can (10-3/4 ounces) condensed French onion soup, undiluted
- 1/4 cup seasoned bread crumbs
- 2 pounds beef stew meat, cut into 1/2-inch cubes
- 1 package (12 ounces) wide egg noodles

- In a 3-qt. slow cooker, combine soups and bread crumbs; mix well. Stir in beef. Cover and cook on low for 8 hours or until meat is tender.

- Cook noodles according to package directions; drain. Serve with beef mixture.

YIELD: 6-8 servings.

SWEET-SOUR BEEF

round steak sauerbraten

COOK TIME: 7 TO 7-1/2 HOURS

Linda Bloom
McHenry, Illinois

It takes only minutes to ready round steak for the slow cooker, then it simmers to a tasty tenderness most of the day. The flavorful beef strips and sauce are good over hot rice.

- 1 envelope brown gravy mix
- 2 tablespoons plus 1-1/2 teaspoons brown sugar
- 2-1/2 cups cold water, *divided*
- 1 cup chopped onion
- 2 tablespoons white vinegar
- 2 teaspoons Worcestershire sauce
- 4 bay leaves
- 2-1/2 pounds boneless beef top round steak, cut into 3-inch x 1/2-inch strips
- 2 teaspoons salt
- 1 teaspoon pepper
- 1/4 cup cornstarch

■ In a 5-qt. slow cooker, combine the gravy mix, brown sugar, 2 cups water, onion, vinegar, Worcestershire sauce and bay leaves.

■ Sprinkle beef with salt and pepper; stir into gravy mixture. Cover and cook on low for 6-1/2 to 7 hours or until meat is tender.

■ Combine cornstarch and remaining water until smooth; stir into beef mixture. Cover and cook on high for 30 minutes or until thickened. Discard bay leaves.

YIELD: 8-10 servings.

sweet-and-sour pot roast

COOK TIME: 4 TO 5 HOURS

Erica Warkentin
Dundas, Ontario

This recipe gives pot roast a new mouth-watering flavor.

- 12 small white potatoes, peeled
- 1 boneless beef chuck roast (about 3 pounds)
- 1 tablespoon vegetable oil
- 1 cup chopped onion
- 1 can (15 ounces) tomato sauce
- 1/4 cup packed brown sugar
- 2 to 3 tablespoons Worcestershire sauce
- 2 tablespoons cider vinegar
- 1 teaspoon salt

■ Place potatoes in a 3-qt. slow cooker. Trim fat from roast; brown in hot oil on all sides in a skillet. Place meat in the slow cooker. Discard all but 1 tablespoon drippings from skillet; saute onion in drippings until tender. Stir in remaining ingredients. Pour over meat and potatoes.

■ Cover; cook on high 4-5 hours or until meat is tender. Before serving, pour sauce into a skillet. Cook and stir over medium-high heat until thickened; serve with potatoes and meat.

YIELD: 6-8 servings.

corned beef and cabbage

COOK TIME: 8 TO 9 HOURS

Karen Waters
Laurel, Maryland

I first tried this fuss-free way to cook traditional corned beef and cabbage for St. Patrick's Day a few years ago. Now it's a regular menu item.

- 1 medium onion, cut into wedges
- 4 medium potatoes, peeled and quartered
- 1 pound baby carrots
- 3 cups water
- 3 garlic cloves, minced
- 1 bay leaf
- 2 tablespoons sugar
- 2 tablespoons cider vinegar
- 1/2 teaspoon pepper
- 1 corned beef brisket with spice packet (2-1/2 to 3 pounds), cut in half
- 1 small head cabbage, cut into wedges

■ Place the onion, potatoes and carrots in a 5-qt. slow cooker. Combine water, garlic, bay leaf, sugar, vinegar, pepper and contents of spice packet; pour over vegetables. Top with brisket and cabbage. Cover and cook on low for 8-9 hours or until meat and vegetables are tender. Remove bay leaf before serving.

YIELD: 6-8 servings.

SWEET-AND-SOUR POT ROAST

CORNED BEEF AND CABBAGE

texas stew

COOK TIME: 4 HOURS

Kim Balstad
Lewisville, Texas

I love to experiment with many different types of recipes. But as a mother of young children, I rely on family friendly ones more and more. Everyone enjoys this stew.

- 1 can (15-1/2 ounces) hominy, drained
- 1 can (15-1/4 ounces) whole kernel corn, drained
- 1 can (15 ounces) sliced carrots, drained
- 1 can (15 ounces) sliced potatoes, drained
- 1 can (15 ounces) ranch-style *or* chili beans, undrained
- 1 can (14-1/2 ounces) diced tomatoes, undrained
- 1 cup water
- 1 beef bouillon cube
- 1/2 teaspoon garlic powder

Chili powder to taste

Dash Worcestershire sauce

Dash hot pepper sauce

1-1/2 pounds ground beef

- 1 medium onion, chopped

■ In a 5-qt. slow cooker, combine the first 12 ingredients. In a skillet, cook beef and onion over medium heat until meat is no longer pink; drain.

■ Transfer to the slow cooker; mix well. Cover and cook on high for 4 hours or until heated through.

YIELD: 10-12 servings.

deviled swiss steak

COOK TIME: 6 TO 8 HOURS

Melissa Gerken
Zumbrota, Minnesota

This main dish is satisfying all by itself. But you can also serve this Swiss steak over hot mashed potatoes, pasta or rice.

- 1/2 cup all-purpose flour
- 1 tablespoon ground mustard
- 1/2 teaspoon salt
- 1/8 teaspoon pepper
- 2 beef flank steaks (1 pound *each*), halved
- 2 tablespoons butter
- 1 cup thinly sliced onion
- 1 can (28 ounces) stewed tomatoes
- 2 tablespoons Worcestershire sauce
- 1 tablespoon brown sugar

■ In a large resealable plastic bag, combine the flour, mustard, salt and pepper. Add steaks and shake to coat. In a large nonstick skillet, brown steaks on both sides in butter.

■ Transfer to a 5-qt. slow cooker. Top with onion. In a bowl, combine the tomatoes, Worcestershire sauce and brown sugar; pour over meat and onion. Cover and cook on low for 6-8 hours or until meat is tender.

YIELD: 8 servings.

slow-cooker lasagna

COOK TIME: 4 TO 5 HOURS

Lisa Micheletti
Collierville, Tennessee

Convenient no-cook lasagna noodles take the work out of this traditional favorite adapted for the slow cooker. We like it accompanied by Parmesan bread or garlic cheese toast.

- 1 pound ground beef
- 1 large onion, chopped
- 2 garlic cloves, minced
- 1 can (29 ounces) tomato sauce
- 1 cup water
- 1 can (6 ounces) tomato paste
- 1 teaspoon salt
- 1 teaspoon dried oregano
- 1 package (8 ounces) no-cook lasagna noodles
- 4 cups (16 ounces) shredded mozzarella cheese
- 1-1/2 cups (12 ounces) small-curd cottage cheese
- 1/2 cup grated Parmesan cheese

■ In a skillet, cook beef, onion and garlic over medium heat until meat is no longer pink; drain. Add the tomato sauce, water, tomato paste, salt and oregano; mix well.

■ Spread a fourth of the meat sauce in an ungreased 5-qt. slow cooker. Arrange a third of the noodles over sauce (break the noodles if necessary). Combine the cheeses; spoon a third of the mixture over noodles. Repeat layers twice. Top with remaining meat sauce. Cover and cook on low for 4-5 hours or until noodles are tender.

YIELD: 6-8 servings.

TEXAS STEW

slow-cooked coffee beef roast
COOK TIME: 8 TO 10 HOURS

Charles Trahan
San Dimas, California

Day-old coffee is the key to this flavorful beef roast that simmers in the slow cooker until it's fall-apart tender.

1 boneless beef sirloin tip roast (2-1/2 pounds), cut in half

2 teaspoons canola oil

1-1/2 cups sliced fresh mushrooms

1/3 cup sliced green onions

2 garlic cloves, minced

1-1/2 cups brewed coffee

1 teaspoon Liquid Smoke, optional

1/2 teaspoon salt

1/2 teaspoon chili powder

1/4 teaspoon pepper

1/4 cup cornstarch

1/3 cup cold water

■ In a large nonstick skillet, brown roast on all sides in oil over medium-high heat. Place in a 5-qt. slow cooker. In the same skillet, saute mushrooms, onions and garlic until tender; stir in coffee, Liquid Smoke if desired, salt, chili powder and pepper. Pour over roast. Cover; cook on low 8-10 hours or until meat is tender.

■ Remove roast and keep warm. Pour cooking juices into a 2-cup measuring cup; skim fat. In a saucepan, combine cornstarch and water until smooth. Gradually stir in 2 cups cooking juices. Bring to a boil; cook and stir for 2 minutes or until thickened. Serve with sliced beef.

YIELD: 6 servings.

easy meat loaf
COOK TIME: 8 TO 9 HOURS

Marna Heitz
Farley, Iowa

This meat loaf retains its shape in the slow cooker and slices beautifully. Because the vegetables cook along with it, the entire dinner is ready at the same time.

1 egg

1/4 cup milk

2 slices day-old bread, cubed

1/4 cup finely chopped onion

2 tablespoons finely chopped green pepper

1 teaspoon salt

1/4 teaspoon pepper

1-1/2 pounds lean ground beef

1/4 cup ketchup

8 medium carrots, cut into 1-inch chunks

8 small red potatoes

■ In a bowl, beat egg and milk. Stir in the bread cubes, onion, green pepper, salt and pepper. Add beef and mix well. Shape into a round loaf.

■ Place in a 5-qt. slow cooker. Spread ketchup on top of loaf. Arrange carrots around loaf. Peel a strip around the center of each potato; place potatoes over carrots.

■ Cover and cook on high for 1 hour. Reduce heat to low; cover and cook 7-8 hours longer or until no pink remains in the meat and the vegetables are tender.

YIELD: 4 servings.

tender round steak
COOK TIME: 7 TO 8 HOURS

Dona McPherson
Spring, Texas

Quick-and-easy slow cooker recipes like this are a real plus around the holidays. Serve these saucy beef slices over mashed potatoes, rice or noodles.

1/4 cup all-purpose flour

1/2 teaspoon salt

1/8 teaspoon pepper

2 pounds boneless beef round steak (3/4 inch thick), cut into serving-size pieces

6 teaspoons vegetable oil, divided

1 medium onion, thinly sliced

1 can (10-3/4 ounces) condensed cream of mushroom soup, undiluted

1/2 teaspoon dried oregano

1/4 teaspoon dried thyme

■ In a large resealable plastic bag, combine the flour, salt and pepper. Add beef, a few pieces at a time, and shake to coat. In a large skillet, brown the meat on both sides in 4 teaspoons oil. Place in a 5-qt. slow cooker.

■ In the same skillet, saute onion in remaining oil until lightly browned; place over beef. Combine the soup, oregano and thyme; pour over onion. Cover and cook on low for 7-8 hours or until meat is tender.

YIELD: 6-8 servings.

SLOW COOKER TIP: Try using whole leaf herbs and spices instead of ground ones. Some spices, especially pepper, can become bitter after cooking for a long time. Add those in the last hour of cooking for best flavor.

SLOW-COOKED COFFEE BEEF ROAST

zippy slow-cooked chili

COOK TIME: 6 TO 8 HOURS

Travis Skroch
Stratford, Wisconsin

Serve up steaming bowls of this chili to warm your family on a cool day...and you'll get plenty of compliments! This nicely spiced chili simmers all day in the slow cooker.

1 pound ground beef

1 can (28 ounces) diced tomatoes, undrained

1 medium onion, chopped

1 medium green pepper, chopped

1 can (15 ounces) vegetarian chili

1 can (8 ounces) tomato sauce

2 tablespoons chili powder

2 tablespoons minced fresh parsley

1 tablespoon dried basil

2 teaspoons ground cumin

4 garlic cloves, minced

1 teaspoon dried oregano

3/4 teaspoon pepper

1/8 teaspoon hot pepper sauce

6 tablespoons shredded cheddar cheese

1 tablespoon minced chives

- In a nonstick skillet, cook beef over medium heat until no longer pink; drain. Transfer to a 3-qt. slow cooker. Add tomatoes, onion, green pepper, chili, tomato sauce, chili powder, parsley, basil, cumin, garlic, oregano, pepper and hot pepper sauce.

- Cover and cook on low for 6-8 hours. Sprinkle with cheese and chives before serving.

YIELD: 6 servings.

egg noodle lasagna

COOK TIME: 4 HOURS

Mary Oberlin
Selinsgrove, Pennsylvania

I was lucky enough to receive this recipe from one of my friends. The perfect take-along for charity events and church potlucks, this crowd-pleaser is sure to warm tummies on the coldest of winter nights.

6-1/2 cups uncooked wide egg noodles

3 tablespoons butter

1-1/2 pounds ground beef

2-1/4 cups spaghetti sauce

6 ounces process cheese (Velveeta), cubed

3 cups (12 ounces) shredded mozzarella cheese

- Cook noodles according to package directions; drain. Add butter and toss to coat. In a skillet, cook beef over medium heat until no longer pink; drain.

- Spread a fourth of the spaghetti sauce in an ungreased 5-qt. slow cooker. Layer with a third of the noodles, a third of the beef, a third of the remaining sauce and a third of the cheeses. Repeat layers twice.

- Cover and cook on low for 4 hours or until cheese is melted and lasagna is heated through.

YIELD: 12-16 servings.

party-pleasing beef dish

COOK TIME: 4 HOURS

Glee Witzke
Crete, Nebraska

I often prepare this mild spaghetti sauce-like mixture when I'm not sure how many guests are coming. It's easy to fix, easy to serve with tortilla chips and toppings and easy to clean up.

1 pound ground beef

1 medium onion, chopped

3/4 cup water

1 can (8 ounces) tomato sauce

1 can (6 ounces) tomato paste

2 teaspoons sugar

1 garlic clove, minced

1 teaspoon chili powder

1 teaspoon ground cumin

1 teaspoon dried oregano

1 cup cooked rice

Tortilla chips

Shredded cheddar cheese, chopped green onions, sliced ripe olives, sour cream, chopped tomato *and/or* taco sauce

- In a large skillet, cook beef and onion over medium heat until meat is no longer pink; drain. Transfer to a 3-qt. slow cooker. Add the next eight ingredients; mix well.

- Cover and cook on low for 4 hours or until heated through. Add rice; cover and cook 10 minutes longer. Serve over tortilla chips with toppings of your choice.

YIELD: 6-8 servings.

Off   Low   High

ZIPPY SLOW-COOKED CHILI

old-fashioned pot roast
COOK TIME: 8 TO 10 HOURS

Joan Airey
Rivers, Manitoba

We raise beef and have a large garden, so I try to find new ways to use these ingredients to make nutritious meals. Simmered in a brown gravy flecked with veggies, this roast is fork-tender when sliced.

- 1 boneless beef rump roast (3-1/2 to 4 pounds)
- 1 tablespoon vegetable oil
- 1 teaspoon pepper
- 2 medium carrots, grated
- 1 medium onion, thinly sliced
- 2 garlic cloves, minced
- 1 can (8 ounces) tomato sauce
- 1/4 cup red wine *or* beef broth
- 1 tablespoon Worcestershire sauce
- 1/2 teaspoon salt
- 1/2 teaspoon *each* dried basil, marjoram, oregano and thyme
- 3 tablespoons cornstarch
- 3 tablespoons cold water

■ Cut roast in half; brown in a Dutch oven in oil on all sides. Sprinkle with pepper. Place the carrots, onion and garlic in a 5-qt. slow cooker; top with the roast.

■ In a bowl, combine the tomato sauce, wine or broth, Worcestershire sauce and seasonings; pour over roast. Cover and cook on low for 8-10 hours or until the meat is tender.

■ Remove meat and keep warm. Skim fat from cooking juices; pour into a saucepan. Bring to a boil. In a small bowl, combine the cornstarch and

water until smooth; stir into cooking juices. Return to a boil; cook and stir for 1-2 minutes or until thickened. Serve with sliced beef.

YIELD: 12-14 servings.

steak 'n' gravy
COOK TIME: 8-1/2 HOURS

Betty Janway
Ruston, Louisiana

Served over rice or mashed potatoes, this nicely spiced steak makes a simple, satisfying meal.

- 1 pound round steak, trimmed
- 1 tablespoon vegetable oil
- 1-1/2 cups water
- 1 can (8 ounces) tomato sauce
- 1 teaspoon ground cumin
- 1 teaspoon garlic powder
- 1/2 teaspoon salt
- 1/4 teaspoon pepper
- 2 tablespoons all-purpose flour
- 1/4 cup cold water

Hot cooked rice *or* mashed potatoes

■ Cut beef into bite-size pieces; brown in oil in a skillet. Transfer to a 3-qt. slow cooker. Cover with water; add tomato sauce and seasonings. Cover and cook on low for 8 hours, or on high for 4 hours, or until meat is tender.

■ In a small bowl, combine flour and cold water to make a paste; stir into liquid in slow cooker. Cover and cook on high 30 minutes longer or until gravy is thickened. Serve over rice or potatoes.

YIELD: 4 servings.

busy day beef stew
COOK TIME: 10 HOURS

Beth Wyatt
Paris, Kentucky

Here's a classic, old-fashioned beef stew that simmers for hours in the slow cooker. I call it my "lazy" stew because it's so easy to make on busy days.

- 1 boneless beef chuck roast (1 to 1-1/2 pounds)
- 1 envelope onion soup mix
- 2 teaspoons browning sauce, optional
- 1/2 teaspoon salt
- 1/2 teaspoon pepper
- 6 cups water
- 2 cups cubed peeled potatoes (1/2-inch pieces)
- 6 to 8 medium carrots, cut into chunks
- 1 medium onion, chopped
- 1 cup frozen peas, thawed
- 1 cup frozen corn, thawed, optional
- 5 tablespoons cornstarch
- 6 tablespoons cold water

■ Cut roast in half and place in a 5-qt. slow cooker; sprinkle with soup mix, browning sauce if desired, salt and pepper. Pour water over meat. Cover and cook on low for 8 hours.

■ Remove roast to a cutting board; let stand for 5 minutes. Add vegetables to slow cooker. Cube beef and return to slow cooker. Cover and cook on low for 1-1/2 hours or until vegetables are tender.

■ Combine cornstarch and cold water until smooth; stir into stew. Cover and cook on high for 30-45 minutes or until thickened.

YIELD: 8-10 servings.

BUSY DAY BEEF STEW

french beef stew

COOK TIME: 9 TO 10 HOURS

Iola Egle
Bella Vista, Arkansas

When it comes to this thick down-home stew, I let my slow cooker do the work. Then I simply toss together a green salad and dinner is ready.

> 3 medium potatoes, peeled and cut into 1/2-inch cubes
>
> 2 pounds beef stew meat
>
> 4 medium carrots, sliced
>
> 2 medium onions, sliced
>
> 3 celery ribs, sliced
>
> 2 cups tomato juice
>
> 1 cup water
>
> 1/3 cup quick-cooking tapioca
>
> 1 tablespoon sugar
>
> 1 tablespoon salt
>
> 1 teaspoon dried basil
>
> 1/2 teaspoon pepper

- Place the potatoes in a greased 5-qt. slow cooker. Top with the beef, carrots, onions and celery. In a bowl, combine the remaining ingredients. Pour over the vegetables.

- Cover and cook on low for 9-10 hours or until vegetables and beef are tender.

YIELD: 8-10 servings.

enchilada casserole

COOK TIME: 6 TO 8 HOURS

Denise Waller
Omaha, Nebraska

Tortilla chips and a side salad turn this casserole into a mouth-watering meal.

> 1 pound ground beef
>
> 2 cans (10 ounces *each*) enchilada sauce
>
> 1 can (10-3/4 ounces) condensed cream of onion soup, undiluted
>
> 1/4 teaspoon salt
>
> 1 package (8-1/2 ounces) flour tortillas, torn
>
> 3 cups (12 ounces) shredded cheddar cheese

- In a skillet, cook beef over medium heat until no longer pink; drain. Stir in the enchilada sauce, soup and salt. In a 3-qt. slow cooker, layer a third of the beef mixture, tortillas and cheese. Repeat the layers twice.

- Cover and cook on low for 6-8 hours or until heated through.

YIELD: 4 servings.

meatball cabbage rolls

COOK TIME: 8 HOURS

Betty Buckmaster
Muskogee, Oklahoma

My mother would often have these cabbage rolls simmering in her slow cooker when my family and I arrived at her house for weekend visits.

> 1 large head cabbage, cored
>
> 2 cans (one 8 ounces, one 15 ounces) tomato sauce, *divided*
>
> 1 small onion, chopped
>
> 1/3 cup uncooked long grain rice
>
> 2 tablespoons chili powder

Salt and garlic powder to taste

> 1 pound ground beef

- In a Dutch oven, cook cabbage in boiling water only until the outer leaves fall off head, about 3 minutes. Remove cabbage from water and remove as many leaves as will come off easily. Reserve 14-16 large leaves for rolls. Return cabbage to water if more leaves are needed. Remove the thick vein from each leaf.

- In a bowl, combine 8 oz. of tomato sauce, onion, rice, chili powder, salt and garlic powder. Crumble beef over mixture; mix well. Shape into 2-in. balls. Place one meatball on each cabbage leaf; fold in sides. Starting at an unfolded edge, roll up leaf to completely enclose meatball. Secure with toothpicks. Place in a 5-qt. slow cooker. Pour remaining tomato sauce over cabbage rolls.

- Cover and cook on low for 8 hours or until meat is no longer pink and cabbage is tender. Discard toothpicks.

YIELD: 4-6 servings.

FRENCH BEEF STEW

sweet and savory brisket

COOK TIME: 8 TO 10 HOURS

Chris Snyder
Boulder, Colorado

I like this recipe not only because it makes such tender and flavorful beef, but because it takes advantage of a slow cooker. It's wonderful to come home from work and have this mouth-watering dish waiting for you.

> 1 beef brisket (3 to 3-1/2 pounds), cut in half
>
> 1 cup ketchup
>
> 1/4 cup grape jelly
>
> 1 envelope onion soup mix
>
> 1/2 teaspoon pepper

- Place half of the brisket in a 5-qt. slow cooker. In a bowl, combine the ketchup, jelly, soup mix and pepper; spread half over meat. Top with remaining meat and ketchup mixture.

- Cover and cook on low for 8-10 hours or until meat is tender. Slice brisket; serve with cooking juices.

YIELD: 8-10 servings.

EDITOR'S NOTE: This is a fresh beef brisket, not corned beef. The meat comes from the first cut of the brisket.

SWEET AND SAVORY BRISKET

moroccan braised beef

COOK TIME: 7 TO 8 HOURS

Taste of Home Test Kitchen

Curry powder is a blend of up to 20 spices, herbs and seeds. Add a pinch of curry to your favorite soups, stews, salads and even rice to add an exotic flavor. In this Moroccan stew, begin by adding 2 teaspoons curry, then adjust to your taste.

> 1/3 cup all-purpose flour
>
> 2 pounds boneless beef chuck roast, cut into 1-inch cubes
>
> 3 tablespoons olive oil
>
> 2 cans (14-1/2 ounces *each*) beef broth
>
> 2 cups chopped onions
>
> 1 can (14-1/2 ounces) diced tomatoes, undrained
>
> 1 cup dry red wine
>
> 1 tablespoon curry powder
>
> 1 tablespoon paprika
>
> 1 teaspoon salt
>
> 1 teaspoon ground cumin
>
> 1 teaspoon ground coriander
>
> 1/2 teaspoon cayenne pepper

1-1/2 cups golden raisins

Hot cooked couscous, optional

- Place flour in a large resealable plastic bag; add beef and toss to coat. In a large skillet, brown beef in oil. Transfer to a 5-qt. slow cooker. Stir in the broth, onions, tomatoes, wine and seasonings. Cover and cook on low for 7-8 hours or until the meat is tender.

- During the last 30 minutes of cooking, stir in the raisins. Serve with couscous if desired.

YIELD: 6 servings.

slow-cooked pepper steak

COOK TIME: 6 TO 7 HOURS

Sue Gronholz
Columbus, Wisconsin

After a long day in our greenhouse raising bedding plants for sale, I appreciate coming in to this hearty beef dish for supper.

> 1-1/2 to 2 pounds beef round steak
>
> 2 tablespoons vegetable oil
>
> 1/4 cup soy sauce
>
> 1 cup chopped onion
>
> 1 garlic clove, minced
>
> 1 teaspoon sugar
>
> 1/2 teaspoon salt
>
> 1/4 teaspoon pepper
>
> 1/4 teaspoon ground ginger
>
> 4 tomatoes, cut into eighths *or* 1 can (16 ounces) tomatoes with liquid, cut up
>
> 1 large green pepper, cut into strips
>
> 1/2 cup cold water
>
> 1 tablespoon cornstarch

Cooked noodles *or* rice

- Cut beef into 3-in. x 1-in. strips; brown in oil in a skillet. Transfer to a 3-qt. slow cooker. Combine the next seven ingredients; pour over beef. Cover and cook on low for 5-6 hours or until meat is tender. Add tomatoes and green peppers; cook on low for 1 hour longer.

- Combine the cold water and cornstarch to make a paste; stir into liquid in slow cooker and cook on high until thickened. Serve over noodles or rice.

YIELD: 6-8 servings.

SLOW-COOKED PEPPER STEAK

vegetable beef stew

COOK TIME: 5-1/2 TO 6-1/2 HOURS

Ruth Rodriguez
Fort Myers Beach, Florida

Here is a variation of a beef stew that I came across. With sweet flavor from apricots and squash, we think it has South American or Cuban flair. Corn makes it even more hearty.

- 3/4 pound lean beef stew meat, cut into 1/2-inch cubes
- 2 teaspoons canola oil
- 1 can (14-1/2 ounces) beef broth
- 1 can (14-1/2 ounces) stewed tomatoes, cut up
- 1-1/2 cups cubed peeled butternut squash
- 1 cup frozen corn, thawed
- 6 dried apricot *or* peach halves, quartered
- 1/2 cup chopped carrot
- 1 teaspoon dried oregano
- 1/4 teaspoon salt
- 1/4 teaspoon pepper
- 2 tablespoons cornstarch
- 1/4 cup water
- 2 tablespoons minced fresh parsley

■ In a nonstick skillet, brown beef in oil over medium heat. Transfer to a 3-qt. slow cooker. Add the broth, tomatoes, squash, corn, apricots, carrot, oregano, salt and pepper. Cover and cook on high for 5-6 hours or until vegetables and meat are tender.

■ Combine cornstarch and water until smooth; stir into stew. Cover and cook on high for 30 minutes or until gravy is thickened. Stir in parsley.

YIELD: 4 servings.

no-bean chili

COOK TIME: 4 HOURS

Molly Butt
Granville, Ohio

I often combine the ingredients for this zesty chili the night before. In the morning, I load up the slow cooker and let it go! It's so easy to prepare.

- 1-1/2 pounds lean ground beef
- 1 can (14-1/2 ounces) stewed tomatoes
- 1 can (8 ounces) tomato sauce
- 1 small onion, chopped
- 1 small green pepper, chopped
- 1 can (4 ounces) chopped green chilies
- 1/2 cup minced fresh parsley
- 1 tablespoon chili powder
- 1 garlic clove, minced
- 1-1/4 teaspoons salt
- 1/2 teaspoon paprika
- 1/4 teaspoon pepper

Hot cooked rice *or* pasta

■ Crumble the beef into a 3-qt. slow cooker. Add the next 11 ingredients and mix well.

■ Cover and cook on high for 4 hours or until heated through. Serve over rice or pasta.

YIELD: 6 servings.

corned beef dinner

COOK TIME: 9 TO 10 HOURS

Michelle Rhodes
Cleveland, Ohio

This flavorful meal is a must for St. Patrick's Day but great any time of the year. It serves four nicely with enough leftover meat for Reuben sandwiches or other dishes.

- 4 to 5 medium red potatoes, quartered
- 2 cups fresh baby carrots, halved lengthwise
- 3 cups chopped cabbage
- 1 corned beef brisket (3-1/2 pounds) with spice packet
- 3 cups water
- 1 tablespoon caraway seeds

■ Place the potatoes, carrots and cabbage in a 5-qt. slow cooker. Cut brisket in half; place over vegetables. Add the water, caraway seeds and contents of spice packet.

■ Cover and cook on low for 9-10 hours or until the meat and vegetables are tender.

YIELD: 8 servings.

VEGETABLE BEEF STEW

spiced pot roast
COOK TIME: 8 TO 9 HOURS

Loren Martin
Big Cabin, Oklahoma

Just pour these ingredients over your pot roast and let the slow cooker do the work. I often serve this roast over noodles or with mashed potatoes, using the juices as a gravy.

- 1 boneless beef chuck roast (2-1/2 pounds)
- 1 medium onion, chopped
- 1 can (14-1/2 ounces) diced tomatoes, undrained
- 1/4 cup white vinegar
- 3 tablespoons tomato puree
- 2 teaspoons Dijon mustard
- 1/2 teaspoon lemon juice
- 4-1/2 teaspoons poppy seeds
- 2 garlic cloves, minced
- 2-1/4 teaspoons sugar
- 1/2 teaspoon ground ginger
- 1/2 teaspoon salt
- 1/2 teaspoon dried rosemary, crushed
- 1/4 teaspoon ground turmeric
- 1/4 teaspoon ground cumin
- 1/4 teaspoon crushed red pepper flakes
- 1/8 teaspoon ground cloves
- 1 bay leaf

Hot cooked noodles

- Place roast in a 3-qt. slow cooker. In a large bowl, combine the onion, tomatoes, vinegar, tomato puree, mustard, lemon juice and seasonings; pour over roast.

- Cover and cook on low for 8-9 hours or until meat is tender. Discard bay leaf. Thicken cooking juices if desired. Serve over noodles.

YIELD: 6-8 servings.

mexican meat loaf
COOK TIME: 6 TO 8 HOURS

Julie Sterchi
Harrisburg, Illinois

An old standby gets fun Mexican flair and an easy new preparation method in my recipe. The round loaf gets extra flavor when served with salsa.

- 1 egg, beaten
- 1/3 cup taco sauce
- 1 cup coarsely crushed corn chips
- 1/3 cup shredded Mexican cheese blend
- 2 tablespoons taco seasoning
- 1/2 teaspoon salt, optional
- 2 pounds lean ground beef

Additional taco sauce *or* salsa

- In a large bowl, combine the first six ingredients. Crumble beef over mixture and mix well. Shape into a round loaf; place in a 3-qt. slow cooker.

- Cover and cook on low for 6-8 hours or until a meat thermometer reads 160°. Serve with taco sauce or salsa.

YIELD: 8 servings.

italian bow tie supper
COOK TIME: 7 TO 8 HOURS

Joy Frey
Kelso, Missouri

This meal might remind you of ravioli. It makes a lot, so I don't have to cook on the night we enjoy the leftovers.

- 1-1/2 pounds ground beef
- 1 medium onion, chopped
- 1 garlic clove, minced
- 2 cans (8 ounces *each*) tomato sauce
- 1 can (14-1/2 ounces) stewed tomatoes, cut up
- 1 teaspoon dried oregano
- 1 teaspoon Italian seasoning

Salt and pepper to taste

- 1 package (16 ounces) bow tie pasta, cooked and drained
- 1 package (10 ounces) frozen chopped spinach, thawed and well drained
- 1-1/2 cups (6 ounces) shredded mozzarella cheese
- 1/2 cup grated Parmesan cheese

- In a skillet, cook beef, onion and garlic over medium heat until meat is no longer pink; drain. Transfer to a 3-qt. slow cooker. Stir in the tomato sauce, tomatoes and seasonings.

- Cover and cook on low for 7-8 hours or until bubbly. Increase heat to high; stir in pasta, spinach and cheeses. Cover and cook for 10 minutes or until heated through and cheese is melted.

YIELD: 6 servings.

SPICED POT ROAST

throw-together short ribs

COOK TIME: 4 TO 5 HOURS

Lamya Asiff
Delburne, Alberta

This recipe takes no time to prepare and results in the most delicious, fall-off-the-bone short ribs. The longer you cook them, the better they get.

1/3 cup water

1/4 cup tomato paste

3 tablespoons brown sugar

1 tablespoon prepared mustard

2 teaspoons seasoned salt

2 teaspoons cider vinegar

1 teaspoon Worcestershire sauce

1 teaspoon beef bouillon granules

2 pounds beef short ribs

1 small tomato, chopped

1 small onion, chopped

1 tablespoon cornstarch

1 tablespoon cold water

■ In a 3-qt. slow cooker, combine the first eight ingredients. Add the ribs, tomato and onion. Cover and cook on low for 4-5 hours or until meat is tender.

■ In a small bowl, combine cornstarch and cold water until smooth; gradually stir into cooking juices. Cover and cook for 10-15 minutes or until thickened.

YIELD: 4-5 servings.

poor man's steak

COOK TIME: 4 HOURS

Susan Wright
Mineral Wells, West Virginia

These flavorful "steaks" fit into everybody's budget. A special friend shared the recipe, and I think of her each time I make this.

1 cup crushed saltine crackers (about 30 crackers)

1/3 cup water

Salt and pepper to taste

2 pounds ground beef

1/4 cup all-purpose flour

2 tablespoons vegetable oil

2 cans (10-3/4 ounces *each*) condensed cream of mushroom soup, undiluted

Hot mashed potatoes *or* noodles

■ In a bowl, combine cracker crumbs, water, salt and pepper. Crumble beef over mixture and mix well. Press into an ungreased 9-in. square pan. Cover and refrigerate for at least 3 hours. Cut into 3-in. squares; dredge in flour. In a skillet, cook the meat squares in oil until browned on both sides.

■ Transfer to a 3-qt. slow cooker with a slotted spatula or spoon. Add soup. Cover and cook on high for 4 hours or until meat is no longer pink. Serve with mashed potatoes or noodles.

YIELD: 9 servings.

taco meat loaf

COOK TIME: 8 HOURS

Diane Essinger
Findlay, Ohio

Our children think there are three basic food groups—pizza, tacos and burgers! They like to doctor up slices of this specially seasoned meat loaf with their favorite taco toppings.

1 egg

1/2 cup sour cream

1/3 cup salsa

2 to 4 tablespoons taco seasoning

1 cup crushed tortilla chips

1/2 cup shredded cheddar cheese

2 pounds lean ground beef

Optional toppings: sour cream, salsa, shredded cheddar cheese, shredded lettuce, sliced ripe olives

■ In a large bowl, combine the first six ingredients. Crumble beef over mixture and mix well. Pat into the bottom of a 3-qt. slow cooker.

■ Cover and cook on low for 8 hours or until a meat thermometer reads 160°. Top with sour cream, salsa, cheese, lettuce and olives if desired.

YIELD: 8 servings.

THROW-TOGETHER SHORT RIBS

chicken & turkey

Take your pick of the best family-favorite poultry recipes created for the slow cooker, such as Mandarin Chicken, page 222. Every dish is a guaranteed winner with your family, too!

Covered cooking in your countertop appliance means juicier chicken and turkey...and more mealtime compliments for you! Because most of these recipes use just one crock for prep and cooking, cleanup is a breeze, even on the busiest days.

herbed chicken and veggies

COOK TIME: 8 TO 9 HOURS

Dorothy Pritchett
Wills Point, Texas

This subtly seasoned dish is a snap to prepare on a hectic working day.

1 broiler/fryer chicken
(3 to 4 pounds), cut up
and skin removed

2 medium tomatoes, chopped

1 medium onion, chopped

2 garlic cloves, minced

1/2 cup chicken broth

2 tablespoons white wine *or*
additional chicken broth

1 bay leaf

1-1/2 teaspoons salt

1 teaspoon dried thyme

1/4 teaspoon pepper

2 cups broccoli florets

Hot cooked rice

■ Place chicken in a 3-qt. slow cooker. Top with tomatoes, onion and garlic. Combine next six ingredients; pour over chicken. Cover and cook on low for 7-8 hours.

■ Add broccoli; cook 45-60 minutes longer or until the chicken juices run clear and the broccoli is tender. Discard bay leaf. Thicken pan juices if desired. Serve over rice.

YIELD: 4-6 servings.

HERBED CHICKEN AND VEGGIES

slow-cooked lemon chicken

COOK TIME: 3-1/2 TO 4-1/2 HOURS

Walter Powell
Wilmington, Delaware

Garlic, oregano and lemon juice give spark to this memorable main dish. It's easy to fix—just brown the chicken in a skillet, then let the slow cooker do the majority of the work. I like to serve this dish to company.

6 bone-in chicken breast
halves (about 3 pounds),
skin removed

1 teaspoon dried oregano

1/2 teaspoon seasoned salt

1/4 teaspoon pepper

2 tablespoons butter

1/4 cup water

3 tablespoons lemon juice

2 garlic cloves, minced

1 teaspoon chicken bouillon
granules

2 teaspoons minced fresh
parsley

Hot cooked rice

■ Pat chicken dry with paper towels. Combine the oregano, seasoned salt and pepper; rub over chicken. In a skillet over medium heat, brown the chicken in butter; transfer to a 5-qt. slow cooker.

■ Add water, lemon juice, garlic and bouillon to the skillet; bring to a boil, stirring to loosen browned bits. Pour over chicken.

■ Cover and cook on low for 3-4 hours. Baste the chicken. Add parsley. Cover and cook 15-30 minutes longer or until meat juices run clear. If desired, thicken cooking juices and serve over chicken and rice.

YIELD: 6 servings.

garlic clove chicken

COOK TIME: 3-1/2 TO 4 HOURS

Ruth Rigoni
Hurley, Wisconsin

This chicken recipe is sure to be a hit with guests and cooks alike. Your company will love the flavorful chicken cooked in a lemon, herb and garlic mixture, and you'll appreciate the stress-free slow cooker preparation. Try this tip for peeling the garlic: Drop the cloves in boiling water for a few seconds; drain and cool. The peels should then slip off easily.

40 garlic cloves, peeled

4 celery ribs, sliced

1 broiler/fryer chicken
(3 to 4 pounds), cut up
and skin removed

1/2 teaspoon salt

1/4 teaspoon pepper

1 tablespoon olive oil

1/4 cup white wine *or* reduced-
sodium chicken broth

3 tablespoons lemon juice

2 tablespoons dry vermouth

2 tablespoons grated lemon
peel

2 tablespoons minced fresh
parsley

2 teaspoons dried basil

1 teaspoon dried oregano

Dash crushed red pepper flakes

■ Place garlic and celery in 5-qt. slow cooker. Sprinkle chicken with salt and pepper. In a large nonstick skillet, brown chicken in oil in batches; transfer to slow cooker.

■ In a small bowl, combine the remaining ingredients. Pour over chicken. Cover and cook on low for 3-1/2 to 4 hours or until chicken juices run clear.

YIELD: 6 servings.

GARLIC CLOVE CHICKEN

cranberry chicken

COOK TIME: 5-1/2 TO 6-1/2 HOURS

Sandy Brooks
Tacoma, Washington

Cooking with cranberries is a happy habit for me. I like to include them because the fruit is filled with vitamin C—and because my husband and son love the flavor. This chicken recipe is the one they request the most.

- 1 cup fresh *or* frozen cranberries
- 3/4 cup chopped onion
- 1/2 teaspoon salt
- 1/4 teaspoon ground cinnamon
- 1/4 teaspoon ground ginger
- 1 broiler/fryer chicken (about 3-1/2 pounds), quartered and skin removed
- 1 cup orange juice
- 1 teaspoon grated orange peel
- 3 tablespoons butter, melted
- 3 tablespoons all-purpose flour
- 2 to 3 tablespoons brown sugar

Hot cooked noodles

- In a 3-qt. slow cooker, combine the first five ingredients; top with chicken. Pour orange juice over chicken and sprinkle with orange peel. Cover and cook on low for 5-6 hours or until meat juices run clear. Remove chicken; debone and cut up the meat. Set aside and keep warm.

- Combine the butter and flour until smooth; add to slow cooker. Cook on high until thickened, about 20 minutes. Stir in chicken and brown sugar; heat through. Serve over noodles.

YIELD: 4-6 servings.

wild rice turkey dinner

COOK TIME: 7 TO 8 HOURS

Tabitha Dodge
Conover, Wisconsin

We live in the northwoods of Wisconsin, and the wild rice, squash and cranberries I use for this dish are locally grown. I combine these ingredients with turkey tenderloins for a complete and satisfying supper.

- 3/4 cup uncooked wild rice
- 1 medium butternut squash, peeled, seeded and cut into 1-inch pieces
- 1 medium onion, cut into 1-inch pieces
- 2 turkey breast tenderloins (1/2 pound *each*)
- 3 cups chicken broth
- 1/2 teaspoon salt
- 1/2 teaspoon pepper
- 1/2 teaspoon dried thyme
- 1/2 cup dried cranberries

- In a 5-qt. slow cooker, layer the rice, squash, onion and turkey. Add broth; sprinkle with salt, pepper and thyme. Cover and cook on low for 7-8 hours or until turkey juices run clear.

- Remove turkey; cut into slices. Stir cranberries into rice mixture; serve with a slotted spoon.

YIELD: 4 servings.

creamy italian chicken

COOK TIME: 4 HOURS

Maura McGee
Tallahassee, Florida

This recipe for tender chicken is in a creamy sauce that gets fast flavor from salad dressing mix.

- 4 boneless skinless chicken breast halves (4 ounces *each*)
- 1 envelope Italian salad dressing mix
- 1/4 cup water
- 1 package (8 ounces) cream cheese, softened
- 1 can (10-3/4 ounces) condensed cream of chicken soup, undiluted
- 1 can (4 ounces) mushroom stems and pieces, drained

Hot cooked pasta *or* rice

Fresh oregano leaves, optional

- Place the chicken in a 3-qt. slow cooker. Combine salad dressing mix and water; pour over chicken. Cover and cook on low for 3 hours.

- In a small mixing bowl, beat cream cheese and soup until blended. Stir in mushrooms. Pour over chicken. Cook 1 hour longer or until chicken juices run clear. Serve over pasta or rice. Garnish with oregano if desired.

YIELD: 4 servings.

WILD RICE TURKEY DINNER

CREAMY ITALIAN CHICKEN

chicken cacciatore

COOK TIME: 6 TO 8 HOURS

Aggie Arnold-Norman
Liberty, Pennsylvania

I've used this recipe for many years, and everyone who tries it likes it. It's very easy to make, but it's also special enough to serve when company comes to call.

> 2 medium onions, thinly sliced
>
> 1 broiler/fryer chicken (2-1/2 to 3 pounds), cut up and skin removed
>
> 2 garlic cloves, minced
>
> 1 to 2 teaspoons dried oregano
>
> 1 teaspoon salt
>
> 1/2 teaspoon dried basil
>
> 1/4 teaspoon pepper
>
> 1 bay leaf
>
> 1 can (14-1/2 ounces) diced tomatoes, unstrained
>
> 1 can (8 ounces) tomato sauce
>
> 1 can (4 ounces) mushrooms stems and pieces, drained
>
> 1/4 cup water *or* dry white wine

Hot cooked spaghetti

■ Place sliced onions in a 5-qt. slow cooker. Add chicken, seasonings, tomatoes, sauce, mushrooms and water.

■ Cover and cook on low for 6-8 hours. Serve chicken with sauce over pasta.

YIELD: 6 servings.

chicken in a pot

COOK TIME: 7 TO 9 HOURS

Alpha Wilson
Roswell, New Mexico

It takes just minutes to get this satisfying supper ready for the slow cooker. And at the end of a busy day, your family will appreciate the simple goodness of tender chicken and vegetables. It's one of our favorite meals.

> 3 medium carrots, cut into 3/4-inch pieces
>
> 2 celery ribs with leaves, cut into 3/4-inch pieces
>
> 2 medium onions, sliced
>
> 1 broiler/fryer chicken (3 to 4 pounds), cut up
>
> 1/2 cup chicken broth
>
> 1-1/2 teaspoons salt
>
> 1 teaspoon dried basil
>
> 1/2 teaspoon pepper

■ In a 5-qt. slow cooker, place carrots, celery and onions. Top with chicken. Combine remaining ingredients; pour over chicken.

■ Cover and cook on low for 7-9 hours or until chicken juices run clear and vegetables are tender. Serve with a slotted spoon.

YIELD: 6 servings.

tangy tender chicken

COOK TIME: 8-1/2 TO 9-1/2 HOURS

Milton Schutz
Pandora, Ohio

Brown sugar, garlic and ginger provide the traditional sweet-sour flavor in this chicken medley. The aroma is heavenly after working outside all day.

> 1 pound baby carrots
>
> 1 medium green pepper, cut into 1/2-inch strips
>
> 1 medium onion, cut into wedges
>
> 6 boneless skinless chicken breast halves
>
> 1 can (20 ounces) pineapple chunks
>
> 1/3 cup packed brown sugar
>
> 1 tablespoon soy sauce
>
> 2 teaspoons chicken bouillon granules
>
> 1/2 teaspoon salt
>
> 1/2 teaspoon ground ginger
>
> 1/4 teaspoon garlic powder
>
> 3 tablespoons cornstarch
>
> 1/4 cup cold water

Hot cooked rice

■ In a 3-qt. slow cooker, layer carrots, green pepper and onion. Top with chicken. Drain pineapple, reserving juice. Place pineapple over chicken. Add the brown sugar, soy sauce, bouillon, salt, ginger and garlic powder to pineapple juice; pour over pineapple. Cover and cook on low for 8-9 hours.

■ Combine cornstarch and water until smooth; gradually stir into cooking juices. Cook 30 minutes longer or until sauce is thickened, stirring once. Serve over rice.

YIELD: 4-6 servings.

CHICKEN CACCIATORE

southwestern chicken

COOK TIME: 3 TO 4 HOURS

Karen Waters
Laurel, Maryland
Prepared salsa and canned corn and beans add fun color, texture and flavor to this savory dish.

- **2 cans (15-1/4 ounces *each*) whole kernel corn, drained**
- **1 can (15 ounces) black beans, rinsed and drained**
- **1 jar (16 ounces) chunky salsa, *divided***
- **6 boneless skinless chicken breast halves**
- **1 cup (4 ounces) shredded cheddar cheese**

- In a 3-qt. slow cooker, combine the corn, black beans and 1/2 cup salsa. Top with chicken; pour the remaining salsa over chicken.

- Cover and cook on high for 3-4 hours or until meat juices run clear. Sprinkle with cheese; cover until cheese is melted, about 5 minutes.

YIELD: 6 servings.

creamy chicken and beef

COOK TIME: 8 TO 9 HOURS

Jane Thocher
Hart, Michigan
Bacon and cream of mushroom soup dress up this tender chicken recipe. I relied on this dish often when our children lived at home. Since it cooked while I was at work, the only thing left to do was prepare noodles and fix a salad.

- **6 bacon strips**
- **1 package (2-1/2 ounces) thinly sliced dried beef**
- **6 boneless skinless chicken breast halves**
- **1/4 cup all-purpose flour**
- **1 can (10-3/4 ounces) condensed cream of mushroom soup, undiluted**
- **1/4 cup sour cream**

Hot cooked noodles

- In a skillet, partially cook bacon over medium heat. Drain on paper towels. Place beef in a greased 3-qt. slow cooker. Fold chicken pieces in half and wrap a bacon strip around each; place over the beef.

- Combine the flour, soup and sour cream until blended; spread over chicken. Cover and cook on low for 8-9 hours or until chicken juices run clear. Serve over noodles.

YIELD: 6 servings.

slow-cooker chicken dinner

COOK TIME: 8-1/2 HOURS

Jenet Cattar
Neptune Beach, Florida
I love using my slow cooker because it's so convenient. This meal-in-one, which includes juicy chicken and tasty veggies in a creamy sauce, is ready to eat when I get home from the office.

- **6 medium red potatoes, cut into chunks**
- **4 medium carrots, cut into 1/2-inch pieces**
- **4 boneless skinless chicken breast halves**
- **1 can (10-3/4 ounces) condensed cream of chicken soup, undiluted**
- **1 can (10-3/4 ounces) condensed cream of mushroom soup, undiluted**
- **1/8 teaspoon garlic salt**
- **2 to 4 tablespoons mashed potato flakes, optional**

- Place potatoes and carrots in a 3-qt. slow cooker. Top with chicken. Combine the soups and garlic salt; pour over chicken.

- Cover and cook on low for 8 hours. To thicken if desired, stir potato flakes into the gravy and cook 30 minutes longer.

YIELD: 4 servings.

SLOW COOKER TIP: For meats to cook evenly in the slow cooker, allow some space between the pieces. That way, the heat can circulate and the seasonings can be nicely distributed.

SOUTHWESTERN CHICKEN

chicken with vegetables

COOK TIME: 5 HOURS

Norlene Razak
Tye, Texas

You'll be surprised at how easily this juicy chicken entree comes together. It's simple and delicious.

- 1 cup sliced fresh mushrooms
- 4 chicken legs, skin removed
- 4 chicken thighs, skin removed
- 4 celery ribs, sliced
- 1 cup sliced zucchini
- 1 cup sliced carrots
- 1 medium onion, sliced
- 1 cup tomato juice
- 1/2 cup chicken broth
- 1 garlic clove, minced
- 1/4 teaspoon paprika

Pepper to taste

- 3 tablespoons cornstarch
- 3 tablespoons cold water

Hot cooked rice

- Place mushrooms and chicken in a 3-qt. slow cooker. Add the next nine ingredients. Cover and cook on low for 5 hours or until meat juices run clear.

- Remove chicken and vegetables and keep warm. Transfer cooking juices to a saucepan; skim fat. Combine the cornstarch and water until smooth; add to the juices. Bring to a boil; cook and stir for 2 minutes or until thickened. Pour over chicken and vegetables; serve over rice.

YIELD: 4 servings.

golden chicken and noodles

COOK TIME: 6 TO 7 HOURS

Charlotte McDaniel
Anniston, Alabama

This tender chicken cooks up in a golden sauce that is nicely flavored with basil. It's great for taking to a potluck supper if you work and don't have time to cook during the day.

- 6 boneless skinless chicken breast halves (1-1/2 pounds)
- 2 cans (10-3/4 ounces each) condensed broccoli cheese soup, undiluted
- 2 cups milk
- 1 small onion, chopped
- 1/2 to 1 teaspoon salt
- 1/2 to 1 teaspoon dried basil
- 1/8 teaspoon pepper

Hot cooked noodles

- Cut chicken pieces in half; place in a 5-qt. slow cooker. Combine the soup, milk, onion, salt, basil and pepper; pour over chicken.

- Cover and cook on high for 1 hour. Reduce heat to low; cover and cook 5-6 hours longer or until the meat juices run clear. Serve over noodles.

YIELD: 6 servings.

red pepper chicken

COOK TIME: 6 HOURS

Piper Spiwak
Vienna, Virginia

Chicken breasts are treated to a bevy of black beans, red peppers and tomatoes in this Southwestern supper. We love this colorful dish over rice cooked in chicken broth.

- 4 boneless skinless chicken breast halves
- 1 can (15 ounces) black beans, rinsed and drained
- 1 jar (15 ounces) roasted red peppers, undrained
- 1 can (14-1/2 ounces) Mexican stewed tomatoes, undrained
- 1 large onion, chopped
- 1/2 teaspoon salt

Pepper to taste

Hot cooked rice

- Place the chicken in a 3-qt. slow cooker. In a bowl, combine the beans, red peppers, tomatoes, onion, salt and pepper. Pour over the chicken.

- Cover and cook on low for 6 hours or until chicken is no longer pink. Serve over rice.

YIELD: 4 servings.

SLOW COOKER TIP: When preparing meat or poultry for the slow cooker, trim off excess fat because it retains heat. Large amounts of fat could raise the temperature of the cooking liquid and cause the meat to overcook.

CHICKEN WITH VEGETABLES

mandarin chicken

COOK TIME: 8 TO 9 HOURS

Aney Chatterson
Soda Springs, Idaho

Oranges and olives are elegantly paired in this different but delicious dish. The chicken is marinated, then cooked slowly in a flavorful sauce, so it stays moist. To trim prep time, ask your butcher to cut up and skin the chicken for you.

- **1 broiler/fryer chicken (3 to 3-1/2 pounds), cut up and skin removed**
- **2 cups water**
- **1 cup ketchup**
- **1/4 cup packed brown sugar**
- **1/4 cup soy sauce**
- **1/4 cup orange juice concentrate**
- **2 teaspoons salt**
- **2 teaspoons ground mustard**
- **1 teaspoon garlic salt**
- **1 teaspoon ground ginger**
- **1 teaspoon pepper**
- **3 tablespoons cornstarch**
- **1/2 cup cold water**
- **1 can (11 ounces) mandarin oranges, drained**
- **1/2 cup whole pitted ripe olives**
- **2 tablespoons chopped green pepper**

Hot cooked rice

- Place chicken in a large resealable plastic bag. In a bowl, combine the water, ketchup, brown sugar, soy sauce, orange juice concentrate, salt, mustard, garlic salt, ginger and pepper. Pour half over the chicken. Seal bag and turn to coat; refrigerate for 8 hours or overnight. Cover and refrigerate remaining marinade. Drain and discard marinade from chicken.

- Place chicken in a 5-qt. slow cooker; add reserved marinade. Cover and cook on low for 7-8 hours. Combine cornstarch and cold water until smooth; stir into the chicken mixture. Add the oranges, olives and green pepper. Cover and cook on high for 30-45 minutes or until thickened. Serve with rice.

YIELD: 4-6 servings.

sweet and tangy chicken

COOK TIME: 8 TO 9 HOURS

Mary Zawlocki
Gig Harbor, Washington

Spicy barbecue sauce blends with sweet pineapple in this quick-to-fix chicken dish. It's tasty enough for a company dinner, just add a salad and rolls.

- **8 boneless skinless chicken breast halves (4 ounces *each*)**
- **2 bottles (18 ounces *each*) barbecue sauce**
- **1 can (20 ounces) pineapple chunks, undrained**
- **1 medium green pepper, chopped**
- **1 medium onion, chopped**
- **2 garlic cloves, minced**

Hot cooked rice

- Place four chicken breasts in a 5-qt. slow cooker. Combine barbecue sauce, pineapple, green pepper, onion and garlic; pour half over the chicken. Top with remaining chicken and sauce.

- Cover and cook on low for 8-9 hours or until chicken is tender. Thicken sauce if desired. Serve the chicken and sauce over rice.

YIELD: 8 servings.

turkey in a pot

COOK TIME: 5 TO 6 HOURS

Lois Woodward
Okeechobee, Florida

I use this recipe often for an easy Sunday dinner. The turkey breast gets a "holiday treatment" when served with cranberry gravy seasoned with cinnamon, cloves and allspice.

- **1 boneless turkey breast (3 to 4 pounds), halved**
- **1 can (16 ounces) whole-berry cranberry sauce**
- **1/2 cup sugar**
- **1/2 cup apple juice**
- **1 tablespoon cider vinegar**
- **2 garlic cloves, minced**
- **1 teaspoon ground mustard**
- **1/2 teaspoon ground cinnamon**
- **1/4 teaspoon ground cloves**
- **1/4 teaspoon ground allspice**
- **2 tablespoons all-purpose flour**
- **1/4 cup cold water**
- **1/4 teaspoon browning sauce, optional**

- Place the turkey skin side up in a 5-qt. slow cooker. Combine the cranberry sauce, sugar, apple juice, vinegar, garlic, mustard, cinnamon, cloves and allspice; pour over turkey. Cover and cook on low for 5-6 hours or until a meat thermometer reads 170°.

- Remove turkey to a cutting board; keep warm. Strain cooking juices. In a saucepan, combine flour and water until smooth; gradually stir in strained juices. Bring to a boil; cook and stir for 2 minutes or until thickened. Stir in browning sauce if desired. Serve with sliced turkey.

YIELD: 12-16 servings.

TURKEY IN A POT

barbecued turkey chili

COOK TIME: 4 HOURS

Melissa Webb
Ellsworth Air Force Base,
South Dakota

The first time I made this, it won first prize at a chili cook-off. It takes just minutes to mix together, and the slow cooker does the rest. It's often requested by friends and family when we all get together.

> 1 can (16 ounces) kidney beans, rinsed and drained
>
> 1 can (15-1/2 ounces) hot chili beans
>
> 1 can (15 ounces) turkey chili with beans
>
> 1 can (14-1/2 ounces) diced tomatoes, undrained
>
> 1/3 cup barbecue sauce

■ In a 3-qt. slow cooker, combine all of the ingredients. Cover and cook on high for 4 hours or until heated through and flavors are blended.

YIELD: 4-6 servings.

turkey in cream sauce

COOK TIME: 7 TO 8 HOURS

Kathy-Jo Winterbottom
Pottstown, Pennsylvania

I've been relying on this recipe for tender turkey since I first moved out on my own years ago. I serve it whenever I have guests to the house, and I'm constantly writing out the recipe.

> 1-1/4 cups white wine *or* chicken broth
>
> 1 medium onion, chopped
>
> 2 garlic cloves, minced
>
> 2 bay leaves
>
> 2 teaspoons dried rosemary, crushed
>
> 1/2 teaspoon pepper
>
> 3 turkey breast tenderloins (3/4 pound *each*)
>
> 3 tablespoons cornstarch
>
> 1/2 cup half-and-half cream *or* milk
>
> 1/2 teaspoon salt

■ In a 3-qt. slow cooker, combine wine or broth, onion, garlic and bay leaves. Combine rosemary and pepper; rub over turkey. Place in slow cooker.

■ Cover and cook on low for 7-8 hours or until meat is tender. Remove turkey and keep warm. Strain cooking juices; pour into a saucepan. Combine cornstarch, cream and salt until smooth; gradually add to juices. Bring to a boil; cook and stir for 2 minutes or until thickened and bubbly. Slice turkey; serve with cream sauce.

YIELD: 9 servings.

turkey with cranberry sauce

COOK TIME: 4 TO 6 HOURS

Marie Ramsden
Fairgrove, Michigan

This is a very tasty and easy way to cook a turkey breast in the slow cooker. The sweet cranberry sauce complements the turkey nicely.

> 2 boneless skinless turkey breast halves (about 4 pounds *each*)
>
> 1 can (14 ounces) jellied cranberry sauce
>
> 1/2 cup plus 2 tablespoons water, *divided*
>
> 1 envelope onion soup mix
>
> 2 tablespoons cornstarch

■ Cut each turkey breast in half; place in a 5-qt. slow cooker. In a bowl, combine the cranberry sauce, 1/2 cup water and soup mix; mix well. Pour over turkey. Cover and cook on low for 4-6 hours or until turkey is no longer pink and a meat thermometer reads 170°. Remove turkey and keep warm.

■ Transfer cranberry mixture to a small saucepan. In a bowl, combine cornstarch and remaining water until smooth. Bring the cranberry mixture to a boil; stir in cornstarch mixture. Cook and stir for 2 minutes or until thickened. Slice turkey; serve with cranberry sauce.

YIELD: 20-25 servings.

BARBECUED TURKEY CHILI

saucy apricot chicken

COOK TIME: 4 TO 5 HOURS

Dee Gray
Kokomo, Indiana

Four ingredients are all you'll need for this tender chicken entree. The tangy glaze is just as wonderful with ham or turkey. Leftovers reheat nicely in the microwave.

> 6 boneless skinless chicken breast halves (about 1-1/2 pounds)
>
> 2 jars (12 ounces *each*) apricot preserves
>
> 1 envelope onion soup mix

Hot cooked rice

- Place chicken in a 3-qt. slow cooker. Combine the preserves and soup mix; spoon over chicken.

- Cover and cook on low for 4-5 hours or until tender. Serve over rice.

YIELD: 6 servings.

colorful chicken stew

COOK TIME: 8 TO 10 HOURS

Ila Alderman
Galax, Virginia

I rely on chili powder to spice up this hearty stew brimming with chicken and fresh-tasting veggies. Since it simmers in a slow cooker all day, it's wonderful to have it ready when you walk in the door.

> 1 pound boneless skinless chicken breasts, cubed
>
> 1 can (14-1/2 ounces) Italian diced tomatoes, undrained
>
> 2 medium potatoes, peeled and cut into 1/2-inch cubes
>
> 5 medium carrots, chopped
>
> 3 celery ribs, chopped
>
> 1 large onion, chopped
>
> 1 medium green pepper, chopped
>
> 2 cans (4 ounces *each*) mushroom stems and pieces, drained
>
> 2 chicken bouillon cubes
>
> 2 teaspoons sugar
>
> 1 teaspoon chili powder
>
> 1/4 teaspoon pepper
>
> 1 tablespoon cornstarch
>
> 2 cups cold water

- In a 5-qt. slow cooker, combine the first 12 ingredients. In a small bowl, combine cornstarch and water until smooth. Stir into chicken mixture.

- Cover and cook on low for 8-10 hours or until vegetables are tender.

YIELD: 10 servings.

tender barbecued chicken

COOK TIME: 8 TO 10 HOURS

Jacqueline Blanton
Gaffney, South Carolina

I'm a teacher and work most of the day, so slow-cooked meals are a great help. One of my family's favorites is this moist, slow-simmered chicken. For an appealing look, choose a darker brown barbecue sauce.

> 1 broiler/fryer chicken (3 to 4 pounds), cut up
>
> 1 medium onion, thinly sliced
>
> 1 medium lemon, thinly sliced
>
> 1 bottle (18 ounces) barbecue sauce
>
> 3/4 cup regular cola

- Place the chicken in a 3-qt. slow cooker. Top with the onion and lemon slices. Combine the barbecue sauce and cola; pour over all.

- Cover and cook on low for 8-10 hours or until chicken juices run clear.

YIELD: 4-6 servings.

EDITOR'S NOTE: This recipe was tested with K.C. Masterpiece brand barbecue sauce.

SAUCY APRICOT CHICKEN

creamy herbed chicken

COOK TIME: 4 TO 5 HOURS

Mary Humeniuk-Smith
Perry Hall, Maryland

I'm a nurse and work nights, so when I get home in the morning, I put this chicken on to cook. At the end of the day, the chicken is moist and tender, and the rich sauce seasoned with garlic and thyme is delicious. This recipe is a real lifesaver for any busy person.

- **4 boneless skinless chicken breast halves**
- **1 can (10-3/4 ounces) condensed cream of chicken soup, undiluted**
- **1 cup milk**
- **1 envelope garlic and herb pasta sauce mix**
- **1 teaspoon dried thyme**
- **1 teaspoon dried parsley flakes**

Hot cooked fettuccine

- Place chicken in a 3-qt. slow cooker. Combine the soup, milk, sauce mix, thyme and parsley; pour over chicken.

- Cover and cook on low for 4-5 hours or until chicken juices run clear. Serve over fettuccine.

YIELD: 4 servings.

rosemary cashew chicken

COOK TIME: 4 TO 5 HOURS

Ruth Andrewson
Leavenworth, Washington

This elegant entree with fresh herb flavor is mouth-watering.

- **1 broiler/fryer chicken (3 to 4 pounds), cut up and skin removed**
- **1 medium onion, thinly sliced**
- **1/3 cup orange juice concentrate**
- **1 teaspoon dried rosemary, crushed**
- **1 teaspoon salt**
- **1/4 teaspoon cayenne pepper**
- **2 tablespoons all-purpose flour**
- **3 tablespoons water**
- **1/4 to 1/2 cup chopped cashews**

Hot cooked pasta

- Place chicken in a 3-qt. slow cooker. Combine next five ingredients; pour over chicken. Cover and cook on low for 4-5 hours or until chicken juices run clear. Remove the chicken and keep warm.

- In a saucepan, combine flour and water. Stir in cooking juices. Bring to a boil; cook and stir 2 minutes or until thickened. Stir in cashews. Pour over chicken. Serve with pasta.

YIELD: 4-6 servings.

chicken saltimbocca

COOK TIME: 4 TO 5 HOURS

Carol McCollough
Missoula, Montana

White wine dresses up cream of chicken soup to make a lovely sauce for chicken, ham and Swiss cheese roll-ups. The tried-and-true recipe comes from my mother.

- **6 boneless skinless chicken breast halves**
- **6 thin slices deli ham**
- **6 slices Swiss cheese**
- **1/4 cup all-purpose flour**
- **1/4 cup grated Parmesan cheese**
- **1/2 teaspoon salt**
- **1/4 teaspoon pepper**
- **2 tablespoons vegetable oil**
- **1 can (10-3/4 ounces) condensed cream of chicken soup, undiluted**
- **1/2 cup dry white wine or chicken broth**

Hot cooked rice

- Flatten chicken to 1/4-in. thickness. Top each piece with a slice of ham and cheese. Roll up tightly; secure with toothpicks. In a shallow bowl, combine the flour, Parmesan cheese, salt and pepper. Roll chicken in flour mixture; refrigerate for 1 hour.

- In a skillet, brown roll-ups in oil on all sides; transfer to a 3-qt. slow cooker. Combine the soup and wine or broth; pour over chicken. Cover and cook on low for 4-5 hours or until a meat thermometer reads 170°. Remove roll-ups and stir sauce. Serve with rice.

YIELD: 6 servings.

ROSEMARY CASHEW CHICKEN

CHICKEN SALTIMBOCCA

sunday chicken supper

COOK TIME: 6 TO 8 HOURS

Ruthann Martin
Louisville, Ohio

I make this slow-cooked sensation with chicken, vegetables and seasonings. It's a hearty, homespun dish that satisfies the biggest appetites.

    4 medium carrots, cut
      into 2-inch pieces

    1 medium onion, chopped

    1 celery rib, cut into 2-inch
      pieces

    2 cups cut fresh green beans
      (2-inch pieces)

    5 small red potatoes,
      quartered

    1 broiler/fryer chicken
      (3 to 3-1/2 pounds), cut up

    4 bacon strips, cooked and
      crumbled

1-1/2 cups hot water

    2 teaspoons chicken bouillon
      granules

    1 teaspoon salt

1/2 teaspoon dried thyme

1/2 teaspoon dried basil

Pinch pepper

- In a 5-qt. slow cooker, layer the first seven ingredients in order listed. In a bowl, combine the remaining ingredients; pour over the top. Do not stir.

- Cover and cook on low for 6-8 hours or until vegetables are tender and chicken juices run clear. Remove chicken and vegetables. Thicken juices for gravy if desired.

YIELD: 4 servings.

chicken with stuffing

COOK TIME: 4 HOURS

Susan Kutz
Stillman Valley, Illinois

You need only five ingredients to create this comforting meal of chicken topped with corn bread stuffing. I sometimes add two cans of soup so there's more sauce.

    4 boneless skinless chicken
      breast halves

    1 can (10-3/4 ounces)
      condensed cream of chicken
      soup, undiluted

1-1/4 cups water

1/4 cup butter, melted

    1 package (6 ounces) corn
      bread stuffing mix

- Place chicken in a greased 3-qt. slow cooker. Top with soup. In a bowl, combine the water, butter and stuffing mix; spoon over the chicken.

- Cover and cook on low for 4 hours or until chicken juices run clear.

YIELD: 4 servings.

chicken stew over biscuits

COOK TIME: 8 TO 9 HOURS

Kathy Garrett
Browns Mills, New Jersey

A pleasant sauce coats this chicken and veggie dinner that's slow-cooked to perfection and served over biscuits.

    2 envelopes chicken
      gravy mix

    2 cups water

3/4 cup white wine *or*
      chicken broth

    2 garlic cloves, minced

    1 tablespoon minced fresh
      parsley

    1 to 2 teaspoons chicken
      bouillon granules

1/2 teaspoon pepper

    5 medium carrots, cut
      into 1-inch chunks

    1 large onion, cut into eight
      wedges

    1 broiler/fryer chicken
      (3 to 4 pounds), cut up

    3 tablespoons all-purpose
      flour

1/3 cup cold water

    1 tube (7-1/2 ounces)
      refrigerated buttermilk
      biscuits

- In a 3-qt. slow cooker, combine gravy mix, water, wine or broth, garlic, parsley, bouillon and pepper. Add carrots, onion and chicken. Cover and cook on low for 7-8 hours.

- Increase heat to high. In a small bowl, combine flour and cold water until smooth; gradually stir into slow cooker. Cover and cook for 1 hour. Meanwhile, bake biscuits according to package directions. Place biscuits in soup bowls; top with stew.

YIELD: 4-6 servings.

Off Low High

SUNDAY CHICKEN SUPPER

sage turkey thighs

COOK TIME: 6 TO 8 HOURS

Natalie Swanson
Catonsville, Maryland

I created this for my boys, who love dark meat. It's more convenient than cooking a whole turkey. It reminds me of our traditional turkey and stuffing seasoned with sage.

> 4 medium carrots, halved
>
> 1 medium onion, chopped
>
> 1/2 cup water
>
> 2 garlic cloves, minced
>
> 1-1/2 teaspoons rubbed sage, *divided*
>
> 2 turkey thighs *or* drumsticks (about 2 pounds), skin removed
>
> 1 teaspoon browning sauce, optional
>
> 1/4 teaspoon salt
>
> 1/8 teaspoon pepper
>
> 1 tablespoon cornstarch
>
> 1/4 cup cold water

■ In a 3-qt. slow cooker, combine the carrots, onion, water, garlic and 1 teaspoon sage. Top with turkey. Sprinkle with remaining sage. Cover and cook on low for 6-8 hours or until a meat thermometer reads 180°.

■ Remove turkey and keep warm. Skim fat from cooking juices; strain and reserve the vegetables. Place vegetables in a food processor; cover and process until smooth. Place in a saucepan; add cooking juices. Bring to a boil. Add browning sauce if desired, salt and pepper. Combine cornstarch and water until smooth; add to juices. Bring to a boil; cook and stir for 2 minutes or until thickened. Serve with the turkey.

YIELD: 4 servings.

turkey with mushroom sauce

COOK TIME: 7 TO 8 HOURS

Myra Innes
Auburn, Kansas

When we were first married, I didn't have an oven, so I made this tender turkey in the slow cooker. These days, I rely on this recipe because it frees up the oven to make other dishes for large get-togethers.

> 1 boneless turkey breast (3 pounds), halved
>
> 2 tablespoons butter, melted
>
> 2 tablespoons dried parsley flakes
>
> 1/2 teaspoon dried tarragon
>
> 1/2 teaspoon salt
>
> 1/8 teaspoon pepper
>
> 1 jar (4-1/2 ounces) sliced mushrooms, drained *or* 1 cup sliced fresh mushrooms
>
> 1/2 cup white wine *or* chicken broth
>
> 2 tablespoons cornstarch
>
> 1/4 cup cold water

■ Place the turkey, skin side up, in a 3-qt. slow cooker. Brush with butter. Sprinkle with parsley, tarragon, salt and pepper. Top with mushrooms. Pour wine or broth over all.

■ Cover and cook on low for 7-8 hours. Remove turkey and keep warm. Skim fat from cooking juices. In a saucepan, combine cornstarch and water until smooth. Gradually add cooking juices. Bring to a boil; cook and stir for 2 minutes or until thickened. Serve with the turkey.

YIELD: 8 servings.

white chili

COOK TIME: 6 TO 7 HOURS

Shari Meissner
Chester, Montana

This specialty is sure to warm you up on winter nights. Cilantro, green chilies and ground cumin make this a winner.

> 3 medium onions, chopped
>
> 2 garlic cloves, minced
>
> 1 tablespoon olive oil
>
> 4 cups cubed cooked chicken *or* turkey
>
> 2 cans (15 ounces *each*) white kidney *or* cannellini beans, rinsed and drained
>
> 1 can (15 ounces) garbanzo beans *or* chickpeas, rinsed and drained
>
> 2 cups chicken broth
>
> 1 can (4 ounces) chopped green chilies
>
> 2 teaspoons ground cumin
>
> 1/2 teaspoon dried oregano
>
> 1/4 teaspoon salt
>
> 1/4 teaspoon cayenne pepper
>
> 1/4 cup minced fresh cilantro
>
> Corn chips, shredded Monterey Jack cheese and sour cream

■ In a skillet, saute onions and garlic in oil until tender. Transfer to a 3-qt. slow cooker. Add the chicken, beans, broth, green chilies, cumin, oregano, salt and cayenne; stir well.

■ Cover and cook on low for 6-7 hours or until bubbly. Stir in cilantro. Serve over corn chips; top with cheese and sour cream.

YIELD: 8 servings (2 quarts).

SAGE TURKEY THIGHS

herbed chicken and shrimp

COOK TIME: 4-1/2 TO 5-1/2 HOURS

Diana Knight
Reno, Nevada

Tender chicken and shrimp make a flavorful combination that's easy to prepare, yet elegant enough to serve at a dinner party. While I clean the house, it practically cooks itself.

- **1 teaspoon salt**
- **1 teaspoon pepper**
- **1 broiler/fryer chicken (3 to 4 pounds), cut up and skin removed**
- **1/4 cup butter**
- **1 large onion, chopped**
- **1 can (8 ounces) tomato sauce**
- **1/2 cup white wine *or* chicken broth**
- **1 garlic clove, minced**
- **1 teaspoon dried basil**
- **1 pound uncooked medium shrimp, peeled and deveined**

■ Combine salt and pepper; rub over the chicken pieces. In a skillet, brown chicken on all sides in butter. Transfer to an ungreased 5-qt. slow cooker. In a bowl, combine the onion, tomato sauce, wine or broth, garlic and basil; pour over chicken.

■ Cover and cook on low for 4-5 hours or until chicken juices run clear. Stir in shrimp. Cover and cook on high for 20-30 minutes or until shrimp turn pink.

YIELD: 4 servings.

creamy chicken fettuccine

COOK TIME: 3 TO 4 HOURS

Melissa Cowser
Greenville, Texas

Convenient canned soup and process cheese hurry along the assembly of this dish that is loaded with delicious chunks of chicken.

- **1-1/2 pounds boneless skinless chicken breasts, cut into cubes**
- **1/2 teaspoon garlic powder**
- **1/2 teaspoon onion powder**
- **1/8 teaspoon pepper**
- **1 can (10-3/4 ounces) condensed cream of chicken soup, undiluted**
- **1 can (10-3/4 ounces) condensed cream of celery soup, undiluted**
- **4 ounces process cheese (Velveeta), cubed**
- **1 can (2-1/4 ounces) sliced ripe olives, drained**
- **1 jar (2 ounces) diced pimientos, drained, optional**
- **1 package (16 ounces) spinach fettuccine *or* spaghetti**

■ Place the chicken in a 3-qt. slow cooker; sprinkle with garlic powder, onion powder and pepper. Top with soups. Cover and cook on high for 3-4 hours or until chicken juices run clear.

■ Stir in cheese, olives and pimientos if desired. Cover and cook until cheese is melted. Meanwhile, cook fettuccine according to package directions; drain. Serve with the chicken.

YIELD: 6 servings.

spicy lemon chicken

COOK TIME: 4 TO 5 HOURS

Nancy Rambo
Riverside, California

I took a favorite recipe and modified it to work in our slow cooker. We enjoy this tender, lemony chicken with rice or buttered noodles.

- **1 medium onion, chopped**
- **1/3 cup water**
- **1/4 cup lemon juice**
- **1 tablespoon vegetable oil**
- **1/2 to 1 teaspoon salt**
- **1/2 teaspoon *each* garlic powder, chili powder and paprika**
- **1/2 teaspoon ground ginger**
- **1/4 teaspoon pepper**
- **4 boneless skinless chicken breast halves (4 ounces *each*)**
- **4-1/2 teaspoons cornstarch**
- **4-1/2 teaspoons cold water**
- **Hot cooked noodles**
- **Chopped fresh parsley, optional**

■ In a greased 3-qt. slow cooker, combine the onion, water, lemon juice, oil and seasonings. Add chicken; turn to coat. Cover and cook on low for 4-5 hours or until a meat thermometer reads 170°. Remove chicken and keep warm.

■ In a saucepan, combine the cornstarch and cold water until smooth. Gradually add the cooking juices. Bring to a boil; cook and stir for 2 minutes or until thickened. Serve with chicken over noodles. Sprinkle with parsley if desired.

YIELD: 4 servings.

HERBED CHICKEN AND SHRIMP

tarragon mushroom chicken

COOK TIME: 4 TO 5 HOURS

Mary Kretschmer
Miami, Florida

Round out this saucy seasoned chicken with some rice or pasta. I often make this dish when my children and grandchildren visit. Using the slow cooker leaves me more time to enjoy their company.

> 6 boneless skinless chicken breast halves (4 ounces each)
>
> 1 can (10-3/4 ounces) condensed cream of chicken soup, undiluted
>
> 1 jar (4-1/2 ounces) sliced mushrooms, drained
>
> 1/2 cup sherry or chicken broth
>
> 2 tablespoons butter, melted
>
> 1 teaspoon dried tarragon
>
> 1 teaspoon Worcestershire sauce
>
> 1/4 teaspoon garlic powder
>
> 1/4 cup all-purpose flour

■ Place the chicken in a 5-qt. slow cooker. In a small bowl, combine the soup, mushrooms, sherry or broth, butter, tarragon, Worcestershire sauce and garlic powder; pour over chicken. Cover and cook on low for 4-5 hours or until chicken juices run clear.

■ Remove chicken and keep warm. Place the flour in a small saucepan; gradually whisk in cooking liquid until blended. Bring to a boil; cook and stir for 2 minutes or until thickened. Serve over chicken.

YIELD: 6 servings.

no-fuss chicken

COOK TIME: 2 TO 2-1/2 HOURS

Mark Twiest
Allendale, Michigan

My mother-in-law devised this recipe when her children were growing up and schedules were hectic. It was a favorite Sunday meal because it could be cooking while the family was at church. When they came home, it didn't take long to finish the preparations and put dinner on the table.

> 2/3 cup all-purpose flour
>
> 1 teaspoon rubbed sage
>
> 1 teaspoon dried basil
>
> 1 teaspoon seasoned salt
>
> 1 broiler/fryer chicken (2-1/2 to 3 pounds), cut up
>
> 1/4 cup butter
>
> 2 cups chicken broth

■ In a shallow bowl, combine flour, sage, basil and seasoned salt; coat chicken. Reserve remaining flour mixture. In a large skillet, melt butter; brown chicken on all sides.

■ Transfer to a 3-qt. slow cooker. Add 1/4 cup reserved flour mixture to the skillet (discarding the rest); stir until smooth. When mixture begins to bubble, stir in chicken broth and bring to a boil; boil for 1 minute. Pour over chicken. Cover and cook on high for 2 to 2-1/2 hours or until chicken juices run clear.

YIELD: 4 servings.

hearty chicken enchiladas

COOK TIME: 8 HOURS

Jenny Miller
Raleigh, North Carolina

My husband, Nathan, and I really like Mexican food, and this is our favorite dish. You can modify it to suit your taste, adding corn, rice or refried beans.

> 1 pound boneless skinless chicken breasts
>
> 2 cans (15 ounces each) enchilada sauce
>
> 1 can (4 ounces) chopped green chilies
>
> 1 can (15 ounces) black beans, rinsed and drained
>
> 8 flour tortillas (6 inches)
>
> 1 cup (4 ounces) shredded Mexican cheese blend

Sour cream, optional

■ In a 3-qt. slow cooker, combine the chicken, enchilada sauce and chilies. Cover and cook on low for 8 hours or until a meat thermometer reads 160°.

■ Remove chicken and shred with two forks. Reserve 1-2/3 cups cooking juices. Pour the remaining cooking juices into a large bowl; add the beans and shredded chicken. Coat two freezer-safe 8-in. square baking dishes with nonstick cooking spray; add 1/2 cup reserved juices to each.

■ Place about 1/3 cup chicken mixture down the center of each tortilla. Roll up and place seam side down in prepared dishes. Pour remaining reserved juices over top; sprinkle with cheese.

■ Cover and freeze one dish for up to 3 months. Cover and bake the second dish at 350° for 20 minutes. Uncover; bake 5 minutes longer or until cheese is lightly browned. Serve with sour cream if desired.

■ To use frozen enchiladas: Thaw in the refrigerator overnight. Remove from the refrigerator 30 minutes before baking. Bake as directed.

YIELD: 4 servings.

HEARTY CHICKEN ENCHILADAS

slow-cooked chicken and stuffing
COOK TIME: 4-1/2 TO 5 HOURS
Angie Marquart
New Washington, Ohio
This no-fuss main dish has a flavorful blend of seasonings and the irresistible duo of tender chicken and moist dressing. It's perfect year-round.

2-1/2 cups chicken broth
1 cup butter, cubed
1/2 cup chopped onion
1/2 cup chopped celery
1 can (4 ounces) mushroom stems and pieces, drained
1/4 cup dried parsley flakes
1-1/2 teaspoons rubbed sage
1 teaspoon poultry seasoning
1 teaspoon salt
1/2 teaspoon pepper
12 cups day-old bread cubes (1/2-inch pieces)
2 eggs
1 can (10-3/4 ounces) condensed cream of chicken soup, undiluted
5 to 6 cups cubed cooked chicken

■ In a large saucepan, combine the first 10 ingredients. Simmer for 10 minutes; remove from the heat. Place bread cubes in a large bowl. Combine eggs and soup; stir into broth mixture until smooth. Pour over bread and toss well.

■ In a 5-qt. slow cooker, layer half of the stuffing and chicken; repeat layers. Cover and cook on low for 4-1/2 to 5 hours or until a meat thermometer inserted into the stuffing reads 160°.

YIELD: 14-16 servings.

chicken a la king
COOK TIME: 7-1/2 TO 8-1/2 HOURS
Eleanor Mielke
Snohomish, Washington
When I know I'll be having a busy day with little time for cooking, I prepare this tasty main dish. Brimming with flavorful chicken and colorful vegetables, it smells so good while cooking.

1 can (10-3/4 ounces) condensed cream of chicken soup, undiluted
3 tablespoons all-purpose flour
1/4 teaspoon pepper
Dash cayenne pepper
1 pound boneless skinless chicken breasts, cut into cubes
1 celery rib, chopped
1/2 cup chopped green pepper
1/4 cup chopped onion
1 package (10 ounces) frozen peas, thawed
2 tablespoons diced pimientos, drained
Hot cooked rice

■ In a slow cooker, combine soup, flour, pepper and cayenne until smooth. Stir in chicken, celery, green pepper and onion. Cover and cook on low for 7-8 hours or until meat juices run clear. Stir in peas and pimientos. Cook 30 minutes longer or until heated through. Serve over rice.

YIELD: 6 servings.

lemony turkey breast
COOK TIME: 5 TO 7 HOURS
Lynn Laux
Ballwin, Missouri
Lemon and a hint of garlic add a lovely touch to these moist slices of turkey.

1 bone-in turkey breast (5 pounds), halved
1 medium lemon, halved
1 teaspoon salt-free lemon-pepper seasoning
1 teaspoon garlic salt
4 teaspoons cornstarch
1/2 cup reduced-sodium chicken broth

■ Remove skin from turkey. Pat turkey dry with paper towels; spray turkey with nonstick cooking spray. Place breast side up in a 3-qt. slow cooker. Squeeze half of the lemon over turkey; sprinkle with lemon-pepper and garlic salt. Place lemon halves under turkey. Cover and cook on low for 5-7 hours or until meat is no longer pink and a meat thermometer reads 170°. Remove turkey and keep warm. Discard lemon.

■ For gravy, pour cooking liquid into a measuring cup; skim fat. In a saucepan, combine cornstarch and broth until smooth. Gradually stir in cooking liquid. Bring to a boil; cook and stir for 2 minutes or until thickened. Serve with turkey.

YIELD: 14 servings.

CHICKEN A LA KING

LEMONY TURKEY BREAST

chicken veggie alfredo

COOK TIME: 6 TO 8 HOURS

Jennifer Jordan
Hubbard, Ohio

My family loves this dinner—it's easy to make and a great way to save time after a busy day. If you like, add other veggies to suit your family's tastes.

- 4 boneless skinless chicken breast halves
- 1 tablespoon vegetable oil
- 1 jar (16 ounces) Alfredo sauce
- 1 can (15-1/4 ounces) whole kernel corn, drained
- 1 cup frozen peas, thawed
- 1 jar (4-1/2 ounces) sliced mushrooms, drained
- 1/2 cup chopped onion
- 1/2 cup water
- 1/2 teaspoon garlic salt
- 1/4 teaspoon pepper

Hot cooked linguine

- In a large skillet, brown chicken in oil. Transfer to a 3-qt. slow cooker. In a bowl, combine the Alfredo sauce, corn, peas, mushrooms, onion, water, garlic salt and pepper. Pour over chicken.

- Cover and cook on low for 6-8 hours. Serve over linguine.

YIELD: 4 servings.

chicken stew

COOK TIME: 4-1/2 HOURS

Linda Emery
Tuckerman, Arkansas

It's convenient to cook and serve this veggie-packed chicken stew from the slow cooker.

- 2 pounds boneless skinless chicken breasts, cut into 1-inch cubes
- 2 cans (14-1/2 ounces *each*) chicken broth
- 3 cups cubed peeled potatoes
- 1 cup chopped onion
- 1 cup sliced celery
- 1 cup thinly sliced carrots
- 1 teaspoon paprika
- 1/2 teaspoon pepper
- 1/2 teaspoon rubbed sage
- 1/2 teaspoon dried thyme
- 1 can (6 ounces) tomato paste
- 1/4 cup cold water
- 3 tablespoons cornstarch

- In a 5-qt. slow cooker, combine the first 11 ingredients; cover and cook on high for 4 hours. Mix water and cornstarch until smooth; stir into stew.

- Cover and cook 30 minutes more or until the vegetables are tender.

YIELD: 10 servings.

king-size drumsticks

COOK TIME: 8 TO 10 HOURS

Let your slow cooker do the work for you when these tender turkey legs make an appearance at your stately supper. Our Test Kitchen staff combined canned enchilada sauce, green chilies and cumin to give this entree a zesty royal treatment.

- 1 can (10 ounces) enchilada sauce
- 1 can (4 ounces) chopped green chilies, drained
- 1 teaspoon dried oregano
- 1/2 teaspoon garlic salt
- 1/2 teaspoon ground cumin
- 6 turkey drumsticks
- 3 tablespoons cornstarch
- 3 tablespoons cold water

- In a bowl, combine the enchilada sauce, chilies, oregano, garlic salt and cumin. Place the drumsticks in a 5-qt. slow cooker; top with sauce. Cover and cook on low for 8-10 hours or until a meat thermometer reads 180°.

- Remove turkey and keep warm. Strain sauce into a saucepan. Combine the cornstarch and water until smooth; stir into the pan. Bring to a boil; cook and stir for 2 minutes or until thickened. Serve with turkey.

YIELD: 6 servings.

SLOW COOKER TIP: You can use your slow cooker to warm rolls or slices of bread to go with a stew or other main dish. Simply wrap them in foil and set them in the covered cooker on top of the hot, cooked food while you set the table to serve.

CHICKEN VEGGIE ALFREDO

ham 'n' swiss chicken

COOK TIME: 4 TO 5 HOURS

Dorothy Witmer
Ephrata, Pennsylvania

This saucy casserole allows you to enjoy all the rich flavor of traditional chicken cordon bleu with less effort. It's a snap to layer the ingredients and let them cook all afternoon.

> 2 eggs
>
> 2 cups milk, *divided*
>
> 1/2 cup butter, melted
>
> 1/2 cup chopped celery
>
> 1 teaspoon finely chopped onion
>
> 8 slices bread, cubed
>
> 12 thin slices deli ham, rolled up
>
> 2 cups (8 ounces) shredded Swiss cheese
>
> 2-1/2 cups cubed cooked chicken
>
> 1 can (10-3/4 ounces) condensed cream of chicken soup, undiluted

- In a large bowl, beat the eggs and 1-1/2 cups milk. Add butter, celery and onion. Stir in bread cubes.

- Place half of the mixture in a greased 3-qt. slow cooker; top with half of the rolled-up ham, cheese and chicken. Combine soup and remaining milk; pour half over the chicken. Repeat layers once.

- Cover and cook on low for 4-5 hours or until a thermometer inserted into bread mixture reads 160°.

YIELD: 6 servings.

chicken in mushroom sauce

COOK TIME: 4 TO 5 HOURS

Kathy Gallagher
La Crosse, Wisconsin

My father thinks a restaurant could make a fortune with this flavorful chicken. Bacon and sour cream add richness to a simple sauce that really dresses up everyday chicken.

> 4 boneless skinless chicken breast halves
>
> 1 can (10-3/4 ounces) condensed cream of mushroom soup, undiluted
>
> 1 cup (8 ounces) sour cream
>
> 4 bacon strips, cooked and crumbled

- Place chicken in a 3-qt. slow cooker. Combine soup and sour cream; pour over chicken.

- Cover and cook on low for 4-5 hours or until chicken is tender. Sprinkle with bacon.

YIELD: 4 servings.

apple chicken stew

COOK TIME: 4 TO 5 HOURS

Carol Mathias
Lincoln, Nebraska

When my husband and I visit the apple orchards in nearby Nebraska City, we always buy cider to use in this sensational, slow-cooked stew.

> 4 medium potatoes, cubed
>
> 4 medium carrots, cut into 1/4-inch slices
>
> 1 medium red onion, halved and sliced
>
> 1 celery rib, thinly sliced
>
> 1-1/2 teaspoons salt
>
> 3/4 teaspoon dried thyme
>
> 1/2 teaspoon pepper
>
> 1/4 to 1/2 teaspoon caraway seeds
>
> 2 pounds boneless skinless chicken breasts, cubed
>
> 2 tablespoons olive oil
>
> 1 large tart apple, peeled and cubed
>
> 1-1/4 cups apple cider *or* juice
>
> 1 tablespoon cider vinegar
>
> 1 bay leaf

- In a 3-qt. slow cooker, layer potatoes, carrots, onion and celery. Combine salt, thyme, pepper and caraway; sprinkle half over vegetables. In a skillet, saute chicken in oil until browned; transfer to slow cooker. Top with apple. Combine apple cider and vinegar; pour over chicken and apple. Sprinkle with remaining salt mixture. Top with bay leaf.

- Cover and cook on high for 4-5 hours or until vegetables are tender and chicken juices run clear. Discard bay leaf. Stir before serving.

YIELD: 6-8 servings.

HAM 'N' SWISS CHICKEN

pork, ham & sausage

Expand your appreciation of the slow cooker by trying these new recipes using standby ingredients and a selection of pork, ham or sausage. Every one has been kitchen-tested for delicious results.

Just a few ingredients is all it takes to turn out Cranberry Pork Roast, page 286, and impress guests. But why save the special dishes for company? Surprise your family with any of these sensational recipes for a weeknight dinner.

saucy pork chop dinner

COOK TIME: 4 TO 5 HOURS

Janet Phillips
Meadville, Pennsylvania

The slow cooker is a wonderful way to save time during the busy holiday season, so this health-conscious delight is sure to come in handy. Family and friends call me the "Crock-Pot Queen." Of my many slow-cooked specialties, this is my husband's favorite.

- **6 pork loin chops (3/4 inch thick)**
- **1 tablespoon vegetable oil**
- **1 large onion, sliced**
- **1 medium green pepper, chopped**
- **1 can (4 ounces) mushroom stems and pieces, drained**
- **1 can (8 ounces) tomato sauce**
- **1 tablespoon brown sugar**
- **2 teaspoons Worcestershire sauce**
- **1-1/2 teaspoons cider vinegar**
- **1/2 teaspoon salt**

Hot cooked rice, optional

- In a skillet, brown pork chops on both sides in oil; drain. Place chops in a 3-qt. slow cooker. Add the onion, green pepper and mushrooms.

- In a bowl, combine the tomato sauce, brown sugar, Worcestershire sauce, vinegar and salt. Pour over meat and vegetables.

- Cover and cook on low for 4-5 hours or until meat is tender. Serve with rice if desired.

YIELD: 6 servings.

sweet and savory ribs

COOK TIME: 8 TO 9 HOURS

Kandy Bingham
Green River, Wyoming

My husband and I love barbecue ribs, but with our busy schedules, we rarely have time to fire up the grill. So we use the slow cooker. By the time we get home from work, the ribs are delicious, juicy and ready to devour.

- **1 large onion, chopped**
- **2-1/2 to 3 pounds boneless country-style pork ribs**
- **1 bottle (18 ounces) honey barbecue sauce**
- **1/3 cup maple syrup**
- **1/4 cup spicy brown mustard**
- **1/2 teaspoon salt**
- **1/4 teaspoon pepper**

- Place onion in a 5-qt. slow cooker. Top with the ribs. Combine the barbecue sauce, syrup, mustard, salt and pepper; pour over ribs. Cover and cook on low for 8-9 hours or until the meat is tender.

YIELD: 6-8 servings.

tender pork roast

COOK TIME: 8 TO 9 HOURS

LaVerne Peterson
Minneapolis, Minnesota

This melt-in-your-mouth, fall-apart-tender pork roast is wonderful to serve to company because it never fails to please anyone who tries it.

- **1 boneless pork roast (about 3 pounds)**
- **1 can (8 ounces) tomato sauce**
- **3/4 cup soy sauce**
- **1/2 cup sugar**
- **2 teaspoons ground mustard**

- Cut roast in half; place in a 5-qt. slow cooker. Combine remaining ingredients; pour over roast. Cover and cook on low for 8-9 hours or until a meat thermometer reads 160°-170°.

- Remove roast to a serving platter and keep warm. If desired, skim fat from pan juices and thicken for gravy.

YIELD: 8 servings.

SWEET AND SAVORY RIBS

TENDER PORK ROAST

barbecued pork chop supper

COOK TIME: 8 TO 9 HOURS

Jacqueline Jones
Round Lake Beach, Illinois

I start this barbecued pork chop recipe in the morning in the slow cooker and enjoy a tasty supper later without any last-minute work.

> 6 small red potatoes, cut into quarters
>
> 6 medium carrots, cut into 1-inch pieces
>
> 8 bone-in pork loin *or* rib chops (1/2 inch thick)
>
> 1 teaspoon salt
>
> 1/4 teaspoon pepper
>
> 1 bottle (28 ounces) barbecue sauce
>
> 1 cup ketchup
>
> 1 cup cola
>
> 2 tablespoons Worcestershire sauce

- Place potatoes and carrots in a 5-qt. slow cooker. Top with pork chops. Sprinkle with salt and pepper. Combine the barbecue sauce, ketchup, cola and Worcestershire sauce; pour over chops.

- Cover and cook on low for 8-9 hours or until meat and vegetables are tender.

YIELD: 8 servings.

chili casserole

COOK TIME: 7-1/2 HOURS

Marietta Slater
Augusta, Kansas

Even people who usually bypass casseroles can't stay away from this zesty meat and rice dish. The seasonings make it irresistible.

> 1 pound bulk pork sausage
>
> 2 cups water
>
> 1 can (15-1/2 ounces) chili beans, undrained
>
> 1 can (14-1/2 ounces) diced tomatoes, undrained
>
> 3/4 cup uncooked long grain rice
>
> 1/4 cup chopped onion
>
> 1 tablespoon chili powder
>
> 1 teaspoon Worcestershire sauce
>
> 1 teaspoon prepared mustard
>
> 3/4 teaspoon salt
>
> 1/8 teaspoon garlic powder
>
> 1 cup (4 ounces) shredded cheddar cheese

- In a skillet, cook the sausage over medium heat until no longer pink; drain. Transfer to a 3-qt. slow cooker. Add the next 10 ingredients; stir well.

- Cover and cook on low for 7 hours or until rice is tender. Stir in cheese; cook 10 minutes longer or until cheese is melted.

YIELD: 6 servings.

ham and hash browns

COOK TIME: 7 TO 8 HOURS

Marlene Muckenhirn
Delano, Minnesota

You just can't beat the slow cooker for convenience...I use mine two or three times a week all year-round. Here's a new way to prepare an old-fashioned favorite.

> 1 package (28 ounces) frozen O'Brien hash brown potatoes
>
> 2 cups cubed fully cooked ham
>
> 1 jar (2 ounces) diced pimientos, drained
>
> 1 can (10-3/4 ounces) condensed cheddar cheese soup, undiluted
>
> 3/4 cup milk
>
> 1/4 teaspoon pepper

- In a 3-qt. slow cooker, combine the potatoes, ham and pimientos. In a bowl, combine the soup, milk and pepper; pour over potato mixture.

- Cover and cook on low for 7-8 hours or until potatoes are tender.

YIELD: 4 servings.

SLOW COOKER TIP: Keep perishable foods refrigerated until preparation time. If you cut up meat and vegetables in advance, store them separately in the refrigerator. Constant refrigeration ensures that bacteria, which multiply rapidly at room temperature, won't get a "head start" during the first few hours of cooking.

BARBECUED PORK CHOP SUPPER

cabbage kielbasa supper

COOK TIME: 8 TO 9 HOURS

Margery Bryan
Moses Lake, Washington

If you're a fan of German food, you'll enjoy this traditional combination of sausage, cabbage and potatoes.

8 cups coarsely shredded cabbage

3 medium potatoes, cut into 1/2-inch cubes

1 medium onion, chopped

1-3/4 teaspoons salt

1/4 teaspoon pepper

1 can (14-1/2 ounces) chicken broth

2 pounds fully cooked kielbasa *or* Polish sausage, cut into serving-size pieces

■ In a 5-qt. slow cooker, combine the cabbage, potatoes, onion, salt and pepper. Pour broth over all. Place sausage on top (slow cooker will be full, but cabbage will cook down).

■ Cover and cook on low for 8-9 hours or until vegetables are tender and sausage is heated through.

YIELD: 6-8 servings.

SLOW COOKER TIP:

Meat in a slow cooker does not brown as if it was cooked in a skillet or oven. You do not have to brown meat before placing it in the slow cooker, but some people prefer the flavor of browned meat. If you're one of them, brown the meat in oil in a skillet or Dutch oven before placing it in the slow cooker.

---

slow-cooked ham

COOK TIME: 8 TO 10 HOURS

Heather Spring
Sheppard Air Force Base, Texas

Entertaining doesn't get much easier than when you serve this tasty five-ingredient entree. I first prepared it for Christmas with great results. Leftovers are delicious in casseroles. I know you'll get recipe requests.

1/2 cup packed brown sugar

1 teaspoon ground mustard

1 teaspoon prepared horseradish

4 tablespoons regular cola, *divided*

1 boneless smoked ham (5 to 6 pounds), cut in half

■ In a bowl, combine the brown sugar, mustard, horseradish and 2 tablespoons cola; mix well. Rub over ham. Place in a 5-qt. slow cooker; pour remaining cola over ham.

■ Cover and cook on low for 8-10 hours or until a meat thermometer reads 140°.

YIELD: 15-20 servings.

---

pork chop dinner

COOK TIME: 6 TO 8 HOURS

Mike Avery
Battle Creek, Michigan

Canned soup creates a comforting gravy for tender pork and potatoes in this simple meal-in-one. Feel free to vary the amount of onion soup mix in the recipe to suit your family's tastes.

6 to 8 medium carrots (1 pound), coarsely chopped

3 to 4 medium potatoes, cubed

4 boneless pork loin chops (3/4 inch thick)

1 large onion, sliced

1 envelope onion soup mix

2 cans (10-3/4 ounces *each*) condensed cream of mushroom soup, undiluted

■ Place carrots and potatoes in a 3-qt. slow cooker. Top with pork chops, onion, soup mix and soup. Cover and cook on low for 6-8 hours or until meat and vegetables are tender.

YIELD: 4 servings.

SLOW-COOKED HAM

PORK CHOP DINNER

sweet 'n' sour ribs

COOK TIME: 8 TO 10 HOURS

Dorothy Voelz
Champaign, Illinois

If you're looking for a change from typical barbecue ribs, you'll enjoy this recipe my mom always prepared on birthdays and special occasions. The tender ribs have a slight sweet-and-sour taste that my family loves. I usually serve them with garlic mashed potatoes and a salad or coleslaw.

> 3 to 4 pounds boneless country-style pork ribs
>
> 1 can (20 ounces) pineapple tidbits, undrained
>
> 2 cans (8 ounces *each*) tomato sauce
>
> 1/2 cup thinly sliced onion
>
> 1/2 cup thinly sliced green pepper
>
> 1/2 cup packed brown sugar
>
> 1/4 cup cider vinegar
>
> 1/4 cup tomato paste
>
> 2 tablespoons Worcestershire sauce
>
> 1 garlic clove, minced

Salt and pepper to taste

■ Place the ribs in an ungreased 5-qt. slow cooker. In a bowl, combine all of the remaining ingredients; pour over the ribs.

■ Cover and cook on low for 8-10 hours or until meat is tender. Thicken the sauce if desired.

YIELD: 8 servings.

creamy potatoes 'n' kielbasa

COOK TIME: 6 TO 8 HOURS

Beth Sine
Faulkner, Maryland

I rely on five ingredients and a slow cooker to create this hearty meal-in-one that my whole family enjoys. Kielbasa beefs up the hash browns and cheese in this comforting main dish.

> 1 package (28 ounces) frozen O'Brien hash brown potatoes
>
> 1 pound fully cooked kielbasa *or* Polish sausage, cut into 1/4-inch slices
>
> 1 can (10-3/4 ounces) condensed cream of mushroom soup, undiluted
>
> 1 cup (4 ounces) shredded cheddar cheese
>
> 1/2 cup water

■ In a 3-qt. slow cooker, combine all of the ingredients. Cover and cook on low for 6-8 hours or until the potatoes are tender.

YIELD: 4-6 servings.

crock o' brats

COOK TIME: 4 TO 6 HOURS

Maryellen Boettcher
Fairchild, Wisconsin

I've taken this filling dish to countless events, and it's popular every time. Slices of bratwurst take center stage alongside potatoes, sauerkraut, apple and onion.

> 5 bratwurst links (about 1-1/4 pounds), cut into 1-inch pieces
>
> 5 medium potatoes, peeled and cubed
>
> 1 can (27 ounces) sauerkraut, rinsed and well drained
>
> 1 medium tart apple, chopped
>
> 1 small onion, chopped
>
> 1/4 cup packed brown sugar
>
> 1/2 teaspoon salt

■ In a large skillet, brown bratwurst on all sides. In a 5-qt. slow cooker, combine all of the remaining ingredients. Stir in bratwurst and pan drippings.

■ Cover and cook on high for 4-6 hours or until the potatoes and apple are tender.

YIELD: 6 servings.

SWEET 'N' SOUR RIBS

slow-cooked ham 'n' broccoli

COOK TIME: 2 TO 3 HOURS

Jill Pennington
Jacksonville, Florida

This sensational dish is so wonderful to come home to, especially on a cool fall or winter day. It's a delicious way to use up leftover holiday ham, too.

3 cups cubed fully cooked ham

1 package (10 ounces) frozen chopped broccoli, thawed

1 can (10-3/4 ounces) condensed cream of mushroom soup, undiluted

1 jar (8 ounces) process cheese sauce

1 can (8 ounces) sliced water chestnuts, drained

1-1/4 cups uncooked instant rice

1 cup milk

1 celery rib, chopped

1 medium onion, chopped

1/8 to 1/4 teaspoon pepper

1/2 teaspoon paprika

■ In a 3-qt. slow cooker, combine the first 10 ingredients; mix well. Cover and cook on high for 2-3 hours or until the rice is tender. Let stand for 10 minutes before serving. Sprinkle with paprika.

YIELD: 6-8 servings.

orange pork roast

COOK TIME: 8 HOURS

Nancy Medeiros
Sparks, Nevada

Overcooking can cause pork roasts to be dry and tough. But this recipe's succulent orange sauce guarantees that the meat turns out moist and tender.

1 pork shoulder roast (3 to 4 pounds), trimmed

1/2 teaspoon salt

1/8 teaspoon pepper

1 can (6 ounces) frozen orange juice concentrate, thawed

1/4 cup honey

1/8 teaspoon ground cloves

1/8 teaspoon ground nutmeg

3 tablespoons all-purpose flour

1/4 cup cold water

■ Sprinkle roast with salt and pepper; place in a 3-qt. slow cooker. Combine orange juice concentrate, honey, cloves and nutmeg; pour over pork.

■ Cover and cook on high for 2 hours. Reduce heat to low and cook 6 hours longer. Remove meat to a serving platter; cover and keep warm. Skim and discard fat from cooking liquid; pour into a saucepan.

■ Combine flour and cold water until smooth; stir into cooking liquid. Bring to a boil; boil and stir for 2 minutes. Serve with roast.

YIELD: 8 servings.

creamy ham and potatoes

COOK TIME: 8 TO 9 HOURS

Peggy Key
Grant, Alabama

Serve this stick-to-your-ribs dish with a green salad and dessert for a complete meal. The creamy mixture of hearty ham and tender potatoes is brimming with homemade flavor.

4 medium red potatoes, thinly sliced

2 medium onions, finely chopped

1-1/2 cups cubed fully cooked ham

2 tablespoons butter

2 tablespoons all-purpose flour

1 teaspoon ground mustard

1/2 teaspoon salt

1/2 teaspoon pepper

1 can (10-3/4 ounces) condensed cream of celery soup, undiluted

1-1/3 cups water

1 cup (4 ounces) shredded cheddar cheese, optional

■ In a 3-qt. slow cooker, layer potatoes, onions and ham. In a saucepan, melt butter. Stir in flour, mustard, salt and pepper until smooth. Combine soup and water; gradually stir into flour mixture. Bring to a boil; cook and stir for 2 minutes or until thickened and bubbly. Pour over ham.

■ Cover and cook on low for 8-9 hours or until potatoes are tender. If desired, sprinkle with cheese before serving.

YIELD: 4 servings.

SLOW-COOKED HAM 'N' BROCCOLI

teriyaki pork roast

COOK TIME: 7 TO 8 HOURS

Roxanne Hulsey
Gainesville, Georgia

I'm always looking for no-fuss recipes, so I was thrilled to find this one. The moist, teriyaki-seasoned pork roast has become a family favorite.

- **3/4 cup unsweetened apple juice**
- **2 tablespoons sugar**
- **2 tablespoons soy sauce**
- **1 tablespoon vinegar**
- **1 teaspoon ground ginger**
- **1/4 teaspoon garlic powder**
- **1/8 teaspoon pepper**
- **1 boneless pork loin roast (about 3 pounds), halved**
- **7-1/2 teaspoons cornstarch**
- **3 tablespoons cold water**

■ Combine the first seven ingredients in a greased 3-qt. slow cooker. Add roast and turn to coat.

■ Cover and cook on low for 7-8 hours or until a thermometer inserted into the roast reads 160°. Remove roast and keep warm.

■ In a saucepan, combine cornstarch and cold water until smooth; stir in cooking juices. Bring to a boil; cook and stir for 2 minutes or until thickened. Serve with the roast.

YIELD: 8 servings.

slow-cooked spaghetti sauce

COOK TIME: 3 TO 4 HOURS

Margaret Shauers
Great Bend, Kansas

This sauce gets a convenient head start from prepared spaghetti sauce. I simply add a few everyday ingredients of my own. Most folks think it's homemade.

- **1 pound bulk Italian sausage**
- **1/4 teaspoon cayenne pepper**
- **1 small onion, sliced**
- **1 medium green pepper, cut into strips**
- **1 jar (28 ounces) spaghetti sauce**

Hot cooked spaghetti

■ In a skillet over medium heat, brown sausage and cayenne for about 5 minutes. Add enough water to cover; bring to a boil. Reduce heat; cover and simmer for 10 minutes. Drain; transfer to a 3-qt. slow cooker. Add onion and green pepper. Pour spaghetti sauce on top.

■ Cover and cook on high for 1 hour. Reduce heat to low and cook 2-3 hours longer. Serve over spaghetti.

YIELD: 4-6 servings.

chops 'n' beans

COOK TIME: 8-1/2 TO 9-1/2 HOURS

Dorothy Pritchett
Wills Point, Texas

This hearty combination of tender pork chops and two kinds of beans makes a satisfying supper in summer or winter.

- **4 pork loin chops (1/2 inch thick)**
- **1/2 teaspoon salt, optional**
- **1/4 teaspoon pepper**
- **1 tablespoon vegetable oil**
- **2 medium onions, chopped**
- **2 garlic cloves, minced**
- **1/4 cup chili sauce**
- **1-1/2 teaspoons brown sugar**
- **1 teaspoon prepared mustard**
- **1 can (16 ounces) kidney beans, rinsed and drained**
- **1 can (15-1/4 ounces) lima beans, rinsed and drained or 1-3/4 cups frozen lima beans**

■ Sprinkle pork chops with salt if desired and pepper. In a skillet, brown chops in oil; transfer chops to a 3-qt. slow cooker. Reserve 1 tablespoon drippings in the skillet; saute onions and garlic until tender. Stir in chili sauce, brown sugar and mustard. Pour over chops.

■ Cover and cook on low for 7-8 hours. Stir in beans. Cover and cook 1 to 1-1/2 hours longer or until meat juices run clear and the beans are heated through.

YIELD: 4 servings.

TERIYAKI PORK ROAST

pork and pinto beans

COOK TIME: 8 HOURS

Darlene Markel
Salem, Oregon
I first tasted this at an office potluck. Now I serve it often for company.

> **1 pound dried pinto beans**
>
> **1 boneless pork loin roast (3 to 4 pounds), halved**
>
> **1 can (14-1/2 ounces) stewed tomatoes**
>
> **5 medium carrots, chopped**
>
> **4 celery ribs, chopped**

1-1/2 cups water

> **2 cans (4 ounces *each*) chopped green chilies**
>
> **2 tablespoons chili powder**
>
> **4 garlic cloves, minced**
>
> **2 teaspoons ground cumin**
>
> **1 teaspoon dried oregano**

Dash pepper

> **2 packages (10-1/2 ounces *each*) corn tortilla chips**

Shredded cheddar cheese and sliced ripe olives, chopped tomatoes, sour cream

■ Place beans in a saucepan; add water to cover by 2 in. Bring to a boil; boil for 2 minutes. Remove from heat; cover and let stand for 1 hour.

■ Drain and rinse beans; discard liquid. Place roast in a 5-qt. slow cooker. In a bowl, combine beans, vegetables, water, chilies and seasonings. Pour over roast. Cover; cook on high 3 hours. Reduce heat to low; cook 5 hours longer or until beans are tender.

■ Remove meat; shred and return to slow cooker. With a slotted spoon, serve meat mixture with corn chips and toppings of your choice.

YIELD: 10 servings.

southwestern stew

COOK TIME: 6 HOURS

Virginia Price
Cheyenne, Wyoming
Slow cooking allows the flavors in this recipe to blend beautifully. Over the past few years, it's become our traditional Super Bowl Sunday meal.

> **1-1/2 pounds boneless pork, trimmed and cut into 1/2-inch cubes**
>
> **2 tablespoons vegetable oil**
>
> **1 medium onion, chopped**
>
> **1 can (15-1/2 ounces) yellow hominy, drained**
>
> **1 can (14-1/2 ounces) diced tomatoes, undrained**
>
> **1 can (4 ounces) chopped green chilies**

1/2 cup water

1/2 teaspoon chili powder

1/4 teaspoon garlic powder

1/4 teaspoon ground cumin

1/4 teaspoon salt

1/4 teaspoon pepper

■ In a large skillet over medium-high heat, brown pork in oil. Add onion and cook for 2 minutes or until tender. Transfer to a 3-qt. slow cooker; add remaining ingredients.

■ Cover and cook on high for 2 hours. Reduce heat to low and cook 4 hours longer.

YIELD: 4-6 servings.

country cassoulet

COOK TIME: 5 TO 6 HOURS

Suzanne McKinley
Lyons, Georgia
This stew goes great with fresh dinner rolls and your favorite green salad.

> **1 pound (2 cups) dried great northern beans**
>
> **2 fresh garlic sausage links**
>
> **3 bacon strips, diced**

1-1/2 pounds boneless pork, cut into 1-inch cubes

> **1 pound boneless lamb, cut into 1-inch cubes**

1-1/2 cups chopped onion

> **3 garlic cloves, minced**
>
> **2 teaspoons salt**
>
> **1 teaspoon dried thyme**
>
> **4 whole cloves**
>
> **2 bay leaves**

2-1/2 cups chicken broth

> **1 can (8 ounces) tomato sauce**

■ Place beans and enough water to cover in a Dutch oven or soup kettle. Bring to a boil; boil for 2 minutes. Remove from heat; let stand 1 hour. Drain beans; discard liquid.

■ In a large skillet over medium-high heat, brown sausage; remove with a slotted spoon to a 3-qt. slow cooker. Add bacon to skillet; cook until crisp. Remove with a slotted spoon to slow cooker. In bacon drippings, cook pork and lamb until browned on all sides. Remove pork and lamb with a slotted spoon to slow cooker. Stir in beans and remaining ingredients.

■ Cover; cook on high 2 hours. Reduce heat to low; cook 3-4 hours longer. Remove cloves, bay leaves. Remove sausage; slice into 1/4-in. pieces. Return to slow cooker, stir gently.

YIELD: 8-10 servings.

PORK AND PINTO BEANS

fruited chops

COOK TIME: 3 TO 3-1/2 HOURS

Cindy Ragan
North Huntingdon, Pennsylvania
I often prepare these tender chops with pineapple sauce for guests.

 3 tablespoons all-purpose flour

1-1/2 teaspoons dried oregano

 3/4 teaspoon salt

 1/4 teaspoon garlic powder

 1/4 teaspoon pepper

 6 lean boneless pork loin chops (5 ounces *each*)

 1 tablespoon olive oil

 1 can (20 ounces) unsweetened pineapple chunks

 3/4 cup unsweetened pineapple juice

 1/4 cup water

 2 tablespoons brown sugar

 2 tablespoons dried minced onion

 2 tablespoons tomato paste

 1/4 cup raisins

- In a large resealable plastic bag, combine the first five ingredients; add pork chops, one at a time, and shake to coat. In a nonstick skillet, brown chops on both sides in oil. Transfer to a 3-qt. slow cooker.

- Drain pineapple; reserve juice. Set pineapple aside. In a bowl, combine 3/4 cup juice with reserved juice. Stir in water, brown sugar, onion and tomato paste; pour over chops. Sprinkle with raisins. Cover; cook on high 3 to 3-1/2 hours or until meat is tender and a meat thermometer reads 160°. Stir in reserved pineapple. Cover; cook 10 minutes longer or until heated through.

YIELD: 6 servings.

mushroom pork tenderloin

COOK TIME: 4 TO 5 HOURS

Donna Hughes
Rochester, New Hampshire
This moist pork tenderloin in a savory gravy is the best you'll ever taste. Prepared with canned soups, it couldn't be easier to assemble.

 2 pork tenderloins (1 pound *each*)

 1 can (10-3/4 ounces) condensed cream of mushroom soup, undiluted

 1 can (10-3/4 ounces) condensed golden mushroom soup, undiluted

 1 can (10-1/2 ounces) condensed French onion soup, undiluted

Hot mashed potatoes, optional

- Place pork in a 3-qt. slow cooker. In a bowl, combine the soups; stir until smooth. Pour over pork.

- Cover and cook on low for 4-5 hours or until the meat is tender. Serve with mashed potatoes if desired.

YIELD: 6 servings.

pot roast 'n' veggies

COOK TIME: 8 HOURS

Donna Wilkinson
Clarksburg, Maryland
I start the pot roast cooking before I leave for church. I add vegetables when I get home and just sit back and relax until it's done.

 2-1/2 to 3 pounds boneless pork shoulder roast

1-1/2 cups beef broth

 1/2 cup sliced green onions

 1 teaspoon dried basil

 1 teaspoon dried marjoram

 1/2 teaspoon salt

 1/2 teaspoon pepper

 1 bay leaf

 6 medium red potatoes, cut into 2-inch chunks

 4 medium carrots, cut into 2-inch chunks

 7 to 8 fresh mushrooms, quartered

 1/4 cup all-purpose flour

 1/2 cup cold water

Browning sauce, optional

- Place roast in a 3-qt. slow cooker; add broth, onions and seasonings. Cover and cook on high for 2 hours. Add potatoes, carrots and mushrooms.

- Cover and cook on low for 6 hours or until vegetables are tender. Remove the meat and vegetables; keep warm. Discard bay leaf. In a saucepan, combine flour and cold water until smooth; stir in 1-1/2 cups cooking juices. Bring to a boil. Cook and stir for 2 minutes or until thickened. Add browning sauce if desired. Serve with roast and vegetables.

YIELD: 6 servings.

FRUITED CHOPS

chicken-fried chops

COOK TIME: 6 TO 8 HOURS

Connie Slocum
Brunswick, Georgia

It takes only a few minutes to brown the meat before assembling this savory meal. The pork chops simmer all day in a flavorful sauce until they're tender.

- 1/2 cup all-purpose flour
- 2 teaspoons salt
- 1-1/2 teaspoons ground mustard
- 1/2 teaspoon garlic powder
- 6 pork loin chops (3/4 inch thick), trimmed
- 2 tablespoons vegetable oil
- 1 can (10-3/4 ounces) condensed cream of chicken soup, undiluted
- 1/3 cup water

■ In a shallow bowl, combine flour, salt, mustard and garlic powder; dredge pork chops. In a skillet, brown the chops on both sides in oil. Place in a 3-qt. slow cooker.

■ Combine soup and water; pour over chops. Cover and cook on low for 6-8 hours or until meat is tender. If desired, thicken pan juices and serve with the pork chops.

YIELD: 6 servings.

> **SLOW COOKER TIP:**
> A quick way to reduce excess liquid at the end of the cooking time is to remove the liquid from the slow cooker, put it into a saucepan and simmer on the stove until it reduces to a desired amount. Add seasonings after the liquid has reduced.

citrus pork roast

COOK TIME: 4 HOURS

Tammy Logan
McComb, Ohio

A delicious hint of orange in the gravy served over thick slices of pork roast makes them stand out from the crowd. Garlic, thyme and ginger further season this easy, family-pleasing entree.

- 1 boneless pork loin roast (3 pounds)
- 1/2 teaspoon garlic powder
- 1/2 teaspoon dried thyme
- 1/2 teaspoon ground ginger
- 1/4 teaspoon pepper
- 1 tablespoon vegetable oil
- 1 cup chicken broth
- 2 tablespoons sugar
- 2 tablespoons lemon juice
- 2 tablespoons soy sauce
- 1-1/2 teaspoons grated orange peel
- 3 tablespoons cornstarch
- 1/2 cup orange juice

■ Cut roast in half. In a small bowl, combine the garlic powder, thyme, ginger and pepper; rub over roast. In a large skillet over medium heat, brown roast on all sides in oil.

■ Place roast in a 5-qt. slow cooker. In a small bowl, combine the broth, sugar, lemon juice, soy sauce and orange peel; pour over roast. Cover and cook on low for 4 hours or until a meat thermometer reads 160°.

■ Remove roast and keep warm. In a saucepan, combine the cornstarch and orange juice until smooth; stir in cooking juices. Bring to a boil; cook and stir for 2 minutes or until thickened. Serve with the roast.

YIELD: 6-8 servings.

cranberry-mustard pork loin

COOK TIME: 4 TO 4-1/2 HOURS

Laura Cook
Wildwood, Missouri

This dressed-up pork loin is so easy that you only have to spend a few minutes in the morning preparing it. It's a favorite of mine because it's so fast and easy!

- 1 boneless whole pork loin roast (2 pounds)
- 1 can (16 ounces) whole-berry cranberry sauce
- 1/4 cup Dijon mustard
- 3 tablespoons brown sugar
- 3 tablespoons lemon juice
- 1 tablespoon cornstarch
- 1/4 cup cold water

■ Place roast in a 3-qt. slow cooker. Combine the cranberry sauce, mustard, brown sugar and lemon juice; pour over roast. Cover and cook on low for 4 to 4-1/2 hours or until a meat thermometer reads 160°.

■ Remove roast and keep warm. Strain cooking juices into a 2-cup measuring cup; add enough water to measure 2 cups. In a saucepan, combine cornstarch and cold water until smooth; stir in cooking juices. Bring to a boil; cook and stir for 2 minutes or until thickened. Serve with pork.

YIELD: 8 servings.

> **SLOW COOKER TIP:**
> Dredging meat in flour and browning in oil before placing in the slow cooker helps thicken the cooking liquid. It can sometimes turn into a ready-made gravy. Skim the fat and season the cooking liquid before serving.

CRANBERRY-MUSTARD PORK LOIN

pork chili

COOK TIME: 6 HOURS

Linda Temple
St. Joseph, Missouri

My husband usually tries to avoid spending time in the kitchen, but he'll frequently offer to prepare this easy chili. Of course, he always eagerly serves as taste-tester!

2-1/2 pounds boneless pork, cut into 1-inch cubes

2 tablespoons vegetable oil

1 can (28 ounces) diced tomatoes, undrained

1 can (15-1/2 ounces) chili beans, undrained

1 can (8 ounces) tomato sauce

1/4 cup salsa

1/4 cup chopped onion

1/4 cup chopped green pepper

1 tablespoon chili powder

1 teaspoon minced jalapeno pepper

1/4 teaspoon garlic powder

1/4 teaspoon cayenne powder

1/4 teaspoon pepper

1/4 teaspoon salt

■ In a large skillet over medium-high heat, brown pork in oil; drain. Place in a 5-qt. slow cooker; add remaining ingredients.

■ Cover and cook on high for 2 hours. Reduce heat to low and cook 4 hours longer.

YIELD: 10-12 servings.

EDITOR'S NOTE: When cutting or seeding hot peppers, use rubber or plastic gloves to protect your hands. Avoid touching your face.

slow-cooker ribs

COOK TIME: 4 TO 5 HOURS

Alpha Wilson
Roswell, New Mexico

These simple-to-prepare ribs call for everyday ingredients. So I never complain when my family asks me to make them. Everyone enjoys their down-home goodness.

3 pounds pork spareribs

1/2 teaspoon salt

1/4 teaspoon pepper

1-3/4 cups sliced onion

1 bottle (18 ounces) barbecue sauce

■ Place ribs, meat side up, on a broiling pan. Sprinkle with salt and pepper. Broil 6 in. from the heat for 15-20 minutes or until browned. Cool; cut into serving-size pieces.

■ Place onion in a 3-qt. slow cooker; top with ribs. Pour barbecue sauce over all. Cover and cook on high for 1 hour; reduce heat to low and cook 3-4 hours or until ribs are tender.

YIELD: 4 servings.

pork and sauerkraut with potatoes

COOK TIME: 5 TO 6 HOURS

Valerie Hay
Longmont, Colorado

This is a wintertime favorite in our home. The down-home flavors of pork and sauerkraut are complemented by potatoes and apples. The aroma is irresistible as it cooks.

2 cans (16 ounces each) sauerkraut, undrained

1 cup thinly sliced onion

2 medium baking apples, peeled and sliced

1/2 cup dark corn syrup

2 bay leaves

1 teaspoon caraway seed

1/2 teaspoon pepper

3 large potatoes, peeled and cut into 2-inch chunks

6 pork chops (3/4 inch thick)

■ In a bowl, combine sauerkraut, onion, apples, corn syrup, bay leaves, caraway and pepper. Spoon half into a 3-qt. slow cooker; top with potatoes. Broil pork chops 6 in. from the heat for 3-4 minutes per side or until browned; place over potatoes. Spoon remaining sauerkraut mixture over pork.

■ Cover and cook on high for 1 hour. Reduce heat to low; cook 4-5 hours longer or until vegetables and meat are tender. Remove bay leaves.

YIELD: 6 servings.

PORK CHILI

ham with cherry sauce

COOK TIME: 4 TO 5 HOURS

Carol Lee Jones
Taylors, South Carolina
I often fix this delicious ham topped with a thick cherry sauce. It's such a favorite that I've served it at Easter dinners, church breakfasts and a friend's wedding brunch.

1 boneless fully cooked ham (3 to 4 pounds)

1/2 cup apple jelly

2 teaspoons prepared mustard

2/3 cup ginger ale, *divided*

1 can (21 ounces) cherry pie filling

2 tablespoons cornstarch

■ Score the surface of ham, making diamond shapes 1/2 in. deep. In a small bowl, combine jelly, mustard and 1 tablespoon ginger ale; rub over scored surface of ham. Cut ham in half; place in a 5-qt. slow cooker.

■ Cover and cook on low for 4-5 hours or until a meat thermometer reads 140° and ham is heated through. Baste with cooking juices toward end of cooking time.

■ For the sauce, place pie filling in a saucepan. Combine cornstarch and remaining ginger ale; stir into pie filling until blended. Bring to a boil; cook and stir for 2 minutes or until thickened. Serve over ham.

YIELD: 12-16 servings.

pizza rigatoni

COOK TIME: 4 HOURS

Marilyn Cowan
North Manchester, Indiana
I turn my slow cooker into a pizzeria with this zesty layered casserole. It is loaded with cheese, Italian sausage, pepperoni and pasta.

1-1/2 pounds bulk Italian sausage

3 cups uncooked rigatoni *or* large tube pasta

4 cups (16 ounces) shredded mozzarella cheese

1 can (10-3/4 ounces) condensed cream of mushroom soup, undiluted

1 small onion, chopped

2 cans (one 15 ounces, one 8 ounces) pizza sauce

1 package (3-1/2 ounces) sliced pepperoni

1 can (6 ounces) pitted ripe olives, drained and halved

■ In a skillet, cook sausage until no longer pink; drain. Cook the pasta according to package directions; drain.

■ In a 5-qt. slow cooker, layer half of the sausage, pasta, cheese, soup, onion, pizza sauce, pepperoni and olives. Repeat layers. Cover and cook on low for 4 hours.

YIELD: 6-8 servings.

ham tetrazzini

COOK TIME: 4 HOURS

Susan Blair
Sterling, Michigan
I've served this tasty dish at parties, family dinners and potlucks. Everyone is surprised by how good it is.

1 can (10-3/4 ounces) condensed cream of mushroom soup, undiluted

1 cup sliced fresh mushrooms

1 cup cubed fully cooked lean ham

1/2 cup evaporated milk

2 tablespoons white wine *or* water

1 teaspoon prepared horseradish

1 package (7 ounces) spaghetti

1/2 cup shredded Parmesan cheese

■ In a 3-qt. slow cooker, combine the soup, mushrooms, ham, milk, wine or water and horseradish.

■ Cover and cook on low for 4 hours. Cook the spaghetti according to package directions; drain. Add the spaghetti and cheese to slow cooker; toss to coat.

YIELD: 6 servings.

SLOW COOKER TIP: Most slow cookers have two or more settings. Foods cook faster on high than on low; however, you may want to use the low setting for all-day cooking or for tougher cuts of meat.

HAM WITH CHERRY SAUCE

sausage sauerkraut supper

COOK TIME: 8 TO 9 HOURS

Joalyce Graham
St. Petersburg, Florida

With big, tender chunks of sausage, potatoes and carrots, this meal-in-one has Old-World flavor that will satisfy even the heartiest of appetites. It always disappears in a hurry, whenever served at a family gathering or at an office potluck.

- 4 cups carrot chunks (2-inch pieces)
- 4 cups red potato chunks
- 2 cans (14 ounces *each*) sauerkraut, rinsed and drained
- 2-1/2 pounds fresh Polish sausage, cut into 3-inch pieces
- 1 medium onion, thinly sliced
- 3 garlic cloves, minced
- 1-1/2 cups dry white wine *or* chicken broth
- 1 teaspoon pepper
- 1/2 teaspoon caraway seed

■ In a 5-qt. slow cooker, layer carrots, potatoes and sauerkraut. In a skillet, brown the sausage; transfer to the slow cooker (slow cooker will be full). Reserve 1 tablespoon drippings in a skillet; saute onion and garlic until tender.

■ Gradually add wine or broth. Bring to a boil; stir to loosen browned bits. Stir in pepper and caraway. Pour over sausage. Cover and cook on low for 8-9 hours or until vegetables are tender and sausage is no longer pink.

YIELD: 10-12 servings.

slow-cooked cherry pork chops

COOK TIME: 3 TO 4 HOURS

Mildred Sherrer
Bay City, Texas

I mixed and matched several recipes to come up with this one. I'm always happy to adapt recipes for my slow cooker. It's so easy to prepare a meal early and let it cook all day.

- 6 bone-in pork loin chops (8 ounces *each* and 3/4-inch thick)
- 1/8 teaspoon salt

Dash pepper

- 1 cup canned cherry pie filling
- 2 teaspoons lemon juice
- 1/2 teaspoon chicken bouillon granules
- 1/8 teaspoon ground mace

■ In a large skillet coated with non-stick cooking spray, brown the pork chops over medium heat on both sides. Season with salt and pepper.

■ In a 3-qt. slow cooker, combine pie filling, lemon juice, bouillon and mace. Add pork chops. Cover and cook on low for 3-4 hours or until meat is no longer pink.

YIELD: 6 servings.

chinese pork ribs

COOK TIME: 6 HOURS

June Ross
Landing, New Jersey

This is one of the only dishes that both of my young boys love—they even come back for seconds.

- 1/4 cup soy sauce
- 1/3 cup orange marmalade
- 3 tablespoons ketchup
- 2 garlic cloves, minced
- 3 to 4 pounds bone-in country-style pork ribs

■ In a bowl, combine the soy sauce, marmalade, ketchup and garlic. Pour half into a 3-qt. slow cooker. Top with ribs; drizzle with remaining sauce. Cover and cook on low for 6 hours or until tender. Thicken cooking juices.

YIELD: 6-8 servings.

SLOW COOKER TIP:
Never stuff a slow cooker full. If the lid doesn't close properly, a seal will not be formed which could greatly extend cooking time. For food safety, only fill a slow cooker between one-half and two-thirds full.

SLOW-COOKED CHERRY PORK CHOPS

CHINESE PORK RIBS

sunday pot roast

COOK TIME: 8 HOURS

Brandy Schaefer
Glen Carbon, Illinois

This recipe proves you don't have to slave over a hot stove to prepare a delicious down-home dinner like Grandma used to make.

- **1 teaspoon dried oregano**
- **1/2 teaspoon onion salt**
- **1/2 teaspoon pepper**
- **1/2 teaspoon caraway seed**
- **1/4 teaspoon garlic salt**
- **1 boneless pork loin roast (3-1/2 to 4 pounds), trimmed**
- **6 medium carrots, peeled and cut into 1-1/2-inchpieces**
- **3 large potatoes, peeled and quartered**
- **3 small onions, quartered**
- **1-1/2 cups beef broth**
- **1/3 cup all-purpose flour**
- **1/3 cup cold water**
- **1/4 teaspoon browning sauce, optional**

■ Combine seasonings; rub over roast. Wrap in plastic wrap and refrigerate overnight. Place carrots, potatoes and onions in a 3-qt. slow cooker; add broth. Unwrap roast and place in the slow cooker.

■ Cover and cook on high for 2 hours. Reduce heat to low and cook 6 hours longer. Transfer roast and vegetables to a serving platter; keep warm. Pour broth into a saucepan. Combine flour and water until smooth; stir into broth. Bring to a boil; boil and whisk for 2 minutes. Add browning sauce if desired. Serve with roast.

YIELD: 12-14 servings.

busy-day barbecued ribs

COOK TIME: 5 TO 6 HOURS

Sherry Smalley
South Milwaukee, Wisconsin

I don't have a lot of time on weekends to spend in the kitchen. That's when this recipe comes in handy. I put all the ingredients in the slow cooker, and before I know it, dinner is ready!

- **3-1/2 to 4 pounds country-style pork ribs**
- **1 can (10-3/4 ounces) condensed tomato soup, undiluted**
- **1/2 cup packed brown sugar**
- **1/3 cup cider vinegar**
- **1 tablespoon soy sauce**
- **1 teaspoon celery seed**
- **1 teaspoon chili powder**

■ Place ribs in a 5-qt. slow cooker. Combine all of the remaining ingredients; pour over the ribs.

■ Cover and cook on high for 1 hour. Reduce heat to low and cook 4-5 hours longer. Thicken sauce for gravy if desired.

YIELD: 6-8 servings.

mushroom pork chops in gravy

COOK TIME: 6 TO 8 HOURS

Vickie Lowe
Lititz, Pennsylvania

Tomato sauce seasoned with oregano, basil and garlic gives Italian flavor to tender chops. This is one of the few ways I will eat pork chops.

- **4 bone-in pork loin chops (1 inch thick)**
- **1/2 pound fresh mushrooms, sliced**
- **1 medium onion, chopped**
- **1 garlic clove, minced**
- **2 cans (8 ounces *each*) tomato sauce**
- **1 tablespoon lemon juice**
- **1/2 teaspoon salt**
- **1/2 teaspoon *each* dried oregano, basil and parsley flakes**
- **1/4 cup cornstarch**
- **1/4 cup cold water**

Green pepper rings, optional

■ In a nonstick skillet, brown pork chops on both sides. In a 3-qt. slow cooker, combine the mushrooms, onion and garlic. Top with the pork chops. In a bowl, combine the tomato sauce, lemon juice, salt, oregano, basil and parsley. Pour over pork. Cover and cook on low for 6-8 hours or until meat is tender.

■ Remove the pork and keep warm. Transfer mushroom mixture to a saucepan. In a small bowl, combine the cornstarch and water until smooth; add to saucepan. Bring to a boil; cook and stir for 2 minutes or until thickened. Serve over the pork chops. Garnish with green pepper rings if desired.

YIELD: 4 servings.

High

SUNDAY POT ROAST

polish kraut and apples

COOK TIME: 4 TO 5 HOURS

Caren Markee
Cary, Illinois

My family loves this hearty, heart-warming meal on cold winter nights. The tender apples, brown sugar and smoked sausage give this dish fantastic flavor. I like making it because the prep time is very short.

- 1 can (14 ounces) sauerkraut, rinsed and well drained
- 1 pound fully cooked Polish sausage *or* kielbasa, cut into 2-inch pieces
- 3 medium tart apples, peeled and cut into eighths
- 1/2 cup packed brown sugar
- 1/2 teaspoon caraway seeds, optional
- 1/8 teaspoon pepper
- 3/4 cup apple juice

■ Place half of the sauerkraut in an ungreased 3-qt. slow cooker. Top with the sausage, apples, brown sugar, caraway seeds if desired and pepper. Top with remaining sauerkraut. Pour apple juice over all.

■ Cover and cook on low for 4-5 hours or until apples are tender.

YIELD: 4 servings.

hot dogs 'n' beans

COOK TIME: 7 TO 8 HOURS

June Formanek
Belle Plaine, Iowa

You'll please kids of all ages with this tasty combination that's good for casual get-togethers. I frequently fix this when the whole family is home.

- 3 cans (two 28 ounces, one 16 ounces) pork and beans
- 1 package (1 pound) hot dogs, halved lengthwise and cut into 1-inch pieces
- 1 large onion, chopped
- 1/2 cup packed brown sugar
- 3 tablespoons prepared mustard
- 4 bacon strips, cooked and crumbled

■ In a 3-qt. slow cooker, combine all of the ingredients; mix well. Cover and cook on low for 7-8 hours.

YIELD: 10 servings.

home-style ribs

COOK TIME: 8 TO 9 HOURS

Roni Goodell
Spanish Fork, Utah

A dear friend gave me the recipe for these tender ribs simmered in a pleasant barbecue sauce. They're great to fix in the summer because you don't have to turn on the oven and heat up the kitchen.

- 4 to 5 pounds boneless pork spareribs, cut into pieces
- 1 medium onion, thinly sliced
- 1 cup ketchup
- 1/2 to 1 cup water
- 1/4 cup packed brown sugar
- 1/4 cup cider vinegar
- 2 tablespoons Worcestershire sauce
- 2 teaspoons ground mustard
- 1-1/2 teaspoons salt
- 1 teaspoon paprika

■ Place half of the ribs in a 5-qt. slow cooker; top with half of the onion. Repeat layers. Combine the remaining ingredients; pour over all.

■ Cover and cook on low for 8-9 hours or until ribs are tender.

YIELD: 6-8 servings.

SLOW COOKER TIP: There are usually two heat settings on a slow cooker: low (200°) and high (300°). You may need to stir some recipes occasionally to prevent scorching. However, you have to add about 20 minutes to the overall cooking time every time the lid is lifted.

POLISH KRAUT AND APPLES

slow-cooked country ribs in gravy

COOK TIME: 4 TO 5 HOURS

Tammi Visser
Uxbridge, Massachusetts

This is a very easy recipe (just the kind I like!) that I got from my sister-in-law. I like to make it in winter as a way to capture the barbecue flavors of summer.

3 pounds country-style pork ribs

1 cup water

1/2 cup ketchup

1 medium onion, chopped

2 tablespoons white vinegar

1 tablespoon sugar

4 teaspoons Worcestershire sauce

1 teaspoon salt

1 teaspoon ground mustard

1 beef bouillon cube

1/4 teaspoon paprika

1/4 teaspoon pepper

■ Place ribs in a 5-qt. slow cooker. Combine remaining ingredients and pour over ribs. Cover and cook on high for 1 hour; reduce heat to low and cook 3-4 hours longer. Remove ribs to serving platter and keep warm. Thicken cooking liquid for gravy.

YIELD: 6 servings.

SLOW COOKER TIP:

If possible, use whole herbs and spices rather than the crushed or powdered variety. A whole leaf or berry can withstand the long cooking time better than the ground version.

herb stuffed chops

COOK TIME: 8 TO 9 HOURS

Diana Seeger
New Springfield, Ohio

Guests will think you stayed home all day when you serve these delicious stuffed chops. I often share this recipe with new brides because I know it will become one of their favorites. It's so convenient, too—I can put the chops in my slow cooker in the morning, then let them cook until dinner.

3/4 cup chopped onion

1/4 cup chopped celery

2 tablespoons butter

2 cups day-old bread cubes

1/2 cup minced fresh parsley

1/3 cup evaporated milk

1 teaspoon fennel seed, crushed

1-1/2 teaspoons salt, divided

1/2 teaspoon pepper, divided

6 rib or loin pork chops (1 inch thick)

1 tablespoon vegetable oil

3/4 cup white wine or chicken broth

■ In a skillet, saute onion and celery in butter until tender. Add bread cubes, parsley, milk, fennel, 1/4 teaspoon salt and 1/8 teaspoon pepper; toss to coat. Cut a pocket in each chop by slicing from the fat side almost to the bone. Spoon about 1/4 cup stuffing into each pocket. Combine the remaining salt and pepper; rub over chops.

■ In a skillet, brown the chops in oil; transfer to a 3-qt. slow cooker. Pour wine or broth over the chops. Cover and cook on low for 8-9 hours or until meat juices run clear.

YIELD: 6 servings.

pork chop potato dinner

COOK TIME: 2-1/2 TO 3 HOURS

Dawn Huizinga
Owatonna, Minnesota

Tender chops cook on a bed of creamy potatoes in this all-in-one meal. It's a snap to assemble, thanks to frozen hash browns, canned soup, shredded cheese and french-fried onions.

6 bone-in pork chops (1/2 inch thick)

1 tablespoon vegetable oil

1 package (30 ounces) frozen shredded hash brown potatoes, thawed

1-1/2 cups (6 ounces) shredded cheddar cheese, divided

1 can (10-3/4 ounces) condensed cream of celery soup, undiluted

1/2 cup milk

1/2 cup sour cream

1/2 teaspoon seasoned salt

1/8 teaspoon pepper

1 can (2.8 ounces) french-fried onions, divided

■ In a large skillet, brown chops in oil on both sides; set aside and keep warm. In a bowl, combine the potatoes, 1 cup cheese, soup, milk, sour cream, seasoned salt and pepper. Stir in half of the onions.

■ Transfer to a greased 5-qt. slow cooker; top with pork chops. Cover and cook on high for 2-1/2 to 3 hours or until meat juices run clear. Sprinkle with remaining cheese and onions. Cover and cook 10 minutes longer or until cheese is melted.

YIELD: 6 servings.

meaty spaghetti sauce

COOK TIME: 8 HOURS

Arlene Sommers
Redmond, Washington
My family always enjoyed my home-made spaghetti sauce, but it's so time-consuming to make on the stovetop. My busy grown daughter adapted my recipe to take advantage of her slow cooker.

- **1 pound bulk Italian sausage**
- **1 pound ground beef**
- **1 medium green pepper, chopped**
- **1 medium onion, chopped**
- **8 garlic cloves, minced**
- **3 cans (14-1/2 ounces *each*) Italian diced tomatoes, drained**
- **2 cans (15 ounces *each*) tomato sauce**
- **2 cans (6 ounces *each*) tomato paste**
- **1/3 cup sugar**
- **2 tablespoons Italian seasoning**
- **1 tablespoon dried basil**
- **2 teaspoons dried marjoram**
- **1 teaspoon salt**
- **1/2 teaspoon pepper**
- **Hot cooked spaghetti**

■ In a large skillet over medium heat, cook the sausage and beef until no longer pink; drain. Transfer to a 5-qt. slow cooker. Stir in green pepper, onion, garlic, tomatoes, tomato sauce, paste, sugar and seasonings; mix well.

■ Cover and cook on low for 8 hours or until bubbly. Serve over spaghetti.

YIELD: 12 servings.

casserole in the cooker

COOK TIME: 4 TO 5 HOURS

Krista Harrison
Brazil, Indiana
For a complete meal-in-one, you'll savor this slow-cooked ham, broccoli and rice dish that has all the goodness of an oven-baked casserole. It's perfect for a Sunday afternoon dinner.

- **1 package (16 ounces) frozen broccoli cuts, thawed and drained**
- **3 cups cubed fully cooked ham**
- **1 can (10-3/4 ounces) condensed cream of mushroom soup, undiluted**
- **1 jar (8 ounces) process cheese sauce**
- **1 cup milk**
- **1 cup uncooked instant rice**
- **1 celery rib, chopped**
- **1 small onion, chopped**

■ In a 3-qt. slow cooker, combine broccoli and ham. Combine the soup, cheese sauce, milk, rice, celery and onion; stir into the broccoli mixture.

■ Cover and cook on low for 4-5 hours or until rice is tender.

YIELD: 4 servings.

fruity pork chops

COOK TIME: 7 TO 8 HOURS

Bonnie Baumgardner
Sylva, North Carolina
I simmer my pork chops in fruit juice, orange peel, mustard and red wine vinegar and top them with a fruit cock-tail sauce.

- **4 bone-in pork loin chops (1 inch thick)**
- **1/2 teaspoon salt**
- **1/4 teaspoon pepper**
- **1/8 teaspoon dried rosemary, crushed**
- **1/8 teaspoon dill weed**
- **1/8 teaspoon ground ginger**
- **2 tablespoons vegetable oil**
- **1 can (15 ounces) fruit cocktail**
- **2 tablespoons red wine vinegar**
- **1 tablespoon prepared mustard**
- **1/4 teaspoon grated orange peel**
- **2 tablespoons cornstarch**
- **2 tablespoons cold water**

■ Sprinkle pork chops with seasonings. In a skillet, brown chops on both sides in oil; transfer to a 3-qt. slow cooker. Drain fruit cocktail, reserving juice. Refrigerate fruit cocktail. In a bowl, combine vinegar, mustard, peel and reserved fruit juice. Pour over pork. Cover; cook on low for 7-8 hours or until meat is tender.

■ Remove chops; keep warm. Strain cooking liquid into a small saucepan. Combine the cornstarch and water until smooth; stir into cooking liquid. Bring to a boil; cook and stir for 2 minutes or until thickened and bubbly. Add fruit cocktail; heat through. Serve over pork chops.

YIELD: 4 servings.

MEATY SPAGHETTI SAUCE

italian pork chop dinner

COOK TIME: 4 TO 6 HOURS

Martina Williams
Grovetown, Georgia

My family loves this meal after church services. I serve it with spaghetti, salad and garlic bread.

- **6 bacon strips, diced**
- **1/2 pound fresh mushrooms, sliced**
- **1 medium onion, finely chopped**
- **1 garlic clove, minced**
- **3/4 cup all-purpose flour**
- **4 teaspoons Italian seasoning, divided**
- **1/4 teaspoon salt**
- **1/4 teaspoon garlic powder**
- **1/8 teaspoon pepper**
- **Dash cayenne pepper**
- **6 bone-in pork loin chops (1 inch thick)**
- **1 can (14-1/2 ounces) diced tomatoes, undrained**
- **1 can (14-1/2 ounces) chicken broth**
- **1 can (6 ounces) tomato paste**
- **1 package (10 ounces) frozen peas, thawed**
- **Hot cooked pasta**

■ In a large skillet, cook the bacon over medium heat until crisp. Using a slotted spoon, remove to paper towels. In the drippings, saute mushrooms, onion and garlic until tender. Transfer to a 5-qt. slow cooker with a slotted spoon.

■ In a shallow bowl, combine the flour, 3 teaspoons Italian seasoning, salt, garlic powder, pepper and cayenne; coat pork chops with flour mixture.

■ In the same skillet, brown the pork chops; transfer to the slow cooker. Top with tomatoes and bacon. Combine the broth, tomato paste and remaining Italian seasoning; add to slow cooker.

■ Cover and cook on low for 4-6 hours or until pork is tender; add peas during the last 30 minutes. Serve with pasta.

YIELD: 6 servings.

ham and bean stew

COOK TIME: 7 HOURS

Teresa D'Amato
East Granby, Connecticut

I need only five ingredients to fix this thick, flavorful stew. It's very easy to make and often requested by my family.

- **2 cans (16 ounces each) baked beans**
- **2 medium potatoes, peeled and cubed**
- **2 cups cubed fully cooked ham**
- **1 celery rib, chopped**
- **1/2 cup water**

■ In a 3-qt. slow cooker, combine all ingredients; mix well. Cover and cook on low for 7 hours or until the potatoes are tender.

YIELD: 6 servings.

> **SLOW COOKER TIP:**
> Always pour liquids over roasts and stews in the slow cooker but don't add any more liquid than specified in the recipe. Slow cooking retains more juices from meats and vegetables than oven or stovetop cooking.

apple-dijon pork roast

COOK TIME: 4 TO 4-1/2 HOURS

Cindy Steffen
Cedarburg, Wisconsin

This is one of my family favorites for cold-weather comfort. This recipe takes less than 5 minutes to assemble and is delicious. I like to serve the roast with rice, then use the tangy sauce as a gravy for both.

- **1 boneless whole pork loin roast (2 to 3 pounds)**
- **1 can (14-1/2 ounces) chicken broth**
- **1 cup unsweetened apple juice**
- **1/2 cup Dijon mustard**
- **6 tablespoons cornstarch**
- **6 tablespoons cold water**

■ Cut roast in half; place in a 5-qt. slow cooker. Combine the broth, apple juice and mustard; pour over roast. Cover and cook on low for 4 to 4-1/2 hours or until a meat thermometer reads 160°.

■ Remove roast and keep warm. For gravy, strain cooking juices and skim fat. Pour juices into a saucepan. Combine cornstarch and water until smooth; gradually stir into juices. Bring to a boil; cook and stir for 2 minutes or until thickened. Serve with pork.

YIELD: 8 servings.

> **SLOW COOKER TIP:**
> Another way to thicken sauces at the end of the cooking time is to add the thickener and turn the heat to high for a short time.

APPLE-DIJON PORK ROAST

saucy scalloped potatoes

COOK TIME: 7 TO 9 HOURS

Elaine Kane
Keizer, Oregon

For old-fashioned flavor, try these scalloped potatoes. They cook up tender, creamy and comforting. Chopped ham adds a hearty touch.

> **4 cups thinly sliced peeled potatoes (about 2 pounds)**
>
> **1 can (10-3/4 ounces) cream of celery *or* mushroom soup, undiluted**
>
> **1 can (12 ounces) evaporated milk**
>
> **1 large onion, sliced**
>
> **2 tablespoons butter**
>
> **1/2 teaspoon salt**
>
> **1/4 teaspoon pepper**
>
> **1-1/2 cups chopped fully cooked ham**

- In a 3-qt. slow cooker, combine the first seven ingredients; mix well. Cover and cook on high for 1 hour.

- Stir in ham. Reduce heat to low; cook 6-8 hours longer or until potatoes are tender.

YIELD: 4-6 main-dish or 8-12 side-dish servings.

cranberry pork chops

COOK TIME: 7 TO 8 HOURS

Robin Czachor
Appleton, Wisconsin

My husband and two kids rave over these moist chops. Use the mild sweet-and-sour sauce to make a gravy that can be served over mashed potatoes or rice. Then add a salad and you have a very satisfying meal that didn't keep you in the kitchen for hours.

> **6 bone-in pork loin chops**
>
> **1 can (16 ounces) jellied cranberry sauce**
>
> **1/2 cup cranberry *or* apple juice**
>
> **1/4 cup sugar**
>
> **2 tablespoons spicy brown mustard**
>
> **2 tablespoons cornstarch**
>
> **1/4 cup cold water**
>
> **1/2 teaspoon salt**

Dash pepper

- Place pork chops in a 3-qt. slow cooker. Combine cranberry sauce, juice, sugar and mustard until smooth; pour over chops.

- Cover and cook on low for 7-8 hours or until meat is tender. Remove chops; keep warm. In a saucepan, combine cornstarch and cold water until smooth; gradually stir in cooking juices. Bring to a boil; cook and stir for 2 minutes or until thickened. Stir in salt and pepper. Serve over chops.

YIELD: 6 servings.

sweet sausage 'n' beans

COOK TIME: 4 HOURS

Doris Heath
Franklin, North Carolina

This is my version of a traditional French dish called cassoulet. It's chock-full of beans, smoked sausage and vegetables.

> **1/2 cup thinly sliced carrots**
>
> **1/2 cup chopped onion**
>
> **2 cups frozen lima beans, thawed**
>
> **2 cups frozen green beans, thawed**
>
> **1 pound fully cooked smoked sausage, cut into 1/4-inch slices**
>
> **1 can (16 ounces) baked beans**
>
> **1/2 cup ketchup**
>
> **1/3 cup packed brown sugar**
>
> **1 tablespoon cider vinegar**
>
> **1 teaspoon prepared mustard**

- In a 3-qt. slow cooker, layer the carrots, onion, lima beans, green beans, sausage and baked beans. Combine ketchup, brown sugar, vinegar and mustard; pour over beans.

- Cover and cook on high for 4 hours or until vegetables are tender. Stir before serving.

YIELD: 4-6 servings.

SAUCY SCALLOPED POTATOES

chalupa

COOK TIME: 8 HOURS

Ginny Becker
Torrington, Wyoming

This is such a refreshing change of pace from traditional chili. It's also fun to serve to guests. Nearly everyone who's sampled it has loved it and requested the recipe.

> 1 cup dried pinto beans
>
> 3-1/2 cups water
>
> 1/4 cup chopped onion
>
> 1 can (4 ounces) chopped green chilies
>
> 1 garlic clove, minced
>
> 1 tablespoon chili powder
>
> 1-1/2 teaspoons salt
>
> 1-1/2 teaspoons ground cumin
>
> 1/2 teaspoon dried oregano
>
> 1 boneless pork shoulder roast (1-1/2 pounds), trimmed
>
> 1 package (10-1/2 ounces) corn chips
>
> 1/4 cup sliced green onions
>
> **Shredded lettuce**
>
> **Shredded cheddar cheese**
>
> **Chopped fresh tomatoes**
>
> **Salsa**

- Place beans and enough water to cover in a 3-qt. saucepan. Bring to a boil; boil for 2 minutes. Remove from the heat; let stand for 1 hour. Drain beans and discard liquid.

- In a 3-qt. slow cooker, combine water, onion, chilies, garlic, chili powder, salt, cumin and oregano. Add roast and beans.

- Cover and cook on high for 2 hours. Reduce heat to low and cook 6 hours longer or until pork is very tender.

- Remove roast and shred with a fork. Drain beans, reserving cooking liquid

in a saucepan. Combine beans and meat; set aside. Skim and discard fat from cooking liquid; bring to a boil.

- Boil, uncovered, for 20 minutes or until reduced to 1-1/2 cups. Add the meat and bean mixture; heat through.

- To serve, spoon meat mixture over corn chips; top with green onions, lettuce, cheese, tomatoes and salsa.

YIELD: 6-8 servings.

shredded pork with beans

COOK TIME: 8 HOURS

Sarah Johnston
Lincoln, Nebraska

A friend gave me this recipe, which my sons say is a keeper. For a refreshing change of pace, spoon the tasty filling into soft tortillas.

> 3 pork tenderloins (1 pound *each*), cut into 3-inch pieces
>
> 2 cans (15 ounces *each*) black beans, rinsed and drained
>
> 1 jar (24 ounces) picante sauce
>
> **Hot cooked rice, optional**

- Place the pork, beans and picante sauce in a 5-qt. slow cooker. Cover and cook on low for 8 hours or until pork is tender. Shred pork; return to slow cooker. Serve with rice if desired.

YIELD: 10-12 servings.

SLOW COOKER TIP:
Flavors are sometimes diluted in the slow cooking process, so it's best to add spices, such as garlic powder and pepper, toward the end of cooking.

baby back ribs

COOK TIME: 6 HOURS

Taste of Home Test Kitchen

Slow cook the ribs during the day and they will be ready to finish on the grill when you get home. We know your family and guests will enjoy these delicious, finger-lickin' ribs.

> 2-1/2 pounds pork baby back ribs, cut into eight pieces
>
> 5 cups water
>
> 1 medium onion, sliced
>
> 2 celery ribs, cut in half
>
> 2 teaspoons minced garlic, *divided*
>
> 1 teaspoon whole peppercorns
>
> 1/2 cup barbecue sauce
>
> 1/4 cup plum sauce
>
> **Dash hot pepper sauce**

- Place the ribs in a 5-qt. slow cooker. Add the water, onion, celery, 1 teaspoon garlic and peppercorns. Cover and cook on low for 6 hours or until meat is tender.

- In a small saucepan, combine the barbecue sauce, plum sauce, hot pepper sauce and remaining garlic. Cook and stir over medium heat for 5 minutes or until heated through. Remove ribs. Discard cooking juices and vegetables.

- Coat grill rack with nonstick cooking spray before starting the grill. Brush ribs with sauce. Grill, uncovered, over medium-low heat for 8-10 minutes or until browned, turning occasionally and brushing with remaining sauce.

YIELD: 4 servings.

taste of home slow cooker classics

BABY BACK RIBS

spaghetti pork chops

COOK TIME: 6 TO 8 HOURS

Ellen Gallavan
Midland, Michigan

The moist chops cook to perfection in a tangy sauce, then are served over pasta. This was one of my mother's most-loved recipes.

- **3 cans (8 ounces *each*) tomato sauce**
- **1 can (10-3/4 ounces) condensed tomato soup, undiluted**
- **1 small onion, finely chopped**
- **1 bay leaf**
- **1 teaspoon celery seed**
- **1/2 teaspoon Italian seasoning**
- **6 bone-in pork chops (1 inch thick)**
- **2 tablespoons olive oil**

Hot cooked spaghetti

- In a 5-qt. slow cooker, combine the tomato sauce, soup, onion, bay leaf, celery seed and Italian seasoning. In a large skillet, brown pork chops in oil. Add to the slow cooker.

- Cover and cook on low for 6-8 hours or until meat is tender. Discard bay leaf. Serve chops and sauce over spaghetti.

YIELD: 6 servings.

lemon pork chops

COOK TIME: 6 HOURS

Barbara De Frang
Hazen, North Dakota

These chops can simmer all day on low and be super-tender by dinnertime. I serve them with a crisp salad and macaroni and cheese as a side dish.

- **4 bone-in pork loin chops (3/4 inch thick)**
- **1/2 teaspoon salt**
- **1/4 teaspoon pepper**
- **1 medium onion, cut into 1/4-inch slices**
- **1 medium lemon, cut into 1/4-inch slices**
- **1/4 cup packed brown sugar**
- **1/4 cup ketchup**

- Place the pork chops in a 3-qt. slow cooker. Sprinkle with salt and pepper. Top with onion and lemon. Sprinkle with brown sugar; drizzle with ketchup.

- Cover and cook on low for 6 hours or until meat juices run clear.

YIELD: 4 servings.

pork and cabbage dinner

COOK TIME: 8 HOURS

Trina Hinkel
Minneapolis, Minnesota

I put on this pork roast in the morning to avoid that evening dinner rush. All I do is fix potatoes, and our family can sit down to a satisfying supper.

- **1 pound carrots**
- **1-1/2 cups water**
- **1 envelope onion soup mix**
- **2 garlic cloves, minced**
- **1/2 teaspoon celery seed**
- **1 boneless pork shoulder roast (4 to 6 pounds)**
- **1/2 teaspoon salt**
- **1/4 teaspoon pepper**
- **1-1/2 pounds cabbage, cut into 2-inch pieces**

- Cut carrots in half lengthwise and then into 2-in. pieces. Place in a 5-qt. slow cooker. Add water, soup mix, garlic and celery seed. Cut roast in half; place over carrot mixture. Sprinkle with salt and pepper. Cover and cook on high for 2 hours.

- Reduce heat to low; cook for 4 hours. Add cabbage; cook 2 hours longer or until the cabbage is tender and a meat thermometer reads 160°. Remove meat and vegetables to a serving plate; keep warm. If desired, thicken pan drippings for gravy and serve with the roast.

YIELD: 8-10 servings.

SPAGHETTI PORK CHOPS

pork carnitas

COOK TIME: 9 TO 11 HOURS

Tracy Byers
Corvallis, Oregon

I use this recipe often when entertaining. I set out all the toppings, and folks have fun assembling their own carnitas..

- **1 boneless pork shoulder *or* loin roast (2 to 3 pounds), trimmed and cut into 3-inch cubes**
- **1/2 cup lime juice**
- **1 teaspoon salt**
- **1/2 teaspoon pepper**
- **1/2 teaspoon crushed red pepper flakes**
- **12 flour tortillas (6 inches), warmed**
- **2 cups (8 ounces) shredded cheddar *or* Monterey Jack cheese**
- **2 medium avocados, peeled and diced**
- **2 medium tomatoes, diced**
- **1 medium onion, diced**

Shredded lettuce

Minced fresh cilantro, optional

Salsa

- In a 5-qt. slow cooker, combine pork, lime juice, salt, pepper and pepper flakes. Cover and cook on high for 1 hour; stir. Reduce heat to low and cook 8-10 hours longer or until meat is very tender.

- Shred pork with a fork (it may look somewhat pink). Spoon about 1/3 cup of filling down the center of each tortilla; top with cheese, avocados, tomatoes, onion, lettuce and cilantro if desired. Fold in bottom and sides of tortilla. Serve with salsa.

YIELD: 12 servings.

chops with fruit stuffing

COOK TIME: 3 HOURS

Suzanne Reyes
Tustin, California

The aroma that fills the house as this pork dish simmers is fabulous. All you need to complete the meal is a green vegetable and maybe a loaf of bread. It's impressive enough for company.

- **6 boneless pork loin chops (1/2 inch thick)**
- **1 tablespoon vegetable oil**
- **1 package (6 ounces) herb stuffing mix**
- **2 celery ribs, chopped**
- **1 medium tart apple, peeled and chopped**
- **1 cup dried cherries *or* cranberries**
- **1/2 cup chopped onion**
- **2/3 cup chicken broth**
- **1/4 cup butter, melted**

- In a large skillet, brown pork chops in oil on both sides. In a large bowl, combine the remaining ingredients.

- Place half of the stuffing mixture in a 3-qt. slow cooker. Top with pork and remaining stuffing mixture. Cover and cook on low for 3 hours or until a meat thermometer reads 160°.

YIELD: 6 servings.

SLOW COOKER TIP:
Slow cookers are best with tougher cuts of meat. Tender cuts, like prime rib roasts and leg of lamb, can be overcooked in a slow cooker.

cranberry pork roast

COOK TIME: 6 TO 8 HOURS

Audrey Thibodeau
Mesa, Arizona

Guests rave about this tender roast, and I love preparing it because it's so simple. The gravy is delicious over creamy mashed potatoes.

- **1 boneless rolled pork loin roast (2-1/2 to 3 pounds)**
- **1 can (16 ounces) jellied cranberry sauce**
- **1/2 cup sugar**
- **1/2 cup cranberry juice**
- **1 teaspoon ground mustard**
- **1/4 teaspoon ground cloves**
- **2 tablespoons cornstarch**
- **2 tablespoons cold water**

Salt to taste

- Place pork roast in a 5-qt. slow cooker. In a small bowl, mash cranberry sauce; stir in the sugar, cranberry juice, mustard and cloves. Pour over roast. Cover and cook on low for 6-8 hours or until meat is tender.

- Remove roast and keep warm. Skim fat from juices. Pour into a 2-cup measuring cup; add water if necessary to measure 2 cups. Pour into a small saucepan. Bring to a boil over medium-high heat.

- Combine cornstarch and cold water until smooth; stir into pan juices. Bring to a boil. Cook and stir for 2 minutes or until thickened. Season with salt. Serve with sliced pork.

YIELD: 4-6 servings.

CRANBERRY PORK ROAST

bread bowl chili

COOK TIME: 7 TO 8 HOURS

Nancy Clancy
Standish, Maine

Instead of having your cake and eating it, too...I say eat chili and the bowl!

- **1 tablespoon all-purpose flour**
- **1/4 teaspoon salt**
- **1/8 teaspoon pepper**
- **1/2 pound *each* boneless pork, boneless skinless chicken breast and lean beef stew meat, cut into cubes**
- **1 tablespoon vegetable oil**
- **1 *each* medium onion and green pepper, chopped**
- **1 can (28 ounces) diced tomatoes, drained**
- **1 can (16 ounces) kidney beans, rinsed and drained**
- **1 can (15-1/2 ounces) navy beans, rinsed and drained**
- **1 can (8 ounces) tomato sauce**
- **1 tablespoon chili powder**
- **1 garlic clove, minced**
- **1-1/2 teaspoons ground cumin**
- **1/2 teaspoon dried basil**
- **1/4 to 1/2 teaspoon cayenne pepper**
- **9 large hard rolls, hollowed out**

Sour cream, chopped green onions and sweet red pepper

- In a resealable plastic bag, combine flour, salt and pepper. Add meat in batches; toss to coat. In a skillet, brown meat in oil. Transfer to a 5-qt. slow cooker. Stir in vegetables, beans, tomato sauce and seasonings.

- Cover; cook on low 7-8 hours or until meat is tender. Spoon chili into rolls and garnish as desired.

YIELD: 9 servings.

san francisco chops

COOK TIME: 7-1/2 TO 8-1/2 HOURS

Tara Bonesteel
Dayton, New Jersey

I find it easy to please friends and family with these fast-to-fix chops. Simmered in a tangy sauce all day, they're so moist and delicious by dinnertime they practically melt in your mouth.

- **4 bone-in pork loin chops (1 inch thick)**
- **1 to 2 tablespoons vegetable oil**
- **1 garlic clove, minced**
- **1/4 cup soy sauce**
- **1/4 cup red wine *or* chicken broth**
- **2 tablespoons brown sugar**
- **1/4 teaspoon crushed red pepper flakes**
- **1 tablespoon cornstarch**
- **1 tablespoon cold water**

Hot cooked rice

- In a skillet, brown pork chops on both sides in oil; transfer to a 3-qt. slow cooker. Add garlic to drippings; cook and stir for about 1 minute or until golden. Stir in soy sauce, wine or broth, brown sugar and red pepper flakes; cook and stir until sugar is dissolved. Pour over chops.

- Cover and cook on low for 7-8 hours or until the meat is tender. Remove chops. Combine cornstarch and cold water until smooth; gradually stir into slow cooker. Return chops to slow cooker. Cover and cook for at least 30 minutes or until slightly thickened. Serve over rice.

YIELD: 4 servings.

golden peach pork chops

COOK TIME: 6 TO 8 HOURS

Adele Durocher
Newport Beach, California

Peach halves add a hint of sweetness to pork chops in this time-tested favorite. The flavorful sauce is nicely seasoned with cinnamon and cloves.

- **1 can (29 ounces) peach halves**
- **5 bone-in pork loin chops (1 inch thick)**
- **1 tablespoon vegetable oil**

Salt and pepper to taste

- **1/4 cup packed brown sugar**
- **1/2 teaspoon ground cinnamon**
- **1/4 teaspoon ground cloves**
- **1 can (8 ounces) tomato sauce**
- **1/4 cup cider vinegar**

- Drain peaches, reserving 1/4 cup juice (discard the remaining juice or save for another use); set fruit and juice aside. In a large skillet, brown pork chops on both sides in oil; transfer to a 3-qt. slow cooker. Sprinkle with salt and pepper.

- In a bowl, combine the brown sugar, cinnamon and cloves; mix well. Add tomato sauce, vinegar and reserved peach juice. Pour over the chops. Arrange peach halves on top. Cover and cook on low for 6-8 hours or until the meat is tender.

YIELD: 5 servings.

BREAD BOWL CHILI

no-fuss pork and sauerkraut

COOK TIME: 4 TO 5 HOURS

Joan Pereira
Avon, Massachusetts

This entree has all the goodness of a big oven-prepared pork roast with sauerkraut but without the fuss. It can cook while you're away. Come home to a mouth-watering dinner.

- **1 boneless whole pork loin roast (4 to 5 pounds), cut into quarters**
- **1/3 cup Dijon mustard**
- **1 teaspoon garlic powder**
- **1 teaspoon rubbed sage**
- **1 can (27 ounces) sauerkraut, rinsed and well drained**
- **2 medium tart apples, sliced**
- **1 cup apple juice**

■ Rub sides of roast with mustard; sprinkle with garlic powder and sage. Place sauerkraut and half of the apples in a 6-qt. slow cooker. Top with roast. Pour apple juice around roast; top with the remaining apples.

■ Cover and cook on high for 4-5 hours or until a meat thermometer reads 160°.

YIELD: 12-16 servings.

tender 'n' tangy ribs

COOK TIME: 4 TO 6 HOURS

Denise Hathaway Valasek
Perrysburg, Ohio

These ribs are so simple to prepare, just brown them, then combine with the sauce ingredients in your slow cooker. Serve them at noon, or let them cook all day for falling-off-the-bone tenderness.

- **3/4 to 1 cup white vinegar**
- **1/2 cup ketchup**
- **2 tablespoons sugar**
- **2 tablespoons Worcestershire sauce**
- **1 garlic clove, minced**
- **1 teaspoon ground mustard**
- **1 teaspoon paprika**
- **1/2 to 1 teaspoon salt**
- **1/8 teaspoon pepper**
- **2 pounds pork spareribs**
- **1 tablespoon vegetable oil**

■ Combine the first nine ingredients in a 3-qt. slow cooker. Cut ribs into serving-size pieces; brown in a skillet in oil. Transfer to slow cooker. Cover and cook on low for 4-6 hours or until tender.

YIELD: 2-3 servings.

TENDER 'N' TANGY RIBS

pizza in a pot

COOK TIME: 8 TO 9 HOURS

Anita Doughty
West Des Moines, Iowa

Since most kids will try anything to do with pizza, I rely on this recipe when one of my two teenage sons has a friend stay for dinner. It's frequently a hit.

- **1 pound bulk Italian sausage**
- **1 can (28 ounces) crushed tomatoes**
- **1 can (15-1/2 ounces) chili beans**
- **1 can (15 ounces) black beans, rinsed and drained**
- **1 can (2-1/4 ounces) sliced ripe olives, drained**
- **1 medium onion, chopped**
- **1 small green pepper, chopped**
- **2 garlic cloves, minced**
- **1/4 cup grated Parmesan cheese**
- **1 tablespoon quick-cooking tapioca**
- **1 tablespoon dried basil**
- **1 bay leaf**
- **1 teaspoon salt**
- **1/2 teaspoon sugar**

Hot cooked pasta

Shredded part-skim mozzarella cheese, optional

■ In a skillet over medium heat, cook the sausage until no longer pink; drain. Transfer to a 3-qt. slow cooker. Add the next 13 ingredients; mix well.

■ Cover and cook on low for 8-9 hours or until slightly thickened. Discard bay leaf. Stir before serving over pasta. Sprinkle with mozzarella cheese if desired.

YIELD: 6 servings.

PIZZA IN A POT

easy and elegant ham
COOK TIME: 6 TO 7 HOURS

Denise DiPace
Medford, New Jersey

I fix this moist, tender ham to serve my large family. It can be readied quickly in the morning, frees up my oven, tastes outstanding and can feed a crowd. Covered with colorful pineapple slices, cherries and orange glaze, its showstopping appearance appeals to both children and adults.

> **2 cans (20 ounces *each*) sliced pineapple**
>
> **1 fully cooked boneless ham (about 6 pounds), halved**
>
> **1 jar (6 ounces) maraschino cherries, well drained**
>
> **1 jar (12 ounces) orange marmalade**

- Drain pineapple, reserving juice; set juice aside. Place half of the pineapple in an ungreased 5-qt. slow cooker. Top with the ham. Add cherries, remaining pineapple and reserved pineapple juice. Spoon marmalade over ham.

- Cover and cook on low for 6-7 hours or until heated through. Remove to a warm serving platter. Let stand for 10-15 minutes before slicing. Serve pineapple and cherries with sliced ham.

YIELD: 18-20 servings.

sesame pork roast
COOK TIME: 9 TO 10 HOURS

Sue Brown
San Miguel, California

I like to marinate a boneless cut of pork in a tangy sauce overnight before cooking it slowly the next day. The result is a tasty roast that's fall-apart tender.

> **1 boneless pork shoulder roast (4 pounds), trimmed**
>
> **2 cups water**
>
> **1/2 cup soy sauce**
>
> **1/4 cup sesame seeds, toasted**
>
> **1/4 cup molasses**
>
> **1/4 cup white wine vinegar**
>
> **4 green onions, sliced**
>
> **2 teaspoons garlic powder**
>
> **1/4 teaspoon cayenne pepper**
>
> **3 tablespoons cornstarch**
>
> **1/4 cup cold water**

- Cut roast in half; place in a large resealable plastic bag or glass dish. In a bowl, combine the water, soy sauce, sesame seeds, molasses, vinegar, onions, garlic powder and cayenne. Pour half over the roast. Cover the pork and remaining marinade; refrigerate overnight. Drain pork, discarding marinade. Place roast in a 5-qt. slow cooker; add the reserved marinade.

- Cover and cook on high for 1 hour. Reduce temperature to low; cook 8-9 hours longer or until meat is tender. Remove the roast and keep warm. In a saucepan, combine cornstarch and cold water until smooth; stir in cooking juices. Bring to a boil; boil and stir for 2 minutes. Serve with the roast.

YIELD: 8 servings.

peachy pork steaks
COOK TIME: 5 HOURS

Sandra McKenzie
Braham, Minnesota

This was my mom's surefire way to get picky children to eat meat. No one can refuse these succulent steaks!

> **4 pork steaks (1/2 inch thick), trimmed**
>
> **2 tablespoons vegetable oil**
>
> **3/4 teaspoon dried basil**
>
> **1/4 teaspoon salt**
>
> **Dash pepper**
>
> **1 can (15-1/4 ounces) peach slices in heavy syrup, undrained**
>
> **2 tablespoons vinegar**
>
> **1 tablespoon beef bouillon granules**
>
> **2 tablespoons cornstarch**
>
> **1/4 cup cold water**
>
> **Hot cooked rice**

- In a skillet, brown steaks in oil; sprinkle with basil, salt and pepper. Drain peaches, reserving juice. Place peaches in a 3-qt. slow cooker; top with steaks. Combine juice, vinegar and bouillon; pour over steaks.

- Cover and cook on high for 1 hour. Reduce heat to low and cook 4 hours longer or until meat is tender. Remove steaks and peaches to a serving platter; keep warm. Skim and discard fat from cooking liquid; pour into a saucepan. Combine cornstarch and cold water until smooth; stir into cooking liquid. Bring to a boil; boil and stir for 2 minutes. Serve steaks, peaches and sauce over rice.

YIELD: 4 servings.

EASY AND ELEGANT HAM

garlic-apple pork roast

COOK TIME: 8 TO 8-1/2 HOURS

Jennifer Loos
Washington Boro, Pennsylvania

This is the meal I have become famous for, and it is so simple. The garlic and apple flavors really complement the pork. It's great with steamed fresh asparagus and roasted red potatoes.

1 boneless whole pork loin roast (3-1/2 to 4 pounds)

1 jar (12 ounces) apple jelly

1/2 cup water

2-1/2 teaspoons minced garlic

1 tablespoon dried parsley flakes

1 to 1-1/2 teaspoons seasoned salt

1 to 1-1/2 teaspoons pepper

■ Cut the roast in half; place in a 5-qt. slow cooker. In a bowl, combine the jelly, water and garlic; pour over roast. Sprinkle with parsley, salt and pepper.

■ Cover and cook on low for 8 to 8-1/2 hours or until a meat thermometer reads 160° and meat is tender. Let stand for 5 minutes before slicing. Serve with cooking juices if desired.

YIELD: 12 servings.

kapuzta

COOK TIME: 6 TO 8 HOURS

Liz Krocak
Montgomery, Minnesota

This is a truly authentic "Old World recipe." Friends who moved here from Poland gave it to my mother years ago. It's been a favorite Sunday dinner with all of us ever since then. It's always a hit at potluck dinners, too.

1-1/2 pounds fresh pork (any type), trimmed, cut into bite-size pieces

1 medium onion, chopped

1-1/2 pounds Polish sausage, sliced into 1/2-inch pieces

1 quart sauerkraut, fresh preferred

1/4 head fresh cabbage, coarsely chopped

1 tablespoon caraway seed

1 can (10-3/4 ounces) condensed cream of mushroom soup

Pepper to taste

■ Cook pork and onion in hot skillet until pork is no longer pink, about 10 minutes. Combine cooked pork and onion with all other ingredients in 5-qt. slow cooker. Mix lightly; cook on low for 6-8 hours or until pork is tender.

YIELD: 6-8 servings.

sausage pasta stew

COOK TIME: 7 TO 9 HOURS

Sarah Bowen
Upland, California

I rely on my slow cooker to prepare this chili-like specialty. It's packed with turkey sausage, pasta and vegetables. My gang gobbles it up without realizing they're eating healthy.

1 pound Italian sausage links, casings removed

4 cups water

1 jar (26 ounces) meatless spaghetti sauce

1 can (16 ounces) kidney beans, rinsed and drained

1 medium yellow summer squash, halved lengthwise and cut into 1-inch pieces

2 medium carrots, cut into 1/4-inch slices

1 medium sweet red *or* green pepper, diced

1/3 cup chopped onion

1-1/2 cups uncooked spiral pasta

1 cup frozen peas

1 teaspoon sugar

1/2 teaspoon salt

1/4 teaspoon pepper

■ In a nonstick skillet, cook sausage over medium heat until no longer pink; drain and place in a 5-qt. slow cooker. Add water, spaghetti sauce, beans, summer squash, carrots, red pepper and onion; mix well. Cover and cook on low for 7-9 hours or until vegetables are tender.

■ Stir in the pasta, peas, sugar, salt and pepper; mix well. Cover and cook on high for 15-20 minutes or until pasta is tender.

YIELD: 8 servings.

GARLIC-APPLE PORK ROAST

SAUSAGE PASTA STEW

desserts

A quick and easy meal doesn't have to end with the main course. Turn on your slow cooker for dessert, too, and serve puddings, cobblers, cakes, fruits or fondues as your final course!

Delight your family with sweet concoctions like Slow-Cooker Bread Pudding found on page 314— a delicious complement to any meal.

chocolate bread pudding

COOK TIME: 2-1/4 TO 2-1/2 HOURS

Becky Foster
Union, Oregon

I love chocolate and I love berries, so I was thrilled to come across this recipe that combines the two. I like to use egg bread when making this dessert. Since it cooks in the slow cooker, I can tend to other things.

- **6 cups cubed day-old bread (3/4-inch cubes)**
- **1-1/2 cups semisweet chocolate chips**
- **1 cup fresh raspberries**
- **4 eggs**
- **1/2 cup heavy whipping cream**
- **1/2 cup milk**
- **1/4 cup sugar**
- **1 teaspoon vanilla extract**
- **Whipped cream and additional raspberries, optional**

- In a greased 3-qt. slow cooker, layer half of the bread cubes, chocolate chips and raspberries. Repeat layers. In a bowl, whisk the eggs, cream, milk, sugar and vanilla. Pour over bread mixture.

- Cover and cook on high for 2-1/4 to 2-1/2 hours or until a thermometer reads 160°. Let stand for 5-10 minutes. Serve with whipped cream and additional raspberries if desired.

YIELD: 6-8 servings.

> **SLOW COOKER TIP:**
> When mixing any sort of batter for a slow cooker recipe, be sure not to over-beat the ingredients.

butterscotch dip

COOK TIME: 45 TO 50 MINUTES

Jeaune Hadl Van Meter
Lexington, Kentucky

If you like the sweetness of butterscotch chips, you'll enjoy this warm, rum-flavored fruit dip. I serve it with apple and pear wedges. It holds up for up to 2 hours in the slow cooker. Try it at your next gathering.

- **2 packages (10 to 11 ounces *each*) butterscotch chips**
- **2/3 cup evaporated milk**
- **2/3 cup chopped pecans**
- **1 tablespoon rum extract**
- **Apple and pear wedges**

- In a mini slow cooker, combine butterscotch chips and milk. Cover and cook on low for 45-50 minutes or until chips are softened; stir until smooth. Stir in pecans and extract. Serve warm with fruit.

YIELD: about 3 cups.

warm fruit compote

COOK TIME: 2 HOURS

Mary Ann Jonns
Midlothian, Illinois

I rely on the convenience of canned goods and my slow cooker to make this old-fashioned dessert.

- **2 cans (29 ounces *each*) sliced peaches, drained**
- **2 cans (29 ounces *each*) pear halves, drained and sliced**
- **1 can (20 ounces) pineapple chunks, drained**
- **1 can (15-1/4 ounces) apricot halves, drained and sliced**
- **1 can (21 ounces) cherry pie filling**

- In a 5-qt. slow cooker, combine peaches, pears, pineapple and apricots. Top with pie filling. Cover; cook on high for 2 hours or until heated through. Serve with a slotted spoon.

YIELD: 14-18 servings.

CHOCOLATE BREAD PUDDING

WARM FRUIT COMPOTE

chocolate-raspberry fondue

SERVE IN A SLOW COOKER

Heather Maxwell
Fort Riley, Kansas

You don't need a fancy fondue pot to make this melt-in-your-mouth concoction. I serve the dip in my small slow cooker. Folks love the chocolate and raspberry combination.

> **1 package (14 ounces) caramels**
>
> **2 cups (12 ounces) semisweet chocolate chips**
>
> **1 can (12 ounces) evaporated milk**
>
> **1/2 cup butter**
>
> **1/2 cup seedless raspberry jam**

Pound cake *and/or* assorted fresh fruit

- In a large saucepan, combine the first five ingredients. Cook over low heat until caramels, chips and butter are melted, about 15 minutes. Stir until smooth.

- Transfer to a small slow cooker. Serve warm with pound cake or fruit.

YIELD: 5 cups.

burgundy pears

COOK TIME: 3 TO 4 HOURS

Elizabeth Hanes
Peralta, New Mexico

These warm spiced pears elevate slow cooking to a new level of elegance, yet they're incredibly easy to make. Your friends won't believe this fancy-looking dessert came from a slow cooker.

> **6 medium ripe pears**
>
> **1/3 cup sugar**
>
> **1/3 cup Burgundy wine *or* grape juice**
>
> **3 tablespoons orange marmalade**
>
> **1 tablespoon lemon juice**
>
> **1/4 teaspoon ground cinnamon**
>
> **1/4 teaspoon ground nutmeg**

Dash salt

Whipped cream cheese

- Peel pears, leaving stems intact. Core from the bottom. Stand pears upright in a 5-qt. slow cooker. In a small bowl, combine the sugar, wine or grape juice, marmalade, lemon juice, cinnamon, nutmeg and salt. Carefully pour over pears.

- Cover and cook on low for 3-4 hours or until tender. To serve, drizzle pears with sauce and garnish with whipped cream cheese.

YIELD: 6 servings.

fruit dessert topping

COOK TIME: 3-1/2 TO 4-1/2 HOURS

Doris Heath
Franklin, North Carolina

You'll quickly warm up to the old-fashioned taste of this fruit topping. Spoon it over vanilla ice cream or slices of pound cake.

> **3 medium tart apples, peeled and sliced**
>
> **3 medium pears, peeled and sliced**
>
> **1 tablespoon lemon juice**
>
> **1/2 cup packed brown sugar**
>
> **1/2 cup maple syrup**
>
> **1/4 cup butter, melted**
>
> **1/2 cup chopped pecans**
>
> **1/4 cup raisins**
>
> **2 cinnamon sticks (3 inches)**
>
> **1 tablespoon cornstarch**
>
> **2 tablespoons cold water**

Pound cake *or* ice cream

- In a 3-qt. slow cooker, toss apples and pears with lemon juice. Combine the brown sugar, maple syrup and butter; pour over fruit. Stir in the pecans, raisins and cinnamon sticks. Cover and cook on low for 3-4 hours.

- Combine cornstarch and water until smooth; gradually stir into slow cooker. Cover and cook on high for 30-40 minutes or until thickened. Discard cinnamon sticks. Serve over pound cake or ice cream.

YIELD: about 6 cups.

CHOCOLATE-RASPBERRY FONDUE

fudgy peanut butter cake

COOK TIME: 1-1/2 TO 2 HOURS

Bonnie Evans
Norcross, Georgia

I clipped this recipe from a newspaper years ago. The house smells great while it's cooking. My husband and son enjoy this warm dessert with vanilla ice cream and nuts on top.

- 3/4 cup sugar, *divided*
- 1/2 cup all-purpose flour
- 3/4 teaspoon baking powder
- 1/3 cup milk
- 1/4 cup peanut butter
- 1 tablespoon vegetable oil
- 1/2 teaspoon vanilla extract
- 2 tablespoons baking cocoa
- 1 cup boiling water

Vanilla ice cream

- In a bowl, combine 1/4 cup sugar, flour and baking powder. In another bowl, combine the milk, peanut butter, oil and vanilla; stir into dry ingredients just until combined. Spread evenly into a 3-qt. slow cooker coated with nonstick cooking spray.

- In a bowl, combine the cocoa and remaining sugar; stir in boiling water. Pour into a 3-qt. slow cooker (do not stir). Cover and cook on high for 1-1/2 to 2 hours or until a toothpick inserted near the center of cake comes out clean. Serve warm with ice cream.

YIELD: 4 servings.

warm apple topping

COOK TIME: 3 HOURS

Rosemary Franta
New Ulm, Minnesota

I have handed out this recipe to more people than any other. It has a delicious nutty flavor. Use it to top waffles or pancakes...or mix with vanilla or plain yogurt for a light and quick dessert.

- 8 tart apples (about 3-1/2 pounds), peeled and sliced
- 1/2 to 1 cup chopped pecans
- 3/4 cup raisins
- 1/2 cup butter, melted
- 1/3 cup sugar
- 1/4 cup old-fashioned oats
- 2 tablespoons lemon juice
- 1/4 teaspoon ground cinnamon

Waffles, pancakes *or* yogurt

- Combine all ingredients in a 3-qt. slow cooker. Cover and cook on high heat for 3 hours, stirring occasionally. Serve warm with waffles, pancakes or yogurt.

YIELD: 5 cups.

raisin bread pudding

COOK TIME: 4 TO 5 HOURS

Sherry Niese
McComb, Ohio

My sister gave me the recipe for this delicious bread pudding. It's a big hit with everyone who's tried it. A home-made vanilla sauce goes together quickly on the stovetop and is yummy drizzled over the warm servings.

- 8 slices bread, cubed
- 4 eggs
- 2 cups milk
- 1/4 cup sugar
- 1/4 cup butter, melted
- 1/4 cup raisins
- 1/2 teaspoon ground cinnamon

SAUCE:

- 2 tablespoons butter
- 2 tablespoons all-purpose flour
- 1 cup water
- 3/4 cup sugar
- 1 teaspoon vanilla extract

- Place bread cubes in a greased 3-qt. slow cooker. In a bowl, beat eggs and milk; stir in sugar, butter, raisins and cinnamon. Pour over bread; stir.

- Cover and cook on high for 1 hour. Reduce heat to low; cook for 3-4 hours or until a thermometer reads 160°. Just before serving, melt butter in a saucepan. Stir in flour until smooth. Gradually add water, sugar and vanilla. Bring to a boil; cook and stir for 2 minutes or until thickened. Serve with the warm bread pudding.

YIELD: 6 servings.

FUDGY PEANUT BUTTER CAKE

hot caramel apples

COOK TIME: 2-1/2 HOURS

Pat Sparks
St. Charles, Missouri

Who ever thinks of making dessert in a slow cooker? This old-time favorite goes together quickly...and it's such a treat to come home to the aroma of cinnamony baked apples just like Mom used to make!

- 4 large tart apples, cored
- 1/2 cup apple juice
- 8 tablespoons brown sugar
- 12 red-hot candies
- 4 tablespoons butter
- 8 caramels
- 1/4 teaspoon ground cinnamon

■ Peel about 3/4 in. off the top of each apple; place in a 3-qt. slow cooker. Pour juice over apples. Fill each with 2 tablespoons of sugar, three red-hot candies, 1 tablespoon butter and two caramels. Sprinkle with cinnamon.

■ Cover and cook on low for 2-1/2 hours or until the apples are tender. Serve immediately.

YIELD: 4 servings.

slow-cooker berry cobbler

COOK TIME: 2 TO 2-1/2 HOURS

Karen Jarocki
Yuma, Arizona

I adapted my mom's yummy cobbler recipe for slow cooking. With the hot summers here in Arizona, we can still enjoy this comforting dessert, and I don't have to turn on the oven.

- 1-1/4 cups all-purpose flour, *divided*
- 2 tablespoons plus 1 cup sugar, *divided*
- 1 teaspoon baking powder
- 1/4 teaspoon ground cinnamon
- 1 egg, lightly beaten
- 1/4 cup milk
- 2 tablespoons canola oil
- 1/8 teaspoon salt
- 2 cups unsweetened raspberries
- 2 cups unsweetened blueberries
- 2 cups frozen vanilla yogurt, optional

■ In a bowl, combine 1 cup flour, 2 tablespoons sugar, baking powder and cinnamon. In another bowl, combine the egg, milk and oil; stir into dry ingredients just until moistened (batter will be thick). Spread batter evenly onto the bottom of a 5-qt. slow cooker coated with nonstick cooking spray.

■ In a bowl, combine salt and remaining flour and sugar; add berries and toss to coat. Spread over batter. Cover and cook on high for 2 to 2-1/2 hours or until a toothpick inserted into cobbler comes out without crumbs. Top each serving with 1/4 cup frozen yogurt if desired.

YIELD: 8 servings.

easy chocolate clusters

COOK TIME: 2 HOURS

Doris Reynolds
Munds Park, Arizona

You can use this simple recipe to make a big batch of chocolate candy without a lot of fuss. I've sent these clusters to my husband's office a number of times...and passed the recipe along as well.

- 2 pounds white candy coating, broken into small pieces
- 2 cups (12 ounces) semisweet chocolate chips
- 1 package (4 ounces) German sweet chocolate
- 1 jar (24 ounces) dry roasted peanuts

■ In a 3-qt. slow cooker, combine candy coating, chocolate chips and German chocolate.

■ Cover and cook on high for 1 hour. Reduce heat to low; cover and cook 1 hour longer or until melted, stirring every 15 minutes. Add peanuts; mix well.

■ Drop by teaspoonfuls onto waxed paper. Let stand until set. Store at room temperature.

YIELD: 3-1/2 dozen.

HOT CARAMEL APPLES

crunchy candy clusters

COOK TIME: 1 HOUR

Faye O'Bryan
Owensboro, Kentucky

These yummy peanut butter bites are so simple. I make them for holidays because my family looks forward to the coated cereal and marshmallow clusters.

- **2 pounds white candy coating, broken into small pieces**
- **1-1/2 cups peanut butter**
- **1/2 teaspoon almond extract, optional**
- **4 cups Cap'n Crunch cereal**
- **4 cups crisp rice cereal**
- **4 cups miniature marshmallows**

■ Place candy coating in a 5-qt. slow cooker. Cover and cook on high for 1 hour. Add peanut butter. Stir in extract if desired. In a large bowl, combine the cereals and marshmallows. Stir in the peanut butter mixture until well coated.

■ Drop by tablespoonfuls onto waxed paper. Let stand until set. Store at room temperature.

YIELD: 6-1/2 dozen.

minister's delight

COOK TIME: 2 TO 3 HOURS

Mary Ann Potter
Blue Springs, Missouri

You'll need just four common ingredients to put together this comforting dessert. A friend gave me this recipe several years ago. She said a local minister's wife fixed it every Sunday, so she named it accordingly.

- **1 can (21 ounces) cherry *or* apple pie filling**
- **1 package (18-1/4 ounces) yellow cake mix**
- **1/2 cup butter, melted**
- **1/3 cup chopped walnuts, optional**

■ Place pie filling in a 3-qt. slow cooker. Combine dry cake mix and butter (mixture will be crumbly); sprinkle over filling. Sprinkle with walnuts if desired.

■ Cover and cook on low for 2-3 hours. Serve in bowls.

YIELD: 10-12 servings.

fruit compote dessert

COOK TIME: 3 TO 4 HOURS

Laura Bryant German
West Warren, Massachusetts

This is one of the first desserts I learned to make in the slow cooker, and it's the one guests still enjoy most. It tastes like it came from a fancy restaurant.

- **2 medium tart apples, peeled**
- **2 medium fresh peaches, peeled and cubed**
- **2 cups unsweetened pineapple chunks**
- **1-1/4 cups unsweetened pineapple juice**
- **1/4 cup honey**
- **2 lemon slices (1/4 inch)**
- **1 cinnamon stick (3-1/2 inches)**
- **1 medium firm banana, thinly sliced**

Whipped cream, sliced almonds and maraschino cherries, optional

■ Cut apples into 1/4-in. slices and then in half; place in a 3-qt. slow cooker. Add the peaches, pineapple, pineapple juice, honey, lemon and cinnamon.

■ Cover and cook on low for 3-4 hours. Just before serving, stir in banana slices. Serve with a slotted spoon if desired. Garnish with whipped cream, almonds and cherries if desired.

YIELD: 8 servings.

SLOW COOKER TIP: A small slow cooker with a removable stoneware insert works great for melting chocolate or candy coating for dipping. It keeps the chocolate or coating at an even temperature for more uniform dipping and easier cleanup.

CRUNCHY CANDY CLUSTERS

chunky applesauce

COOK TIME: 6 TO 8 HOURS

Lisa Roessner
Ft. Recovery, Ohio

My mother gave me the recipe for this warm and cinnamony apple dish. Simmering it in a slow cooker fills the house with a wonderful aroma. You can also serve it with cream for dessert.

8 to 10 large tart apples, peeled and cut into chunks

1/2 to 1 cup sugar

1/2 cup water

1 teaspoon ground cinnamon

Vanilla ice cream

■ Combine apples, sugar, water and cinnamon in a 3-qt. slow cooker; stir gently.

■ Cover and cook on low for 6-8 hours or until apples are tender. Serve with ice cream.

YIELD: 5 cups.

chocolate pudding cake

COOK TIME: 6 TO 7 HOURS

Paige Arnette
Lawrenceville, Georgia

This rich, fudgy dessert is a cross between pudding and cake. I like to serve it warm with a scoop of vanilla ice cream. Whenever I take it to parties, everybody wants the recipe.

1 package (18-1/4 ounces) chocolate cake mix

1 package (3.9 ounces) instant chocolate pudding mix

2 cups (16 ounces) sour cream

4 eggs

1 cup water

3/4 cup vegetable oil

1 cup (6 ounces) semisweet chocolate chips

Whipped cream *or* ice cream, optional

■ In a mixing bowl, combine the first six ingredients. Beat on medium speed for 2 minutes. Stir in chocolate chips. Pour into a 5-qt. slow cooker that has been coated with nonstick cooking spray.

■ Cover and cook on low for 6-7 hours or until a toothpick inserted near the center comes out with moist crumbs. Serve in bowls with whipped cream or ice cream if desired.

YIELD: 10-12 servings.

apple-nut bread pudding

COOK TIME: 3 TO 4 HOURS

Lori Fox
Menomonee Falls, Wisconsin

Traditional bread pudding gives way to autumn's influences in this comforting treat. I add apples and pecans to my slow-cooked version, then I top warm servings with ice cream.

8 slices raisin bread, cubed

2 medium tart apples, peeled and sliced

1 cup chopped pecans, toasted

1 cup sugar

1 teaspoon ground cinnamon

1/2 teaspoon ground nutmeg

3 eggs, lightly beaten

2 cups half-and-half cream

1/4 cup apple juice

1/4 cup butter, melted

Vanilla ice cream

■ Place the bread cubes, apples and pecans in a greased 3-qt. slow cooker. In a bowl, combine the sugar, cinnamon and nutmeg. Add the eggs, cream, apple juice and butter; mix well. Pour over bread mixture.

■ Cover and cook on low for 3-4 hours or until a knife inserted in the center comes out clean. Serve with ice cream.

YIELD: 6-8 servings.

SLOW COOKER TIP: If you're not home during the entire slow-cooking process and there was a power outage, it's best to throw away the food that is in your slow cooker. Even if it looks done, discard it for food-safety reasons.

CHUNKY APPLESAUCE

strawberry rhubarb sauce

COOK TIME: 6 TO 7 HOURS

Judith Waxman
Harkers Island, North Carolina

This tart and tangy fruit sauce is excellent over angel food cake or ice cream. I've served this rosy-colored mixture many times and gotten rave reviews from friends and family.

- **6 cups chopped rhubarb (1/2-inch pieces)**
- **1 cup sugar**
- **1/2 teaspoon grated orange peel**
- **1/2 teaspoon ground ginger**
- **1 cinnamon stick (3 inches)**
- **1/2 cup white grape juice**
- **2 cups halved unsweetened strawberries**

Angel food cake *or* vanilla ice cream

- Place rhubarb in a 3-qt. slow cooker. Combine sugar, orange peel and ginger; sprinkle over rhubarb. Add cinnamon stick and grape juice.

- Cover and cook on low for 5-6 hours or until rhubarb is tender. Stir in strawberries; cook 1 hour longer. Discard cinnamon stick. Serve over cake or ice cream.

YIELD: 10 servings.

granola apple crisp

COOK TIME: 5 TO 6 HOURS

Barbara Schindler
Napoleon, Ohio

Tender apple slices are tucked beneath a sweet and crunchy topping in this comforting crisp. For variety, replace the apples with your favorite fruit.

- **8 medium tart apples, peeled and sliced**
- **1/4 cup lemon juice**
- **1-1/2 teaspoons grated lemon peel**
- **2-1/2 cups granola cereal with fruit and nuts**
- **1 cup sugar**
- **1 teaspoon ground cinnamon**
- **1/2 cup butter, melted**

- In a large bowl, toss apples, lemon juice and peel. Transfer to a greased 3-qt. slow cooker. Combine cereal, sugar and cinnamon; sprinkle over apples. Drizzle with butter.

- Cover and cook on low for 5-6 hours or until the apples are tender. Serve warm.

YIELD: 6-8 servings.

chocolate pecan fondue

SERVE IN A SLOW COOKER

Suzanne Cleveland
Lyons, Georgia

When our kids have friends sleep over, I like to surprise them with this chocolate treat. Our favorite dippers include fruit, marshmallows, cookies and pound cake.

- **1/2 cup half-and-half cream**
- **2 tablespoons honey**
- **9 ounces semisweet chocolate, broken into small pieces**
- **1/4 cup finely chopped pecans**
- **1 teaspoon vanilla extract**

Fresh fruit and shortbread cookies

- In a heavy saucepan over low heat, combine cream and honey; heat until warm. Add the chocolate; stir until melted. Stir in pecans and vanilla.

- Transfer to a small slow cooker and keep warm. Serve with fruit and cookies.

YIELD: 1-1/3 cups.

STRAWBERRY RHUBARB SAUCE

apple granola dessert

COOK TIME: 6 TO 8 HOURS

Janis Lawrence
Childress, Texas

I would be lost without my slow cooker. Besides using it to prepare our evening meal, I often make desserts in it, including these tender apples that get a tasty treatment from granola cereal, honey, cinnamon and nutmeg.

- **4 medium tart apples, peeled and sliced**
- **2 cups granola cereal with fruit and nuts**
- **1/4 cup honey**
- **2 tablespoons butter, melted**
- **1 teaspoon ground cinnamon**
- **1/2 teaspoon ground nutmeg**

Vanilla ice cream *or* whipped topping, optional

■ In a 3-qt. slow cooker, combine apples and cereal. In a bowl, combine honey, butter, cinnamon and nutmeg; pour over apple mixture and mix well. Cover and cook on low for 6-8 hours. Serve with ice cream or whipped topping if desired.

YIELD: 4-6 servings.

SLOW COOKER TIP:
Spray your stoneware insert with nonstick cooking spray before adding dessert ingredients. You'll have nicer scooping and easier cleanup after the meal.

---

butterscotch apple crisp

COOK TIME: 5 HOURS

Jolanthe Erb
Harrisonburg, Virginia

This sweet treat is a cozy way to warm up winter nights. Sliced apples are sprinkled with a tasty topping made with oats, brown sugar and butterscotch pudding mix.

- **6 cups sliced peeled tart apples (about 5 large)**
- **3/4 cup packed brown sugar**
- **1/2 cup all-purpose flour**
- **1/2 cup quick-cooking oats**
- **1 package (3-1/2 ounces) cook-and-serve butterscotch pudding mix**
- **1 teaspoon ground cinnamon**
- **1/2 cup butter**

Vanilla ice cream, optional

■ Place apples in a 3-qt. slow cooker. In a bowl, combine the brown sugar, flour, oats, pudding mix and cinnamon. Cut in butter until mixture resembles coarse crumbs. Sprinkle over apples. Cover and cook on low 5 hours or until apples are tender. Serve with ice cream if desired.

YIELD: 6 servings.

---

pumpkin pie pudding

COOK TIME: 6 TO 7 HOURS

Andrea Schaak
Bloomington, Minnesota

My husband loves anything pumpkin, and this creamy, comforting dessert is one of his favorites. We make this super easy pudding year-round, but it's especially nice in fall.

- **1 can (15 ounces) solid-pack pumpkin**
- **1 can (12 ounces) evaporated milk**
- **3/4 cup sugar**
- **1/2 cup biscuit/baking mix**
- **2 eggs, beaten**
- **2 tablespoons butter, melted**
- **2-1/2 teaspoons pumpkin pie spice**
- **2 teaspoons vanilla extract**

Whipped topping, optional

■ In a large bowl, combine the first eight ingredients. Transfer to a 3-qt. slow cooker coated with nonstick cooking spray. Cover and cook on low for 6-7 hours or until a thermometer reads 160°. Serve in bowls with whipped topping if desired.

YIELD: 6 servings.

BUTTERSCOTCH APPLE CRISP

PUMPKIN PIE PUDDING

slow-cooker bread pudding

COOK TIME: 3 HOURS

Edna Hoffman
Hebron, Indiana

I use my slow cooker to turn day-old cinnamon rolls into a comforting, old-fashioned dessert. It tastes wonderful topped with lemon or vanilla sauce or whipped cream.

> **8 cups cubed day-old unfrosted cinnamon rolls**
>
> **4 eggs**
>
> **2 cups milk**
>
> **1/4 cup sugar**
>
> **1/4 cup butter, melted**
>
> **1/2 teaspoon vanilla extract**
>
> **1/4 teaspoon ground nutmeg**
>
> **1 cup raisins**

■ Place cubed cinnamon rolls in a 3-qt. slow cooker. In a small mixing bowl, combine the eggs, milk, sugar, butter, vanilla and nutmeg; beat until smooth. Stir in raisins. Pour over cinnamon rolls; stir gently. Cover and cook on low for 3 hours or until a knife comes out clean.

YIELD: 6 servings.

warm strawberry fondue

COOK TIME: SERVE IN A SLOW COOKER

Sharon Mensing
Greenfield, Iowa

For a delightful dessert, I only need a handful of ingredients to fix this unusual fruit fondue. Use grapes, bananas, strawberries and angel food cake cubes as dippers.

> **1 package (10 ounces) frozen sweetened sliced strawberries, thawed**
>
> **1/4 cup half-and-half cream**
>
> **1 teaspoon cornstarch**
>
> **1/2 teaspoon lemon juice**

Angel food cake cubes and fresh fruit

■ In a food processor or blender, combine the strawberries, cream, cornstarch and lemon juice; cover and process until smooth.

■ Pour into saucepan. Bring to a boil; cook and stir for 2 minutes or until slightly thickened. Transfer to a fondue pot or mini slow cooker; keep warm. Serve with cake and fruit.

YIELD: 1-1/2 cups.

butterscotch fondue

COOK TIME: SERVE IN A SLOW COOKER

Taste of Home
Test Kitchen

Folks of all ages will enjoy dipping into a pot filled with this yummy concoction. The combination of brown sugar, sweetened condensed milk and toffee bits has lovely flavor. Use it to cap off a meal, or serve it as a sweet snack.

> **1/2 cup butter, cubed**
>
> **2 cups packed brown sugar**
>
> **1 can (14 ounces) sweetened condensed milk**
>
> **1 cup light corn syrup**
>
> **2 tablespoons water**
>
> **1/4 cup English toffee bits *or* almond brickle chips**
>
> **1 teaspoon vanilla extract**

Angel food cake cubes and fresh fruit

■ In a large saucepan, combine the butter, brown sugar, milk, corn syrup and water. Cook and stir over medium heat until smooth.

■ Remove from the heat. Stir in toffee bits and vanilla. Transfer to a fondue pot or mini slow cooker; keep warm. Serve with cake and fruit.

YIELD: 4 cups.

SLOW-COOKER BREAD PUDDING

SLOW COOKER TIP:
Bread puddings, cobblers and cakes taste even better served up warm from the slow cooker. Time the end of cooking with the end of your meal so dessert can be served up fresh.

BUTTERSCOTCH FONDUE AND WARM STRAWBERRY FONDUE

breads & salads

Complete your family's slow-cooked meals with fresh-from-the-oven breads and toss-together salads. Round Cheese Bread, page 354, which starts with baking mix, is a delectable addition to hearty chili, steaming bowls of soup or saucy stews.

Have fun and mix and match these tasty breads and crisp, crunchy salads with the fabulous entrees in this book.

chili corn bread wedges

Taste of Home Test Kitchen

With a little help from a boxed mix and a can of green chilies, you'll have no trouble baking a pan of this sweet, moist corn bread. Serve these thick slices alongside bowls of your family's favorite soup or chili.

- 1 package (8-1/2 ounces) corn bread/muffin mix
- 1 egg
- 1/3 cup milk
- 1 can (4 ounces) chopped green chilies
- 2 tablespoons sugar
- 3/4 cup frozen corn, thawed

■ Place corn bread mix in a large bowl. Combine the egg, milk, chilies and sugar; stir into mix just until moistened. Fold in corn.

■ Pour into a greased 9-in. round baking pan. Bake at 400° for 20-25 minutes or until a toothpick inserted near the center comes out clean. Cool on a wire rack for 5 minutes. Cut into wedges; serve warm.

YIELD: 6-8 servings.

sour cream 'n' chive biscuits

Lucile Proctor
Panguitch, Utah

I grow chives in my front yard and like to use them in as many recipes as I can. These moist, tender biscuits are delectable as well as attractive.

- 2 cups all-purpose flour
- 1 tablespoon baking powder
- 1/2 teaspoon salt
- 1/4 teaspoon baking soda
- 1/3 cup shortening
- 3/4 cup sour cream
- 1/4 cup milk
- 1/4 cup minced chives

■ In a bowl, combine dry ingredients. Cut in shortening until mixture resembles coarse crumbs. With a fork, stir in sour cream, milk and chives until the mixture forms a ball.

■ On a lightly floured surface, knead five to six times. Roll to 3/4-in. thickness; cut with a 2-in. biscuit cutter. Place on an ungreased baking sheet. Bake at 350° for 12-15 minutes or until golden brown.

YIELD: 12-15 biscuits.

calico salad

Joanne Neuendorf
Potosi, Wisconsin

This is a light, colorful and tasty salad for the holidays and during "veggie season." It travels well and is an expected dish at family reunions.

- 2 cups fresh broccoli florets
- 2 cups fresh cauliflowerets
- 1 cup cherry *or* grape tomatoes
- 1/2 cup chopped red onion
- 1/2 cup chopped celery
- 1/4 cup chopped sweet red pepper
- 1/4 cup chopped green pepper
- 1/2 cup sour cream
- 2 tablespoons milk
- 1 tablespoon ranch salad dressing mix
- 1/4 cup unsalted sunflower kernels
- 3 bacon strips, cooked and crumbled

■ In a large bowl, combine the first seven ingredients. In another bowl, combine the sour cream, milk and salad dressing mix. Pour over vegetables; toss to coat. Refrigerate until serving. Stir in sunflower kernels and bacon.

YIELD: 8 servings.

> **COOKING TIP:**
> Use the convenient fully cooked bacon strips available in the grocery store when recipes call for only a few strips. It saves time and makes preparing the recipe —and cleaning up afterwards—so much easier.

CHILI CORN BREAD WEDGES

CALICO SALAD

salad with egg dressing

Mary Bloom
Titusville, Pennsylvania

Egg sparks the taste of this pleasantly sweet cooked dressing. It's also good over fresh spinach or cabbage.

2 eggs, beaten

1/2 cup sugar

1/4 cup water

1/4 cup white vinegar

8 cups mixed salad greens

1 small onion, chopped

4 bacon strips, cooked and crumbled

1 medium tomato, cut into wedges

1/2 cup sliced cucumber

■ In a microwave-safe bowl, combine the eggs, sugar and water. Microwave, uncovered, on high for 1 minute. Stir in vinegar; cook for 1 to 1-1/2 minutes or until a thermometer reads 160°.

■ In a salad bowl, combine greens, onion, bacon, tomato and cucumber. Drizzle with warm dressing; toss to coat.

YIELD: 6-8 servings.

EDITOR'S NOTE: This recipe was tested with an 850-watt microwave.

ready-to-serve salad

Gaylene Anderson
Sandy, Utah

A mixture of delightful ingredients, like bacon, mandarin oranges, almonds and mozzarella cheese, and a simple dressing transform packaged salad greens into a special side dish.

1 package (16 ounces) ready-to-serve salad

8 bacon strips, cooked and crumbled

1 can (11 ounces) mandarin oranges, drained

1/2 cup chopped red onion

1/4 cup sliced almonds

1 cup (4 ounces) shredded part-skim mozzarella cheese

1/2 cup vegetable oil

2 tablespoons sugar

2 tablespoons white vinegar

1/4 to 1/2 teaspoon salt

■ In a large salad bowl, toss the first six ingredients. Combine the remaining ingredients in a jar with a tight-fitting lid; shake well. Pour over salad and toss to coat.

YIELD: 6 servings.

soft italian breadsticks

Christy Eichelberger
Jesup, Iowa

I use the "dough only" cycle on my bread machine to prepare these melt-in-your-mouth breadsticks that my family of five gobbles up! The soft, chewy breadsticks are irresistible when brushed with butter and sprinkled with Parmesan cheese.

1 cup water (70° to 80°)

3 tablespoons butter, softened

1-1/2 teaspoons salt

3 cups bread flour

2 tablespoons sugar

1 teaspoon Italian seasoning

1 teaspoon garlic powder

2-1/4 teaspoons active dry yeast

TOPPING:

1 tablespoon butter, melted

1 tablespoon grated Parmesan cheese

■ In bread machine pan, place the water, butter, salt, flour, sugar, Italian seasoning, garlic powder and yeast in order suggested by manufacturer. Select dough setting (check dough after 5 minutes of mixing; add 1 to 2 tablespoons of water or flour if needed).

■ When cycle is completed, turn dough onto a lightly floured surface; divide in half. Cut each portion into 12 pieces; roll each into a 4-in. to 6-in. rope. Place 2 in. apart on greased baking sheets. Cover and let rise in a warm place until doubled, about 20 minutes.

■ Bake at 350° for 15-18 minutes or until golden brown. Immediately brush with butter; sprinkle with Parmesan cheese. Serve warm.

YIELD: 2 dozen.

SALAD WITH EGG DRESSING

SOFT ITALIAN BREADSTICKS

confetti corn muffins

Dolores Hurtt
Florence, Montana

Green pepper and shredded carrot add color to these homemade corn muffins.

1-1/4 cups all-purpose flour

3/4 cup cornmeal

2 tablespoons sugar

3 teaspoons baking powder

1 teaspoon salt

1 egg

1 cup milk

1/4 cup butter, melted

1 medium carrot, shredded

1/3 cup chopped green pepper

■ In a large bowl, combine flour, cornmeal, sugar, baking powder and salt. In another bowl, combine egg, milk and butter; stir into dry ingredients just until moistened. Fold in carrot and green pepper.

■ Fill greased or paper-lined muffin cups two-thirds full. Bake at 425° for 14-18 minutes or until a toothpick comes out clean. Cool for 5 minutes before removing from pan to a wire rack. Serve warm.

YIELD: 1 dozen.

ale bread

Jeannine Norder
Eaton Rapids, Michigan

For a tender white loaf that's a bit moister and denser than other breads, try this simple recipe. It's equally good whether you use beer or ginger ale. Try slices warm with butter alongside a hearty slow-cooked meal.

1 cup warm beer *or* ginger ale (70° to 80°)

1/3 cup water (70° to 80°)

2 tablespoons vegetable oil

3 tablespoons sugar

1-1/2 teaspoons salt

3 cups bread flour

2-1/4 teaspoons active dry yeast

■ In bread machine pan, place all ingredients in order suggested by manufacturer. Select basic bread setting. Choose crust color and loaf size if available.

■ Bake according to bread machine directions (check dough after 5 minutes of mixing; add 1 to 2 tablespoons of water or flour if needed).

YIELD: 1 loaf (about 1-1/2 pounds).

tortellini caesar salad

Tammy Steenbock
Sembach Air Base, Germany

This salad was served at a dear friend's baby shower by a health-conscious friend, who suggested the dressing be prepared with low-fat or fat-free ingredients. Either way, the creamy dressing has plenty of garlic flavor and coats the pasta, romaine and croutons nicely. This deliciously different salad is so tasty and satisfying. It's great for potlucks.

1 package (9 ounces) frozen cheese tortellini

1/2 cup mayonnaise

1/4 cup milk

1/4 cup plus 1/3 cup shredded Parmesan cheese, *divided*

2 tablespoons lemon juice

2 garlic cloves, minced

8 cups torn romaine

1 cup seasoned salad croutons

Halved cherry tomatoes, optional

■ Cook tortellini according to package directions. Meanwhile, in a small bowl, combine the mayonnaise, milk, 1/4 cup Parmesan cheese, lemon juice and garlic; mix well.

■ Drain tortellini and rinse in cold water; place in a large bowl. Add the romaine and remaining Parmesan.

■ Just before serving, drizzle with dressing and toss to coat. Top with croutons and tomatoes if desired.

YIELD: 10 servings.

CONFETTI CORN MUFFINS

TORTELLINI CAESAR SALAD

cauliflower romaine salad

Eileen Blick
Andale, Kansas

I brown bread crumbs and grate fresh cauliflower for the top layer of this sensational salad that features a fast-to-fix Parmesan dressing. I make this unique side dish for everything from potlucks to special occasions.

1 cup dry bread crumbs

3 tablespoons butter

10 cups torn romaine

1 cup mayonnaise

2 tablespoons grated Parmesan cheese

1 tablespoon lemon juice

1 garlic clove, minced

1/4 teaspoon salt

1/8 teaspoon pepper

1-3/4 cups coarsely grated cauliflower

■ In a small skillet, brown bread crumbs in butter; set aside. Place the romaine in a large salad bowl. In a small bowl, combine mayonnaise, Parmesan cheese, lemon juice, garlic, salt and pepper. Pour over romaine and toss to coat. Top with cauliflower and reserved crumbs. Serve immediately.

YIELD: 8-10 servings.

> **COOKING TIP:**
> Nothing beats fresh garlic, but when in a time crunch, why take the time to peel and mince garlic when you can buy it in a jar? Minced garlic is available on grocery store shelves, but once opened, it needs to be kept in the refrigerator.

couscous salad

Debbie Graber
Eureka, Nevada

I created this salad one weekend to take to a friend's house, and everybody loved it. It's become a much-requested favorite at gatherings. Dice up some pepperoni and add it to the salad.

1-1/4 cups water

1 cup uncooked couscous

1/2 teaspoon salt

1/2 cup Italian salad dressing

3/4 cup chopped fresh mushrooms

1 can (2-1/4 ounces) sliced ripe olives, drained

1/2 cup diced cucumber

1/3 cup *each* diced onion, green pepper and sweet red pepper

■ In a small saucepan, bring water to a boil. Stir in couscous and salt. Cover and remove from the heat; let stand for 5 minutes. Fluff with a fork.

■ In a large bowl, combine the couscous, salad dressing, mushrooms, olives, cucumber, onion and peppers. Cover and refrigerate for 20 minutes or until chilled.

YIELD: 6 servings.

herbed garlic bread

Wendy Smith
Hartford, Wisconsin

I use either French or Vienna bread for this recipe. The Parmesan cheese complements the garlic nicely. Try this bread with a bowl of minestrone or a plate of spaghetti.

1 unsliced loaf (1 pound) French bread

1/2 cup butter, softened

2 tablespoons grated Parmesan cheese

2 tablespoons minced fresh parsley

4 garlic cloves, minced

1/2 teaspoon dried oregano

1/8 teaspoon garlic salt

■ Slice bread, but not all the way through, leaving slices attached at the bottom. In a small mixing bowl, cream butter. Add the Parmesan cheese, parsley, garlic, oregano and garlic salt; mix well. Spread between slices.

■ Wrap loaf in a large piece of heavy-duty foil (about 28 in. x 18 in.). Bake at 325° for 15-20 minutes or until heated through.

YIELD: 8-10 servings.

COUSCOUS SALAD

HERBED GARLIC BREAD

cornmeal drop biscuits

Rhonda McKee
Greensburg, Kansas

I like to stir up a batch of these light, golden biscuits that are flecked with cheese. They taste so delicious warm and spread with butter.

- 1-1/3 cups all-purpose flour
- 1/2 cup cornmeal
- 2-1/2 teaspoons baking powder
- 1/2 teaspoon salt
- 1/2 teaspoon ground mustard
- 1/2 cup shortening
- 1/2 cup shredded cheddar cheese
- 1 cup milk

- In a bowl, combine the flour, cornmeal, baking powder, salt and mustard; cut in shortening until crumbly. Stir in cheese and milk just until moistened.

- Drop by 1/4 cupfuls 2 in. apart onto a greased baking sheet. Bake at 375° for 26-28 minutes or until golden brown. Serve warm.

YIELD: 10 servings.

rosemary focaccia

Shelley Ross
Bow, Washington

With rosemary and lots of cheese, these savory bread squares will make an everyday dinner seem like a festive occasion.

- 1 loaf (1 pound) frozen bread dough, thawed
- 2 tablespoons olive oil
- 1/4 cup thinly sliced onion
- 1-1/2 teaspoons minced garlic
- 1 cup (4 ounces) shredded part-skim mozzarella cheese
- 2 tablespoons minced fresh rosemary

- Roll the dough into an ungreased 15-in. x 10-in. x 1-in. baking pan; build up edges slightly. Brush with oil; top with the onion, garlic, cheese and rosemary.

- Bake at 400° for 15-20 minutes or until cheese is melted and golden brown. Let stand for 5 minutes before slicing.

YIELD: 15 servings.

antipasto salad

Crystal Ranft
Forestville, New York

I frequently toss together this zippy salad. It's always a hit at family gatherings and social dinners, and it's so flexible. I've used spinach instead of lettuce and pepperoni in place of salami.

- 6 cups torn leaf lettuce
- 8 ounces hard salami, julienned
- 6 ounces provolone cheese, julienned
- 1 cup (4 ounces) shredded part-skim mozzarella cheese
- 2 medium tomatoes, chopped
- 1 can (6 ounces) pitted ripe olives, drained and halved
- 1 tablespoon minced chives
- 1 can (8 ounces) tomato sauce
- 1/2 cup vegetable oil
- 1/4 cup red wine vinegar
- 1 teaspoon sugar
- 1 teaspoon salt
- 1 teaspoon dried oregano
- 1/2 teaspoon garlic powder
- 1/4 teaspoon pepper

- Place the lettuce on a large serving platter. Arrange the salami, cheeses, tomatoes and olives over top. Sprinkle with chives. In a blender, combine remaining ingredients; cover; process until smooth. Drizzle over salad.

YIELD: 8-10 servings.

> **COOKING TIP:**
> Speed up salad preparations by using pre-packaged greens. It's more expensive than fresh lettuce, but sometimes the convenience helps you have more time to make a recipe.

CORNMEAL DROP BISCUITS

ANTIPASTO SALAD

herb vegetable orzo salad

Taste of Home Test Kitchen
Sweet golden corn, grape tomatoes and fresh basil in this salad bring the very best flavors to the table. Subtly salty olives add an interesting contrast.

- **1 cup uncooked orzo pasta**
- **2 cups frozen corn, thawed**
- **1/2 cup chopped sweet red pepper**
- **1/2 cup grape *or* cherry tomatoes**
- **1/2 cup pitted Greek olives, halved**
- **1/4 cup chopped sweet onion**
- **1/4 cup minced fresh basil *or* 4 teaspoons dried basil**
- **2 tablespoons minced fresh parsley**
- **3 tablespoons olive oil**
- **2 tablespoons balsamic vinegar**
- **1/4 teaspoon salt**
- **1/4 teaspoon pepper**

■ Cook pasta according to package directions; drain and rinse in cold water. Place in a large serving bowl; add the corn, red pepper, tomatoes, olives, onion, basil and parsley.

■ In a jar with a tight-fitting lid, combine the oil, vinegar, salt and pepper; shake well. Pour over salad and toss to coat.

YIELD: 8 servings.

COOKING TIP:
Fresh parsley trumps dried parsley for best flavor. It's an easy-to-grow, hardy herb. One tablespoon fresh parsley equals one teaspoon dried parsley.

raspberry vinaigrette

Dorothy Smith
El Dorado, Arkansas
This fruity salad dressing gets its beautiful, rich red color from raspberries. A hint of Dijon mustard gives it just the right touch of tartness.

- **1-1/3 cups fresh *or* frozen unsweetened raspberries**
- **1/3 cup reduced-sodium chicken broth**
- **2 tablespoons sugar**
- **1 tablespoon cider vinegar**
- **2-1/2 teaspoons olive oil**
- **2 teaspoons Dijon mustard**
- **Mixed salad greens**

■ Press raspberries through a sieve, reserving juice; discard seeds. In a jar with a tight-fitting lid, combine the broth, sugar, vinegar, oil, mustard and reserved juice. Refrigerate. Shake before serving over salad greens.

YIELD: 1 cup.

swiss onion crescents

Joy McMillan
The Woodlands, Texas
I put a special spin on these golden crescents by filling them with Swiss cheese, green onions and Dijon mustard. They're a snap to prepare because I use refrigerated dough.

- **1 tube (8 ounces) refrigerated crescent rolls**
- **3 tablespoons shredded Swiss cheese, *divided***
- **2 tablespoons chopped green onion**
- **1-1/2 teaspoons Dijon mustard**

■ Unroll crescent dough and separate into eight triangles. Combine 2 tablespoons cheese, green onion and mustard; spread about 1 teaspoon over each triangle.

■ Roll up from the short side. Place point side down on an ungreased baking sheet and curve into a crescent shape. Sprinkle with remaining cheese. Bake at 375° for 11-13 minutes or until golden brown.

YIELD: 8 rolls.

RASPBERRY VINAIGRETTE

SWISS ONION CRESCENTS

beet spinach salad

Marguerite Shaeffer
Sewell, New Jersey

It's great to have another way to serve beets. The tender beet strips are tangy and tasty marinated in this super salad recipe.

2 large fresh beets

2 tablespoons red wine vinegar

1 teaspoon Dijon mustard

1/4 cup olive oil

1-1/2 teaspoons sugar

1/8 teaspoon salt

Dash pepper

1/2 cup chopped green onions

1/2 teaspoon minced fresh mint

4 cups torn fresh spinach

1 medium navel orange, peeled and sectioned

1/2 cup fresh raspberries

■ Place beets in a large saucepan and cover with water. Bring to a boil. Reduce heat; cover and simmer for 30 minutes or until tender. Cool; peel and cut into 1/4-in. strips.

■ In a small bowl, whisk vinegar and mustard until blended; gradually whisk in oil. Add the sugar, salt and pepper.

■ In a large bowl, combine the beets, onions, mint and 2 tablespoons vinaigrette. Cover and refrigerate for 30 minutes.

■ In a large salad bowl, combine the spinach, orange sections, beet mixture and remaining vinaigrette; toss. Top with the raspberries and serve immediately.

YIELD: 4 servings.

cheesy texas toast

LaDonna Reed
Ponca City, Oklahoma

My husband and I love garlic bread, but it's such a waste for just the two of us, so I came up with this cheesy recipe. You can prepare it in a few minutes, and it's tasty, too!

2 tablespoons butter, softened

4 slices French bread (1 inch thick)

1/4 to 1/2 teaspoon garlic powder

1 cup (4 ounces) shredded part-skim mozzarella cheese

Chopped green onions or parsley, optional

■ Spread butter over bread. Sprinkle with garlic powder and cheese. Place on an ungreased baking sheet. Bake at 400° for 5-7 minutes or until cheese is melted. Sprinkle with onions or parsley if desired. Serve warm.

YIELD: 2 servings.

bacon-tomato spinach salad

Jeanne Voss
Anaheim Hills, California

This lovely salad combines spinach, tomatoes, red onion and bacon, served with a creamy homemade dressing. It's a classic we've enjoyed for years.

16 cups torn fresh spinach (about 12 ounces)

12 cherry tomatoes, halved

6 bacon strips, cooked and crumbled

1/4 cup julienned red onion

CREAMY OREGANO DRESSING:

1 cup mayonnaise

1 to 2 tablespoons white vinegar

2 teaspoons dried oregano

Salt and pepper to taste

■ In a large bowl, combine the spinach, tomatoes, bacon and onion. In a small bowl, whisk dressing ingredients until smooth. Serve with salad.

YIELD: 8 servings.

CHEESY TEXAS TOAST

BACON-TOMATO SPINACH SALAD

creamy french dressing

Ruth Ann Stelfox
Raymond, Alberta

This dressing has home-style goodness that always draws compliments.

- 1/2 cup mayonnaise
- 1/2 cup ketchup
- 1/4 cup white vinegar
- 1/2 cup sugar
- 1 small onion, cut into wedges
- 1/2 teaspoon salt
- 1/4 teaspoon pepper
- 1 cup vegetable oil

Salad greens, tomato wedges and cucumber slices *or* vegetables of your choice

- In a blender, place the mayonnaise, ketchup, vinegar, sugar, onion, salt and pepper. Cover; process until smooth. While processing, add oil in a steady stream. Serve over salad. Refrigerate leftover dressing.

YIELD: 2-1/2 cups.

caesar salad

Barbara Wheeler
Sparks Glencoe, Maryland

This classic recipe can't be beat! When Mom's cooking, our whole family looks forward to this refreshing salad that's tossed with a tangy homemade dressing. Store-bought can't compete! I know you'll enjoy it.

- 3 tablespoons olive oil
- 4-1/2 teaspoons lemon juice
- 1 teaspoon prepared mustard
- 1 garlic clove, minced
- 6 cups torn romaine
- 2/3 cup Caesar salad croutons
- 1/2 cup shredded Parmesan cheese

Coarsely ground pepper to taste

- In a jar with a tight-fitting lid, combine the oil, lemon juice, mustard and garlic; shake well. In a salad bowl, combine the romaine, croutons, Parmesan cheese and pepper. Drizzle with dressing and toss to coat.

YIELD: 4 servings.

italian herb muffins

Cyndee Page
Reno, Nevada

My husband enjoys garlic bread with spaghetti. While preparing spaghetti for dinner one day, I realized I was out of bread and thought, "Why not make an herb muffin instead?" I created this recipe, and it was a hit.

- 2 cups all-purpose flour
- 2 tablespoons grated Parmesan cheese
- 1 tablespoon sugar
- 1 tablespoon Italian seasoning
- 3 teaspoons baking powder
- 1 teaspoon salt
- 1 egg
- 3/4 cup milk
- 1/2 cup vegetable oil
- 1/4 cup butter, softened
- 1/2 teaspoon garlic powder

- In a bowl, combine the flour, Parmesan cheese, sugar, Italian seasoning, baking powder and salt. In another bowl, whisk the egg, milk and oil; stir into dry ingredients just until moistened.

- Fill greased or paper-lined muffin cups three-fourths full. Bake at 400° for 15-20 minutes or until a toothpick comes out clean. Cool for 5 minutes before removing from pan to a wire rack.

- In a small bowl, combine the butter and garlic powder. Serve with warm muffins.

YIELD: 10 muffins.

CAESAR SALAD

ITALIAN HERB MUFFINS

crescent rolls

Joyce Guth
Mohnton, Pennsylvania

My mother-in-law bakes these buttery rolls for holiday meals. If you're not careful, the plate will be empty before it's on the table!

3/4 cup plus 2 tablespoons
    warm milk (70° to 80°)

1/4 cup water (70° to 80°)

1 egg

6 tablespoons butter,
    softened, *divided*

3 cups bread flour

2 tablespoons sugar

1 teaspoon salt

2 teaspoons active dry yeast

- In bread machine pan, place the milk, water, egg, 4 tablespoons butter, flour, sugar, salt and yeast in order suggested by manufacturer. Select dough setting (check dough after 5 minutes of mixing; add 1 to 2 tablespoons of water or flour if needed).

- When cycle is completed, turn dough onto a lightly floured surface. Roll into a 12-in. circle. Melt remaining butter; brush over dough. Cut into 12 wedges. Roll up wedges from the wide end and place pointed side down 2 in. apart on greased baking sheets. Curve ends to form a crescent shape.

- Cover and let rise in a warm place until doubled, about 20 minutes. Bake at 375° for 17-20 minutes. Remove to wire racks.

YIELD: 1 dozen.

cheesy onion breadsticks

Taste of Home Test Kitchen

Basic biscuit mix gets a makeover with cheese, green onions and garlic powder. Brushing the breadsticks with melted butter when they come out of the oven adds to the eye appeal. Consider fixing a double batch—these won't last long.

1 cup biscuit/baking mix

1/4 cup milk

1/2 cup shredded cheddar
    cheese

2 green onions, finely chopped

1/4 teaspoon garlic powder

1 tablespoon butter, melted

- In a bowl, combine the biscuit mix, milk, cheese, onions and garlic powder. Turn onto a lightly floured surface; knead 8-10 times. Roll into an 8-in. x 6-in. rectangle.

- Cut lengthwise into eight strips. Place on a greased baking sheet. Bake at 375° for 12-15 minutes or until golden brown. Brush with butter.

YIELD: 8 breadsticks.

CHEESY ONION BREADSTICKS

asparagus berry salad

Trisha Kruse
Eagle, Idaho

When strawberries and asparagus are at their peak, this salad is sensational! I like to serve it for brunch or dinner. Sometimes I add grilled chicken or salmon to create a refreshing but filling main-dish salad.

1 pound fresh asparagus,
    trimmed and cut into 1-inch
    pieces

3 tablespoons olive oil,
    divided

1/4 teaspoon salt

1/4 teaspoon coarsely ground
    pepper

8 cups spring mix salad
    greens

3 cups sliced fresh
    strawberries

1/2 small red onion, thinly sliced

1/2 cup chopped walnuts,
    toasted

2 tablespoons balsamic
    vinegar

2 teaspoons sugar

- In a bowl, toss the asparagus with 1 tablespoon oil. Spread in a single layer in a greased 15-in. x 10-in. x 1-in. baking pan. Sprinkle with salt and pepper. Bake at 400° for 15-20 minutes or until tender.

- In a large bowl, toss greens, strawberries, onion, walnuts and asparagus. In a small bowl, whisk the vinegar, sugar and remaining oil. Drizzle over salad and toss to coat.

YIELD: 6-8 servings.

ASPARAGUS BERRY SALAD

bacon-onion pan rolls

Liz Vaughn
Mt. Prospect, Illinois
These buttery bacon-filled rolls are a favorite item at family get-togethers.

1 loaf (1 pound) frozen bread dough, thawed

1/4 cup butter, melted, *divided*

1/2 pound sliced bacon, cooked and crumbled

1/2 cup chopped onion

■ On a lightly floured surface, roll out dough to 1/4-in. thickness. Cut with a 2-1/2-in. biscuit cutter; brush with 3 tablespoons butter. Place 1 teaspoon of bacon and onion on half of each roll. Fold over and pinch to seal.

■ Place, pinched edge up, in a greased 9-in. square baking pan, forming three rows of six. Brush tops with remaining butter. Let rise until doubled, about 30 minutes. Bake at 350° for 25-30 minutes or until golden brown.

YIELD: 1-1/2 dozen.

zesty garden salad

Melissa Mosness
Loveland, Colorado
Olives and pickled pepper rings give a basic salad a fun, new twist. It's a great side salad for a family meal. It's also easy to double to serve at a picnic or potuck dinner. It's one of my best-loved recipes.

4 cups torn romaine

1 can (2-1/4 ounces) sliced ripe olives, drained

1/2 cup chopped tomato

1/2 cup shredded cheddar cheese

1/4 cup pickled pepper rings

1/2 cup Italian salad dressing

■ In a large salad bowl, toss the romaine, olives, tomato, cheese and pepper rings. Just before serving, drizzle with dressing and toss to coat.

YIELD: 4 servings.

crisp cheese breadsticks

Elizabeth Tonn
Waukesha, Wisconsin
This recipe transforms strips of day-old bread into a crunchy, tasty side.

1 jar (5 ounces) sharp American cheese spread

1/2 cup butter, softened

1 egg white

1 teaspoon Italian seasoning

1/4 teaspoon garlic powder

1 unsliced loaf (1 pound) day-old white *or* wheat bread

■ In a small mixing bowl, combine the cheese spread, butter, egg white, Italian seasoning and garlic powder; beat until fluffy and blended.

■ Remove crust from bread. Cut loaf in half widthwise. Cut each half horizontally into thirds; cut each portion lengthwise into fourths. (Strips will measure about 4 in. x 1 in. x 1 in.)

■ Spread cheese mixture over strips; place 2 in. apart on a greased baking sheet. Bake at 350° for 12-15 minutes or until lightly browned.

YIELD: 2 dozen.

ZESTY GARDEN SALAD

> **COOKING TIP:**
> Make your own Italian seasoning. Combine 3 tablespoons *each* dried basil, oregano and parsley flakes; 1 tablespoon garlic powder; 1 teaspoon dried thyme; 1 teaspoon dried rosemary, crushed; 1/4 teaspoon pepper; and 1/4 teaspoon crushed red pepper flakes. Grind until mixture is a coarse powder. Store in an airtight container for up to 6 months.

CRISP CHEESE BREADSTICKS

cheddar zucchini wedges

Vevie Clarke
Camano Island, Washington

I stir together biscuit mix, tender zucchini, cheddar cheese and toasted almonds to create this flavorful round bread. The golden wedges look as appealing as they taste.

- **1 medium onion, chopped**
- **1/4 cup butter**
- **2-1/2 cups biscuit/baking mix**
- **1 tablespoon minced fresh parsley**
- **1/2 teaspoon dried basil**
- **1/2 teaspoon dried thyme**
- **3 eggs, beaten**
- **1/4 cup milk**
- **1-1/2 cups shredded zucchini**
- **1 cup (4 ounces) shredded cheddar cheese**
- **3/4 cup chopped almonds, toasted**

■ In a skillet, saute onion in butter until tender. In a bowl, combine the biscuit mix, parsley, basil, thyme and onion mixture. Stir in eggs and milk just until combined. Fold in the zucchini, cheese and almonds.

■ Transfer to a greased 9-in. round baking pan. Bake at 400° for 25-30 minutes or until a toothpick inserted near the center comes out clean. Cut into wedges.

YIELD: 6-8 servings.

italian salad dressing

Maxine Johnson
Fenton, Michigan

I always have this dressing on hand since it yields a large jar and has wonderful, fresh homemade flavor. Italian salad dressing is very versatile. It even can be used to marinate chicken breasts.

- **1/3 cup sugar**
- **1 envelope Italian salad dressing mix**
- **3 garlic cloves, minced**
- **3/4 cup cider vinegar**
- **3/4 cup water**
- **3/4 cup vegetable oil**

■ In a small bowl, combine the sugar, salad dressing mix, garlic, vinegar and water; gradually whisk in oil. Store in the refrigerator. Stir before serving.

YIELD: 2-1/3 cups.

ITALIAN SALAD DRESSING

berry peach tossed salad

Maryvonne Martin
Orangevale, California

Loaded with fresh peaches and berries, this salad says "summer." It is a wonderful accompaniment to grilled meats, poultry or seafood.

- **3 tablespoons olive oil**
- **3 tablespoons orange juice**
- **3 tablespoons lemon juice**
- **1/4 teaspoon salt**
- **1/4 teaspoon pepper**
- **3 romaine hearts, torn**
- **1 medium red onion, halved and thinly sliced**
- **1/2 cup crumbled feta cheese**
- **2 medium fresh peaches, thinly sliced**
- **1 cup fresh raspberries**
- **1 cup fresh blackberries**

■ For dressing, in a small bowl, whisk the first five ingredients. In a large salad bowl, combine the romaine, onion, feta cheese and peaches.

■ Drizzle with dressing and toss gently. Sprinkle with raspberries and blackberries. Serve immediately.

YIELD: 6 servings.

COOKING TIP:
If fresh peaches and berries are not in season, try using frozen fruit which is readily available in the freezer section of your supermarket.

BERRY PEACH TOSSED SALAD

artichoke tossed salad

Melissa Mosness
Loveland, Colorado

Marinaed artichoke hearts make everything taste better. They star in this crisp, tossed salad. Why have plain lettuce when a dressed-up salad like this is so easy? It's a satisfying side dish with any meaty entree.

> 2 cups *each* torn romaine, leaf and iceberg lettuce
>
> 1 jar (6-1/2 ounces) marinated artichoke hearts, drained and chopped
>
> 1 cup sliced fresh mushrooms
>
> 1 can (2-1/4 ounces) sliced ripe olives, drained
>
> 1/2 cup Italian salad dressing

■ In a salad bowl, combine the lettuce, artichokes, mushrooms and olives. Drizzle with salad dressing; toss to coat. Serve immediately.

YIELD: 6 servings.

ARTICHOKE TOSSED SALAD

marinated salad

Susan Branch
Kalamazoo, Michigan

This chilled pasta salad is pleasing to the eye and the palate. I like to serve it when sweet corn, tomatoes and zucchini are in season. The make-ahead favorite is lightly dressed with tarragon vinegar, olive oil and dill weed.

> 3-1/4 cups fresh whole kernel corn, cooked and drained
>
> 2 cups cherry tomatoes, halved
>
> 1-1/2 cups cooked rigatoni *or* large tube pasta
>
> 1 medium zucchini, halved lengthwise and thinly sliced
>
> 1/2 cup pitted ripe olives
>
> 1/3 cup tarragon vinegar
>
> 2 tablespoons olive oil
>
> 1-1/2 teaspoons dill weed
>
> 1 teaspoon salt
>
> 1/2 teaspoon ground mustard
>
> 1/4 teaspoon garlic powder
>
> 1/4 teaspoon pepper

■ In a large bowl, combine the corn, tomatoes, rigatoni, zucchini and olives.

■ In a small bowl, whisk together the vinegar, oil, dill, salt, mustard, garlic powder and pepper. Pour over corn mixture; toss to coat. Cover and refrigerate for at least 2 hours.

YIELD: 7 servings.

crunchy onion sticks

Leora Muellerleile
Turtle Lake, Wisconsin

Although I've been collecting recipes for more than 50 years, I never tire of tried-and-true ones like this.

> 2 eggs, lightly beaten
>
> 2 tablespoons butter, melted
>
> 1 teaspoon all-purpose flour
>
> 1/2 teaspoon garlic salt
>
> 1/2 teaspoon dried parsley flakes
>
> 1/4 teaspoon onion salt
>
> 2 cans (2.8 ounces *each*) french-fried onions, crushed
>
> 1 tube (8 ounces) refrigerated crescent rolls

■ In a shallow bowl, combine the first six ingredients. Place the onions in another shallow bowl. Separate crescent dough into four rectangles; seal perforations. Cut each rectangle into eight strips. Dip each strip in egg mixture, then roll in onions.

■ Place 2 in. apart on ungreased baking sheets. Bake at 375° for 10-12 minutes or until golden brown. Immediately remove from baking sheets. Serve warm.

YIELD: 32 breadsticks.

COOKING TIP:
To save time, purchase fresh pre-sliced mushrooms instead of whole mushrooms. Generally, they are more expensive than whole mushrooms, but the convenience greatly helps speed along food preparation.

CRUNCHY ONION STICKS

crusty french rolls

Donna Washburn
Mallorytown, Ontario

Save time by letting your bread machine knead the dough for these hearty, chewy rolls with a wonderful golden crust. They're the best eaten the day they're baked or frozen for a later date.

1-1/4 cups water (70° to 80°)

2 teaspoons sugar

1 teaspoon salt

3-1/2 cups bread flour

1-1/4 teaspoons active dry yeast

1 tablespoon cornmeal

1 egg white

1 tablespoon water

- In bread machine pan, place the first five ingredients in order suggested by manufacturer. Select dough setting (check dough after 5 minutes of mixing; add 1 to 2 tablespoons of water or flour if needed).

- When cycle is completed, turn dough onto a lightly floured surface. Divide into 18 portions; shape each into a round ball.

- Place on lightly greased baking sheets; sprinkle with cornmeal. Cover and let rise in a warm place until doubled, about 45 minutes.

- Beat egg white and water; brush over dough. Bake at 375° for 15 minutes; brush again with glaze. Bake 10 minutes longer or until golden brown.

YIELD: 1-1/2 dozen.

garlic herb twists

Peggy Rosamond
Jacksonville, Texas

I'm a busy wife, mother and grandmother who also works full time as an accounts payable clerk, so I need quick dinner ideas. These three-ingredient breadsticks are good at church meetings, at potlucks or anytime. They're so tasty and a snap to assemble and bake as a slow-cooked entree finishes simmering. Try these twists with beef.

1 tube (8 ounces)
refrigerated crescent rolls

1/3 cup sour cream

1 to 2 tablespoons herb with garlic soup mix

- Unroll crescent dough into one long rectangle; seal seams and perforations. Combine sour cream and soup mix; spread over dough.

- Cut into 1-in. strips. Loosely twist strips and place on an ungreased baking sheet. Bake at 375° for 11-13 minutes or until golden brown. Serve warm.

YIELD: 1 dozen.

olive-cucumber tossed salad

Sundra Hauck
Bogalusa, Louisiana

You get lots of flavor from just a few ingredients in this easy-to-fix salad.

1 cup Italian salad dressing

2 medium cucumbers, peeled, halved, seeded and sliced

1 cup pimiento-stuffed olives, halved

1 teaspoon Creole seasoning

2 packages (10 ounces *each*) ready-to-serve salad greens

- In a bowl, combine salad dressing, cucumbers, olives and Creole seasoning. Cover; refrigerate for at least 30 minutes. Just before serving, place salad greens in a large bowl; add cucumber mixture. Toss to coat.

YIELD: 8 servings.

EDITOR'S NOTE: The following spices may be substituted for the Creole seasoning—1/2 teaspoon *each* paprika and garlic powder, and a pinch *each* cayenne pepper, dried thyme and ground cumin.

GARLIC HERB TWISTS

OLIVE-CUCUMBER TOSSED SALAD

ranch garlic bread

John Palmer
Cottonwood, California

I've worked as a manager of a fast food restaurant for 12 years. At home, I like to cook up different things using everyday ingredients. I give a buttery loaf of French bread plenty of flavor simply with salad dressing mix and garlic powder.

- **1 cup butter, softened**
- **2 to 3 tablespoons ranch salad dressing mix**
- **2 teaspoons garlic powder**
- **1 loaf (1 pound) French bread, halved lengthwise**

■ In a small mixing bowl, combine butter, dressing mix and garlic powder; beat until combined. Spread over cut sides of bread. Place on a baking sheet.

■ Broil 4-6 in. from the heat for 3-4 minutes or until golden brown.

YIELD: 8 servings.

EDITOR'S NOTE: Chili seasoning mix, taco seasoning or onion soup mix may be substituted for the ranch salad dressing mix.

COOKING TIP:

Garlic powder packs a lot of flavor, but sometimes the consistency of freshly minced garlic is perfect for a recipe. Use fresh garlic when you have the time and you will taste the difference.

---

fruit 'n' nut tossed salad

Sue Stewart
Hales Corners, Wisconsin

With its sweet lemony dressing, this green salad comes together in only 15 minutes. Even my picky 6-year-old will eat this.

- **1 head romaine, torn**
- **1 can (11 ounces) mandarin oranges, drained**
- **1 cup seedless red grapes, halved**
- **1/2 cup slivered almonds, toasted**

DRESSING:

- **1/4 cup vegetable oil**
- **3 tablespoons sugar**
- **3 tablespoons lemon juice**
- **1/4 teaspoon grated lemon peel**

Dash salt and pepper

■ In a large bowl, gently toss the romaine, oranges, grapes and almonds. In a small bowl, whisk the dressing ingredients. Drizzle over salad and toss to coat.

YIELD: 10 servings.

FRUIT 'N' NUT TOSSED SALAD

---

onion-garlic bubble bread

Charlene Bzdok
Little Falls, Minnesota

I've relied on this bread recipe often over the years. Frozen dough hurries along the golden, pull-apart loaf. It's wonderful with Italian dishes.

- **1 loaf (1 pound) frozen bread dough, thawed**
- **1/2 cup finely chopped sweet onion**
- **1/2 cup butter, melted**
- **2 garlic cloves, minced**
- **1 teaspoon dried parsley flakes**
- **1/4 teaspoon salt**

■ Divide dough into 24 pieces. In a small bowl, combine the remaining ingredients. Dip each piece of dough into butter mixture; place in a 10-in. fluted tube pan coated with nonstick cooking spray.

■ Cover and let rise in a warm place until doubled, about 1 hour. Bake at 375° for 20-25 minutes or until golden brown. Serve warm.

YIELD: 1 loaf (24 pieces).

ONION-GARLIC BUBBLE BREAD

buttery corn bread

Nicole Callen
Auburn, California

I got this recipe from a long-time friend several years ago and it's my most-used. I love to serve this melt-in-your-mouth corn bread hot from the oven with butter and syrup. It gets rave reviews on holidays and at potluck dinners.

2/3 cup butter, softened
1 cup sugar
3 eggs
1-2/3 cups milk
2-1/3 cups all-purpose flour
1 cup cornmeal
4-1/2 teaspoons baking powder
1 teaspoon salt

- In a mixing bowl, cream butter and sugar. Combine the eggs and milk. Combine flour, cornmeal, baking powder and salt; add to creamed mixture alternately with the egg mixture.

- Pour into a greased 13-in. x 9-in. x 2-in. baking pan. Bake at 400° for 22-27 minutes or until a toothpick inserted near the center comes out clean. Cut into squares; serve warm.

YIELD: 12-15 servings.

mushroom spinach salad

Patty Kile
Greentown, Pennsylvania

I've made this salad for my husband and me for years. I don't like cooked spinach, so I was looking for an alternative way to prepare this nutritious vegetable. This salad is especially delicious made with fresh spinach from the garden.

3 cups torn fresh spinach
1/2 cup sliced fresh mushrooms
1/2 cup seasoned croutons
2 tablespoons vegetable oil
1 tablespoon white wine vinegar
1-1/2 teaspoons sugar
1 teaspoon lemon juice
1/8 teaspoon salt
1/8 teaspoon pepper
1 tablespoon crumbled cooked bacon

- In a bowl, combine the spinach, mushrooms and croutons. In a jar with a tight-fitting lid, combine oil, vinegar, sugar, lemon juice, salt and pepper; shake well. Drizzle over salad and toss to coat. Sprinkle with bacon.

YIELD: 2 servings.

dilly romaine salad

Catherine Dawe
Kent, Ohio

Fresh dill gives a nice zing and flavor to the dressing for this refreshing salad. I seldom use store-bought dressings anymore, now that I know how easy it is to mix up my own special home-made versions.

8 cups torn romaine
1 medium cucumber, sliced
1 cup halved cherry tomatoes
1 small red onion, sliced and separated into rings

CREAMY DILL DRESSING:

1/2 cup evaporated milk
1/2 cup vegetable oil
3 tablespoons cider vinegar
2 teaspoons minced fresh dill
1/2 teaspoon onion salt
1/2 teaspoon dried minced onion
1/2 teaspoon salt
1/2 teaspoon ground mustard
1/8 teaspoon white pepper

- In a large salad bowl, toss the romaine, cucumber, tomatoes and onion. In a jar with a tight-fitting lid, combine the dressing ingredients; cover and shake well. Serve with salad. Refrigerate any leftover dressing.

YIELD: 12 servings (1 cup dressing).

> **COOKING TIP:**
> Remember to always check expiration dates on pantry ingredients. Using baking powder past its expiration date could result in a flat biscuit instead of a fluffy one.

BUTTERY CORN BREAD

DILLY ROMAINE SALAD

corn bread confetti salad

Jennifer Horst
Goose Creek, South Carolina

Corn bread salads have long been popular in the South but may be new to people in other regions. No matter where you live, I think you'll like this one!

- **1 package (8-1/2 ounces) corn bread/muffin mix**
- **2 cans (15-1/2 ounces *each*) whole kernel corn, drained**
- **2 cans (15 ounces *each*) pinto beans, rinsed and drained**
- **1 can (15 ounces) black beans, rinsed and drained**
- **3 small tomatoes, chopped**
- **1 medium green pepper, chopped**
- **1 medium sweet red pepper, chopped**
- **1/2 cup chopped green onions**
- **10 bacon strips, cooked and crumbled**
- **2 cups (8 ounces) shredded cheddar cheese**

DRESSING:

- **1 cup (8 ounces) sour cream**
- **1 cup mayonnaise**
- **1 envelope ranch salad dressing mix**

■ Prepare corn bread according to package directions. Cool completely; crumble. In a large bowl, combine the corn, beans, tomatoes, peppers, onions, bacon, cheese and crumbled corn bread.

■ In a small bowl, combine the dressing ingredients until well blended. Just before serving, pour dressing over salad and toss.

YIELD: 20-22 servings.

nectarine arugula salad

Christine Laba
Arlington, Virginia

Here's a summer salad that brightens any supper. The homemade dressing has a hint of raspberry.

- **4 cups fresh arugula *or* baby spinach**
- **4 cups torn Bibb *or* Boston lettuce**
- **3 medium nectarines, sliced**
- **2 tablespoons pine nuts, toasted**
- **2 tablespoons crumbled blue cheese**
- **2 tablespoons raspberry vinegar**
- **2 teaspoons sugar**
- **1 teaspoon Dijon mustard**
- **1/8 teaspoon salt**

Dash pepper

- **3 tablespoons olive oil**

■ In a large salad bowl, combine the first five ingredients. In a small bowl, whisk the vinegar, sugar, mustard, salt and pepper until blended. Gradually whisk in oil until dressing thickens. Drizzle over salad; toss to coat.

YIELD: 8 servings.

fluffy biscuits

Nancy Horsburgh
Everett, Ontario

If you're looking for a flaky basic biscuit, this recipe is the best. These golden-brown rolls bake up tall, light and tender. Their mild flavor tastes even better when the warm biscuits are spread with butter or jam.

- **2 cups all-purpose flour**
- **4 teaspoons baking powder**
- **3 teaspoons sugar**
- **1/2 teaspoon salt**
- **1/2 cup shortening**
- **1 egg**
- **2/3 cup milk**

■ In a small bowl, combine the flour, baking powder, sugar and salt. Cut in shortening until the mixture resembles coarse crumbs. Beat egg with milk; stir into dry ingredients just until moistened.

■ Turn onto a well-floured surface; knead 20 times. Roll to 3/4-in. thickness; cut with a floured 2-1/2-in. biscuit cutter. Place on a lightly greased baking sheet. Bake at 450° for 8-10 minutes or until golden brown. Serve warm.

YIELD: 1 dozen.

NECTARINE ARUGULA SALAD

FLUFFY BISCUITS

blue cheese salad dressing

Christy Freeman
Central Point, Oregon

This distinctively flavored dressing, makes a great accompaniment to any mix of fresh greens. The thick, creamy dressing does double duty at our house, as I often serve it as a dip with fresh vegetables.

- **2 cups mayonnaise**
- **1 cup (8 ounces) sour cream**
- **1/4 cup white wine vinegar**
- **1/4 cup minced fresh parsley**
- **1 garlic clove, crushed**
- **1/2 teaspoon ground mustard**
- **1/2 teaspoon salt**
- **1/4 teaspoon pepper**
- **4 ounces crumbled blue cheese**

■ Place all the ingredients in a blender; cover and process until smooth. Store in the refrigerator.

YIELD: 3 cups.

BLUE CHEESE SALAD DRESSING

dressed-up salad

Karen Bailey
Golden, Colorado

Convenient bagged salad greens are easily turned into a dazzling salad with fresh crunchy vegetables and a tangy Dijon vinaigrette.

- **1 package (8 ounces) ready-to-serve salad greens**
- **1 cup sliced cucumber**
- **1 cup julienned sweet red pepper**
- **1 cup julienned green pepper**
- **1/2 cup sliced radishes**
- **1/3 cup sliced green onions**
- **1/4 cup minced fresh parsley**

DIJON VINAIGRETTE:

- **1/4 cup olive oil**
- **1/3 cup red wine vinegar**
- **1 teaspoon sugar**
- **1 teaspoon minced fresh tarragon or 1/4 teaspoon dried tarragon**
- **1 teaspoon Dijon mustard**
- **1/4 teaspoon salt**
- **1/8 teaspoon pepper**

■ In a large salad bowl, combine the greens, cucumber, peppers, radishes, onions and parsley. In a jar with a tight-fitting lid, combine the vinaigrette ingredients; shake well. Drizzle over salad just before serving.

YIELD: 6 servings.

COOKING TIP:
Freshly ground pepper is great in salads. Whole peppercorns are available in the supermarket spice section and a peppercorn grinder can be found in cooking shops and in the kitchen section of department and discount stores.

mostaccioli veggie salad

Julie Sterchi
Harrisburg, Illinois

I first sampled this refreshing salad several years ago. The mix of pasta, zucchini, summer squash, cucumber, sweet peppers and black olives is coated with a light vinaigrette.

- **3 cups uncooked mostaccioli or large tube pasta**
- **1 medium cucumber, thinly sliced**
- **1 small yellow summer squash, quartered and sliced**
- **1 small zucchini, halved and sliced**
- **1/2 cup diced sweet red pepper**
- **1/2 cup diced green pepper**
- **1/2 cup sliced ripe olives**
- **3 to 4 green onions, chopped**

DRESSING:

- **1/3 cup sugar**
- **1/3 cup white wine vinegar**
- **1/3 cup vegetable oil**
- **1-1/2 teaspoons prepared mustard**
- **3/4 teaspoon dried minced onion**
- **3/4 teaspoon garlic powder**
- **1/2 teaspoon salt**
- **1/2 teaspoon pepper**

■ Cook pasta according to package directions. Drain and rinse in cold water. Place in a large bowl; add the cucumbers, summer squash, zucchini, peppers, olives and onions.

■ In a jar with a tight-fitting lid, combine the dressing ingredients; shake well. Pour over pasta mixture; toss to coat. Cover and refrigerate for 8 hours. Toss again before serving. Serve with a slotted spoon.

YIELD: 10 servings.

MOSTACCIOLI VEGGIE SALAD

fiesta mixed greens

Sherri Parks
Silver Springs, Florida
Precut ingredients take the effort out of making this fantastic salad. It's a colorful and refreshing side dish. Add leftover turkey, chicken or ham for a hearty lunch salad or cool summer main course.

- 4 cups torn mixed salad greens
- 1 large tomato, chopped
- 1 medium sweet yellow pepper, chopped
- 3/4 cup pimiento-stuffed olives
- 1 celery rib, chopped
- 1 green onion, chopped
- 1/4 cup olive oil
- 2 tablespoons plus 1-1/2 teaspoons white wine vinegar
- 1 tablespoon salsa
- 1/8 teaspoon garlic salt
- 1/8 teaspoon dried oregano
- 1/8 teaspoon dried cilantro flakes
- 1/8 teaspoon ground cumin
- 1/8 teaspoon pepper

■ In a salad bowl, combine the greens, tomato, yellow pepper, olives, celery and onion. In a jar with a tight-fitting lid, combine the remaining ingredients; shake well. Just before serving, drizzle over salad and toss to coat.

YIELD: 4 servings.

mixed green salad

Brenda Lancaster
Grand Blanc, Michigan
I frequently toss together this pretty medley of greens, mushrooms, red pepper, onion and oranges. I use raspberry vinegar in the homemade dressing, but cider vinegar also works nicely in a pinch.

- 3-1/2 cups baby spinach
- 2 cups torn leaf lettuce
- 1/2 cup chopped sweet red pepper
- 1/2 cup sliced red onion
- 1/4 cup mandarin oranges
- 1/4 cup sliced fresh mushrooms

DRESSING:
- 2 tablespoons olive oil
- 1 tablespoon raspberry vinegar
- 1 teaspoon sugar
- 1/4 teaspoon minced fresh parsley
- 1/4 teaspoon minced fresh basil

Pepper to taste

■ In a large salad bowl, combine spinach, lettuce, red pepper, onion, oranges and mushrooms. In a jar with a tight-fitting lid, combine the dressing ingredients; shake well. Drizzle over salad; toss to coat.

YIELD: 4 servings.

poppy seed biscuit ring

Elnora Willhite
Ontario, California
It takes just a few simple ingredients to dress up refrigerated biscuits and form this pretty ring. My daughter Robin first brought these bread rings to a family celebration. Now they're a must at special occasions and family get-togethers.

- 1/3 cup butter, melted
- 1 teaspoon dried minced onion
- 1 teaspoon poppy seeds
- 1/2 teaspoon dried minced garlic
- 2 tubes (12 ounces *each*) refrigerated buttermilk biscuits

■ In a bowl, combine butter, onion, poppy seeds and garlic. Separate each tube of biscuits into 10 biscuits; dip in butter mixture and stand up on end in a lightly greased 10-in. fluted tube pan.

■ Bake at 400° for 14-16 minutes or until golden brown. Immediately invert onto a serving plate. Serve warm.

YIELD: 10-15 servings.

MIXED GREEN SALAD

POPPY SEED BISCUIT RING

make-ahead vegetable salad

Kathy Berndt
El Campo, Texas

This tangy salad is simply chock-full of garden-fresh goodies. Storing it in the fridge overnight helps blend the delectable flavors.

- 6 medium tomatoes, cut into eighths
- 1 medium green pepper, thinly sliced
- 1 medium red onion, thinly sliced
- 1 medium cucumber, thinly sliced
- 3/4 cup cider vinegar
- 1/4 cup water
- 2 tablespoons sugar
- 1-1/2 teaspoons celery salt
- 1-1/2 teaspoons mustard seed
- 1/4 teaspoon salt
- 1/8 to 1/4 teaspoon cayenne pepper
- 1/8 teaspoon pepper

- In a large bowl, combine the tomatoes, green pepper, onion and cucumber; set aside. In a saucepan, combine the remaining ingredients.

- Bring to a boil; boil for 1 minute. Pour over vegetables and toss to coat. Cover and refrigerate for 8 hours or overnight. Serve with a slotted spoon.

YIELD: 10-12 servings.

round cheese bread

Deborah Bitz
Medicine Hat, Alberta

I often share the recipe for this savory round loaf with Italian flair. Warm buttered wedges are tasty with a pasta dinner or tossed salad.

- 1-1/2 cups biscuit/baking mix
- 1 cup (4 ounces) shredded part-skim mozzarella cheese
- 1/4 cup grated Parmesan cheese
- 1/2 teaspoon dried oregano
- 1/2 cup milk
- 1 egg, beaten
- 2 tablespoons butter, melted

Additional Parmesan cheese

- In a bowl, combine the first six ingredients (batter will be thick). Spoon into a greased 8-in. round baking pan. Drizzle with butter; sprinkle with additional Parmesan cheese.

- Bake at 400° for 20-25 minutes or until a toothpick inserted near the center comes out clean. Cool for 10 minutes. Cut into wedges. Serve warm.

YIELD: 6-8 servings.

ROUND CHEESE BREAD

black-eyed pea salad

Melinda Ewbank
Fairfield, Ohio

To create a more interesting pasta salad, I added pasta to my favorite black-eyed pea salad. The result is different and delicious. Cucumber and green pepper give this picnic side dish a satisfying crunch.

- 6 ounces small shell pasta, cooked and drained
- 1 can (15 ounces) black-eyed peas, rinsed and drained
- 1 cup sliced green onions
- 3/4 cup diced seeded peeled cucumber
- 3/4 cup diced green pepper
- 3/4 cup diced seeded tomato
- 1 small jalapeno pepper, seeded and finely chopped

DRESSING:
- 3 tablespoons canola oil
- 1/4 cup red wine vinegar
- 1 teaspoon sugar
- 1 teaspoon dried basil
- 1 teaspoon chili powder
- 1 teaspoon hot pepper sauce
- 1/2 teaspoon seasoned salt

- In a salad bowl, combine the first seven ingredients. In a jar with a tight-fitting lid, combine the oil, vinegar, sugar, basil, chili powder, hot pepper sauce and seasoned salt; shake well. Pour over salad and stir to coat. Cover and refrigerate for at least 2 hours before serving.

YIELD: 6 servings.

EDITOR'S NOTE: When cutting or seeding hot peppers, use rubber or plastic gloves to protect your hands. Avoid touching your face.

BLACK-EYED PEA SALAD

thousand island salad dressing

Kim Orr
Louisville, Kentucky

This comforting homemade dressing is chock-full of tasty ingredients, including chopped onion, celery and hard-cooked eggs. It's a delightful topping for any crisp green salad.

1 cup mayonnaise

1/4 cup chili sauce

2 hard-cooked eggs, chopped

2 tablespoons chopped green onion

2 tablespoons chopped celery

4-1/2 teaspoons finely chopped onion

1 teaspoon paprika

1/2 teaspoon salt

■ In a bowl, combine all ingredients; mix well. Cover and refrigerate until serving. Serve over salad greens.

YIELD: 1-1/2 cups.

endive salad with potatoes

Lisa Radelet
Boulder, Colorado

Endive and red potatoes are the unusual combo in this refreshing green salad. The tart dressing brings out the best of both flavors.

2 bunches curly endive, torn (about 8 cups)

3 small red potatoes, cooked and sliced

1/4 cup olive oil

3 tablespoons cider vinegar

2 teaspoons sugar

1 teaspoon salt

1/8 teaspoon pepper

■ In a large salad bowl, combine endive and potatoes. In a jar with a tight-fitting lid, combine the remaining ingredients; shake well. Drizzle over salad and toss to coat; serve immediately.

YIELD: 8-10 servings.

broccoli muffins

Theresa Rentfro
Cedar Creek, Texas

Because my family loves muffins, I'm always on the lookout for new variations. When I tried these nutritional muffins the first time, they were really a hit and became a favorite addition to our big family meals.

1-3/4 cups all-purpose flour

1 cup quick-cooking oats

1/4 cup sugar

2 teaspoons baking powder

1/4 teaspoon salt

1 cup milk

1/3 cup vegetable oil

1 egg, lightly beaten

1 cup chopped fresh broccoli, blanched

1/2 cup shredded cheddar cheese

■ In a large bowl, combine flour, oats, sugar, baking powder and salt. In a small bowl, mix milk, oil and egg; stir into dry ingredients just until moistened. Fold in broccoli and cheese.

■ Spoon into greased or paper-lined muffin cups. Bake at 400° for 18-20 minutes or until top springs back when lightly touched.

YIELD: 1 dozen.

> **COOKING TIP:**
> Consider using extra-virgin olive oil in salad dressings. Extra-virgin olive oil is made from the first pressing of the olives and is considered the finest and fruitiest of the olive oils. In general, the darker the color the more intense the flavor.

THOUSAND ISLAND SALAD DRESSING

BROCCOLI MUFFINS

easy veggie salad

Julie Scott
Pratt, Kansas

If I'm especially short on time, I'll buy sliced vegetables from the salad bar at the grocery store. The light, flavorful dressing whisks together in a snap and tastes better than bottled dressing. Since this recipe makes a lot, we can enjoy the salad the next day, too.

- 1 can (16 ounces) kidney beans, rinsed and drained
- 1 can (14-1/2 ounces) cut green beans, drained
- 1 small cucumber, halved and thinly sliced
- 2 cups thinly sliced carrots
- 1/2 cup chopped green pepper
- 1/4 cup sliced radishes
- 1/2 cup red wine vinegar
- 1/3 cup sugar
- 2 tablespoons vegetable oil
- 1 teaspoon ground mustard
- 1 teaspoon salt

Dash pepper

- In a large bowl, combine the beans, cucumber, carrots, green pepper and radishes. In a small bowl, combine the remaining ingredients; mix well. Pour over vegetables and toss to coat. Serve with a slotted spoon. Refrigerate leftovers up to 2 days.

YIELD: 12-14 servings.

COOKING TIP:
For a different flavor in Mozzarella Wedges, try substituting shredded cheddar, Swiss or Monterey Jack in place of the mozzarella.

mozzarella wedges

Lisa Keesee
Temperance, Michigan

I invented this recipe one night as an alternative to plain crescent rolls, and my family loved it. The cheesy wedges can be served as an appetizer or an accompaniment to soup or salad.

- 1 tube (8 ounces) refrigerated crescent rolls
- 1 tablespoon butter, melted
- 1/4 to 1/2 teaspoon garlic powder
- 2 cups (8 ounces) shredded part-skim mozzarella cheese

- Separate crescent dough into eight triangles; place on a greased 12-in. round pizza pan with points toward the center. Press dough onto the bottom and up the sides of pan; seal perforations.

- Brush with butter; sprinkle with garlic powder and cheese. Bake at 375° for 15-17 minutes or until crust is golden brown and cheese is lightly browned. Cut into wedges.

YIELD: 8 servings.

MOZZARELLA WEDGES

two-cheese tossed salad

Barbara Birk
American Fork, Utah

Colorful, hearty ingredients and a delectable dressing make second helpings of this salad hard to resist. Cottage cheese is an unusual but tasty addition. I never have to worry about storing leftovers.

- 1/2 cup vegetable oil
- 1/2 cup chopped red onion
- 1/4 cup sugar
- 1/4 cup white vinegar
- 1 teaspoon poppy seeds
- 1/2 teaspoon dried minced onion
- 1/4 to 1/2 teaspoon prepared mustard
- 1/8 to 1/4 teaspoon salt
- 5 cups torn fresh spinach
- 5 cups torn iceberg lettuce
- 1/2 pound fresh mushrooms, sliced
- 1 carton (8 ounces) cottage cheese
- 1 cup (4 ounces) shredded Swiss cheese
- 2 bacon strips, cooked and crumbled

- In a jar with tight-fitting lid, combine the first eight ingredients. Refrigerate overnight. Just before serving, toss spinach, lettuce, mushrooms and cheeses in a large salad bowl. Shake dressing and pour over salad. Sprinkle with bacon.

YIELD: 12-14 servings.

TWO-CHEESE TOSSED SALAD

indexes

Alphabetical Index

This index lists every recipe in alphabetical order, so you can easily find your favorites.

General Index

This index lists every recipe by food category and/or major ingredient,
so you can easily find recipes to suit your needs.

Cook Time Index

This index lists every recipe by cook time, so you can easily find recipes that fit your schedule. Recipes are listed under the minimum cook time. Many have ranges, shown in parentheses, and may cook longer.

serve in a slow cooker
appetizers
cheddar fondue, 22
creamy chipped beef fondue, 36
meaty chili dip, 32
nacho rice dip, 20
parmesan fondue, 26
pizza spread, 34
sweet 'n' spicy meatballs, 30
tangy pork meatballs, 22
tomato fondue, 28

desserts
butterscotch fondue, 314
chocolate pecan fondue, 310
chocolate-raspberry fondue, 300
warm strawberry fondue, 314

1 hour
appetizers
hot chili dip
    (1 to 2 hours), 28
party sausages
    (1 to 2 hours), 18
pizza dip
    (1-1/2 to 2 hours), 16

desserts
butterscotch dip
    (45 to 50 minutes), 298
crunchy candy clusters
    (1 hour), 306
fudgy peanut butter cake
    (1-1/2 to 2 hours), 302

2 hours
appetizers & beverages
barbecue sausage bites
    (2-1/2 to 3 hours), 20
cranberry apple cider
    (2 hours), 32
fruit salsa
    (2 hours), 18
hearty broccoli dip
    (2 to 3 hours), 14
hot bacon cheese dip
    (2 hours), 12
hot spiced lemon drink
    (2 to 3 hours), 20
orange spiced cider
    (2 to 3 hours), 18
paddy's reuben dip
    (2 hours), 24
peppered meatballs
    (2-1/2 hours), 28
reuben spread
    (2 hours), 14
slow-cooked salsa
    (2-1/2 to 3 hours), 30
spiced apricot cider
    (2 hours), 30
tropical tea
    (2 to 4 hours), 26

desserts
chocolate bread pudding
    (2-1/4 to 2-1/2 hours), 298
easy chocolate clusters
    (2 hours), 304
hot caramel apples
    (2-1/2 hours), 304
minister's delight
    (2 to 3 hours), 306
slow-cooker berry cobbler
    (2 to 2-1/2 hours), 304
warm fruit compote
    (2 hours), 298

main dishes
no-fuss chicken
    (2 to 2-1/2 hours), 236
pork chop potato dinner
    (2-1/2 to 3 hours), 274
slow-cooked ham 'n' broccoli
    (2 to 3 hours), 254
slow-cooker pizza casserole
    (2 to 3 hours), 136

side dishes
cheddar spirals
    (2-1/2 hours), 120
lemon red potatoes
    (2-1/2 to 3 hours), 100
mashed potatoes
    (2 to 4 hours), 126
rich spinach casserole
    (2-1/2 hours), 124
slow-cooked beans
    (2 hours), 124
slow-cooked broccoli
    (2-1/2 to 3 hours), 100

3 hours
appetizers & beverages
hot crab dip
    (3 to 4 hours), 26
marinated chicken wings
    (3-1/2 to 4 hours), 34
mulled grape cider
    (3 hours), 14
slow-cooker party mix
    (3 hours), 36
tangy barbecue wings
    (3 to 4 hours), 24

beef & ground beef
main dishes
slow-cooked sirloin
    (3-1/2 to 4-1/2 hours), 140